Temporal Politics

New Horizons

Series editors: Clayton Chin, Paul Patton, Lasse Thomassen

The Analytic-Continental divide continues to be a significant fracture in contemporary Western political thought. At the same time, the divide is widely recognized as deeply problematic and unproductive, and there is a growing interest in work across this division in political thought today.
This series supports political philosophy and political theory that works across the Analytic-Continental divide. Books in the series provide a home for exciting new work in political philosophy and political theory that reflects on, moves beyond and experiments with this once intractable division.

Books available:
Adrian Little, *Temporal Politics: Contested Pasts, Uncertain Futures*

Books forthcoming:
David Howarth, *The Political Philosophy of William Connolly: Revitalizing Democracy and Radical Politics*
Visit the series page: edinburghuniversitypress.com/series-new-horizons

Temporal Politics

Contested Pasts, Uncertain Futures

Adrian Little

EDINBURGH
University Press

Edinburgh University Press is one of the leading university presses in the UK. We publish academic books and journals in our selected subject areas across the humanities and social sciences, combining cutting-edge scholarship with high editorial and production values to produce academic works of lasting importance. For more information visit our website: edinburghuniversitypress.com

Edinburgh University Press Ltd
The Tun – Holyrood Road
12(2f) Jackson's Entry
Edinburgh EH8 8PJ

First published in hardback by Edinburgh University Press 2022

Typeset in 11/13 Foundry Sans and Foundry Old Style
by Manila Typesetting Company, and
printed and bound by CPI Group (UK) Ltd,
Croydon, CR0 4YY

A CIP record for this book is available from the British Library

ISBN 978 1 3995 0464 5 (hardback)
ISBN 978 1 3995 0465 2 (paperback)
ISBN 978 1 3995 0466 9 (webready PDF)
ISBN 978 1 3995 0467 6 (epub)

Contents

Preface

Political theorists face three particular challenges in the contemporary academy which this book addresses. First, there is the internal schism between the analytical and continental traditions which has resulted in a bifurcation of theoretical debates between these differing methodologies to the detriment of all in my view. Second, there is the marginalisation of the sub-discipline of political theory within the larger discipline of political science, a trend that has developed and strengthened over the last twenty years. Third, there is considerable pressure in many societies – including the one I live and work in – to demonstrate relevance to something colloquially referred to as 'the real world'. While the first question is primarily an internal matter for the practice of political theorists, the second and third present as existential challenges for theory and its place in our academic community of practice. *Temporal Politics* will address all three questions at different points and, in so doing, make the case that the three are related. Specifically, the challenges of communicating the importance of political theory outside of the sub-discipline is exacerbated by our inability to share our theories and methods with each other internally. Arresting this situation does not have to be focused on internal harmony, but rather on providing recognition that there is value in the work that both analytical and continental philosophers do and that engagement between them will enhance both. It will also provide a stronger foundation on which to tackle the second and third challenges.

In political theory, most scholars – even in traditions that may straddle the analytical-continental division like pragmatism or critical theory – will end up being categorised on one side of the analytical-continental divide or the other. This is perhaps inevitable, and, from my previous work, I am well aware that I will generally be regarded as being more on the continental side of the division. Regardless of these categorisations, however, I don't think it is important in challenging the analytical-continental divide to straddle the fence or to seek to synthesise the differing approaches across the divide. Instead, my view of the analytical-continental divide is that it is something that we as political theorists should cut across in our *practice*. Instead of merely writing about our willingness to engage with multiple traditions – think here of some of those theory journals which purport to welcome contributions from all approaches, but only seem to publish papers which reflect a certain disposition! – I think it is far better that we incorporate our engagement with multiple traditions *into our practice* as theorists. This openness to approaches and methodologies which may take us out of our comfort zone makes us more interesting theorists from my perspective, with a more rounded position from which to engage with the material problems that we try to tackle. Certainly, first-class political theorists can stay within a certain theoretical-methodological approach and many/most do, but the extent to which they can engage in a meaningful way with substantive issues as they manifest in material politics is a different question. Therefore, in keeping with the argument of the book, my proposition is that, if theorists want to engage with material problems, the strongest foundation is a genuine openness to multiple traditions that can be incorporated into our *theoretical practice*.

Openness to multiplicity also extends beyond the analytical-continental divide. In recent years, I have become engaged with debates in comparative political theory and the associated methodology (Little 2018). Some of those methodological reflections are implicit in what follows, and with them comes further recognition that there are multiple ways of knowing the world and engaging politically within it. I have presented elements of this work in a variety of papers on six continents over the last seven years and that geographical diversity has also been an element in the argument for openness in the book and a desire to maximise the inputs to my thinking from a number of different perspectives. Importantly for me, I think political theorists need to be careful about assuming that our place at the heart of the political science discipline is unquestioned. I won't dwell here on the evidence to the contrary, but there is plenty of it. I want to emphasise that an openness to other sub-disciplines is also vital in reminding the discipline of the centrality of political theory. Again, thinking about this point in terms of my practice as a political theorist has led to me working with a number of colleagues (including some of those listed below) in the fields of Indigenous politics, international relations and public policy. In my humble opinion, working across sub-disciplinary divisions also helps to generate thinking about political theory as a scholarly practice that can challenge the analytical-continental divide through what we do (with colleagues) in addressing particular political problems as much as it is done by solely theoretical reflection.

It is a pleasure to be able to include *Temporal Politics* in this new series from Edinburgh University Press. While I refer explicitly to the analytical-continental divide at different points in the book, my challenge to the division is often implicit and embedded in the methodological dimension of the book. After setting out the conceptual focus of temporal politics in the first part of the book in a way that exemplifies the importance of moving beyond theoretical and sub-disciplinary silos, in the second part I move towards the practice of temporal politics by discussing three illustrative cases of how a temporal approach to political issues may shift the nature of the debates in question. The idea is not so much to resolve the complex issues I discuss in Chapters 4 to 6, but rather to show that a shift towards temporal analysis potentially changes the nature of these debates in not entirely predictable ways. The final part of the book returns to more theoretical/methodological questions. It demonstrates the ways in which a concern for political temporality married with the examination of illustrative cases generates new ways of thinking about political theory, political action and the practice of bringing the two together based on the application of process philosophy to our discussion of material issues.

A range of interlocutors over the last six or seven years have helped to shape my thinking (whether they realise it or not), though none can be blamed for any idiosyncratic positions I have ended up adopting as a result of these engagements. The diversity of these scholars reflects my approach to the practice of political theory as one that is open to multiple perspectives. In alphabetical order (though I single out a smaller number of individuals for particular thanks below), they include Lawrie Balfour, Peter Balint, Adrian Blau, Clayton Chin, Hastings Donnan, Keith Dowding, Erik Doxtader, John Dryzek, Robyn Eckersley, Selen Ercan, Alan Finlayson, Jonathan Floyd, Michael Freeden, Matthew Gibney, Hamza Bin Jehangir, Mathias Koenig-Archibugi, Patti Lenard, Kate Macdonald, Terry Macdonald, Mark McMillan, Anne McNevin, Sarah Maddison, Paul Muldoon, Sana Nakata, David Owen, Umut Ozguc, Paul Patton, Juliet Rogers, Andy Schaap, Adam Sheingate, Lasse Thomassen, Simon Tormey, Nick Vaughan-Williams and Melissa Williams.

Special thanks go to a few collaborators that have made the journey particularly enjoyable and intellectually stimulating. Back in 2012, I was awarded an Australian Research Council Discovery grant with Mark McMillan, Paul Muldoon and Juliet Rogers (and Partner Investigators Erik Doxtader and Andy Schaap). Little did we know then what was in front of us – from Cape Town to Belfast and too many nights that went on much longer than they needed to back in Melbourne. Mark, Paul and Juliet have been major influences on my thinking as well as great mates. I thank all three for their intellectual support, but must recognise the importance of Mark's thinking in particular in helping me to learn about Indigenous knowledge in Australia and infusing my thoughts that appear in Chapter 4 with his insights. Mark's connection to Wiradjuri land and his cultural heritage provided me with greater awareness than I could ever have gleaned from purely academic research as a non-Indigenous scholar. Terry Macdonald and Kate Macdonald have been important influences in challenging collaborations that demonstrate that it is often much easier to stay within the comfort zone of who and what we know; needless to say, for those of us that engage in work across the analytical-continental divide, it is a difficult – sometimes arduous – practice that often takes time to bear fruit. Keeping it within the family probably isn't to be recommended either! Hamza Bin Jehangir read the entire manuscript and provided incisive commentary. My understanding of comparative political theory is all the better for my work with Hamza and I hope that will continue in future years.

I am very grateful to Clayton Chin, Paul Patton and Lasse Thomassen for the invitation to participate in this new series. In practice, I think there are not that many political theorists that really do challenge the analytical-continental divide, but Clayton, Paul and Lasse are exemplars of what can be achieved. At Edinburgh University Press, Carol Macdonald was a thoughtful and supportive Commissioning Editor and the entire production team was a pleasure to work with.

I am also grateful to the *European Journal of Political Theory* for permission to include Chapter 5, which is an amended version of 'The Complex Temporality of Borders: Contingency and Normativity', *European Journal of Political Theory* 14(4): 429–47 (2015). One section of Chapter 6 is adapted with permission from 'Performing the Demos: Towards a Processive Theory of Global Democracy', *Critical Review of International Social and Political Philosophy* 18(6): 620–41 (2015).

Finally, all authors should be aware of the forbearance they ask of their families, but also of the very welcome diversions they can provide when the writing process is not as productive as it might be. In this respect, special thanks and love to Kate, Jude, Milo and Niamh.

Temporal Politics is dedicated to the memory of Andy Little, who died during the writing of the book. He touched the lives of so many he came into contact with, not so much through what he thought or said, but what he did.

PART ONE

1

The Context of Temporal Politics

Contemporary politics around the world abounds with discussions of disillusionment, populism and the shortcomings of political systems especially within established democracies (Foa and Mounk 2016, Norris 2014, Runciman 2018). While there have been plentiful historical challenges to the modern democratic nation-state, most of the critique and opposition to liberal democracies has been from external parties. For example, liberal democratic states have had to withstand pressure from states aligned with different ideological traditions such as communism and fascism, while the rise of globalisation, with its attendant pressures on nation-state structures and practices in a more interdependent world, has given rise to consciousness of the proximity of critical global movements that challenge the foundations of liberal democratic societies. More recently still, in the twenty-first century the threats posed by 'internal outsiders' – that is, potentially violent opponents of the liberal democratic order living within the confines of the nation-state – have become a prominent feature of political discourse.

In the last decade, however, a substantial literature has emerged in liberal democracies which provides an immanent critique of the structures and practices of liberal democracy itself. That is, this emergent challenge is not provided by a 'dangerous outsider' with an axe to grind against liberal democracy (though undoubtedly those actors exist too), but rather the critique comes from within, from those often aligned with the broad foundations of liberal democratic societies. This is a form of critique which holds a mirror up to the liberal democratic nation-state and argues – from within – that the state's institutions or practices, or the people involved in delivering government, have fundamental shortcomings which are failing to deliver on democracy's promise. The argument suggests that the line between democratic theory and practice has been fundamentally ruptured and that something needs to be done to reverse this decline of democracy and the troublesome trajectory it provides for the future. This is a systemic critique, trapped in a statist imaginary, that points to the failings of democratic institutions – and the leadership and governments they produce – to deliver on democratic values (however they are conceived). Like older forms of 'declinism' (Elchardus and Spruyt 2016, English and Kenny 1999), this perspective is often accompanied with a melancholic wistfulness about the past of liberal democracy where things seemingly functioned better. This yearning creates a past that is only half-remembered and an ideal-typical picture of democracy that has become distorted over the passage of time (Little 2008, Diamond and Plattner 2016). It also plays into what Paul Gilroy (2019: 372) has called 'restorative fantasies of making the country great again'.

The evidence of such decline is seemingly all around us in the political literature on this topic. Political scientists in various parts of the world typically point to lower levels of electoral participation, declining faith in politicians and political parties, the failings of old political systems and the ascendancy of new types of political figures challenging established democratic orders and institutions (Norris 2014, Norris and Inglehart 2019). Various explanations of these phenomena have been advanced, ranging from structural explanations of the shortcomings of parliamentary political systems or the inadequacy of the nation-state in the face of globalising pressures, through to the relationship between the media and politics or the emergence of new types of political actors and the rise of populism (Tormey 2014, Moffitt 2016). While partially related to these accounts (at least insofar as it provides an alternative immanent critique to those already established), this book proposes a different perspective that encompasses both the structural and agential dimensions in the differing explanations mentioned above. The novelty lies in the focus on the analysis of political temporality as both an explanatory factor in arguments about decline, and a means of navigating through accounts of a contemporary malaise to envisage a new temporally informed understanding of politics that might help to renew faith in political processes once again. As such, the book builds from an explanatory critique of the shortcomings of modern democratic politics (more normally associated with post-structural and post-foundational accounts) to argue for an approach to political analysis through the lens of temporal methods. The ensuing method of 'temporal politics' clearly has normative implications for how we practise theoretical analysis in politics and engages with contextual and grounded forms of normative theory (more normally associated with analytical traditions).

Temporal Politics makes the case that a major part of the melancholic disquiet about contemporary politics lies in the failure to understand the temporality of political processes. This tendency is melancholic because it tends to hark back to a bygone political age when systems and demo-cratic institutions were thought to function in a more efficient fashion, where political actors were less dishonest and opportunistic, or where the operation of democratic systems was less susceptible to pressures of glo-balisation (Little 2010; for related accounts see Hooker 2016, Roy 2009, Traverso 2017). Such a melancholic outlook is ahistorical on two counts. First, it is based upon a nostalgic view of a morally superior past which serves to make invisible previous critiques of democratic shortcomings both from within democratic systems and from ideological opponents on the outside, as well as the ways in which democracies have developed and changed over time. Second, it compresses temporal discussion into a phase of post-enlightenment, Western politics that does a disservice to the lon-ger emergence of modern democratic systems and the possibilities for dif-ferent kinds of formulations of democracy in the future. This melancholia also feeds into a misrepresentation of the future as a phase of inevitable demise because of the failings of the present. *Temporal Politics* suggests that an alternative understanding of temporality may help us to develop a processive account of politics that facilitates a more positive orientation towards political action and change in the future and a less melancholic disposition towards the institutions and systems of the past. This argu-ment constructs the present as a space of possibility, of emergent political change from our historical legacies towards a still to be defined future that will be shaped by the actions we take.

More significantly still, while the main objective of the book is to establish a new theory of political temporality, Chapter 7 contends that political temporality invokes a processive approach to politics – informed by a better understanding of temporality – that potentially helps us to rethink some of the most significant issues that characterise contemporary politics. As the title of the book implies, the theory of political tempo-rality developed herein builds upon the idea of contested understandings of the past alongside an embrace of the uncertainty of political futures. It uses these understandings of the nature of the past and future to develop alternative accounts to some of the most pressing issues in contemporary politics such as the transformation of societies characterised by histori-cal injustices, contemporary debates about borders and migration, and the declining faith in democratic structures, institutions and practices. While the book examines these cases in some detail, I contend that the theory and methodology of temporal analysis in politics can be applied more generally to cast new light on a much wider range of divisive issues, such as climate change, the impact of new technology, and racial and cultural discrimina-tion in the contemporary world.

Why Is Time and Temporality So Important?

Although there has been some limited engagement with the concept of time in contemporary political theory (Widder 2008, Hutchings 2013, Shapiro 2016, Downey 2020), political science analysis has traditionally tended to focus on more tangible objects such as institutions (for example, the nature of bureaucracy, the political role of markets, the organisational role of particular bodies), policies (including processes affecting the full range of matters of interest and control to different layers of government), and a fairly narrow range of actors (voters, citizens, politicians, political parties, pressure groups and so forth). Placed alongside these traditional subjects and objects of political analysis, time and temporality seem quite abstract and ill-defined. Indeed, for many commentators, the notion of time and its passage would not be remotely politically controversial.

This book contends that time is in fact deeply political and that, in order to comprehend this, we need to differentiate between traditional concepts of time (with defined and uncritical understandings of the past, present and future) and the idea of temporality. This move from time to temporality helps us to grasp the political significance of temporal change in politics. Therefore, I define temporality in politics as being not only about the passage of time, but also, and more importantly, about the pace and/or tempo of political change. Temporal analysis helps us to grapple with the fact that the past, present and future are not settled entities, but rather they are matters of interpretation, partly grounded in the lived experience of time, with the result that these phases of social life often overlap with one another in the interpretations of different people. Moreover, because temporality in politics is interpretive, there will often be contention over the pace of change from one era to the next and disagreement about whether the pace of change between them has been too fast or too slow. Essentially, and most fundamentally, what differentiates temporality from traditional accounts of time is that the former is intrinsically centred upon *the lived experience of time*, that is, temporality focuses on the multitudinous conceptions of how humans experience the movement of time.

From this perspective, political temporality is inherently controversial because it is grounded in the inevitably competing temporal understandings of different phenomena. It enables the past to live into the future, when many people might like to confine the past to the past, to move on from past events or injustices without having to deal with the contemporary and future ramifications of the past for politics. Political temporality demands that when we tackle contemporary issues, we need to understand competing historical trajectories as well as disagreement about the implications of political action on how particular issues or problems will ensue and mani-fest in the future. As such, it resists ahistorical thinking about politics – as if there are not contested narratives of how contemporary societies came to be as they are – and legitimises futurology as a political strategy (as we will see in Chapter 6 on democracy), albeit accepting that projections of the future will often be speculative and that remembrance of the past will be contested. As the subtitle to the book makes clear, a temporal approach to politics therefore embraces both political contestation and the challenge of uncertainty.

What should be clear is that the notion of political temporality makes the movement of time in politics a much more controversial issue than traditional conceptions permit. It undermines the linearity of many depic-tions of time in politics – we move from x to y to z through a clear sequence with distinct causality, or policy a had impact b which then created a new problem c – and allows for much more disorderly and complex renderings of things like progression and causality. To be clear, it does not reject the existence of progression and causality, but it permits greater conflict about the nature of them and the linear sequencing that these explanations often assume, primarily because it places a premium on understanding all enti-ties as relational. Political temporality embraces a wider range of political subjects and multiplies the complicated ways in which they might interact with one another to generate the challenges that have to be addressed in politics (see Gaus 2019 for related thoughts from a more analytical perspective). And just as this facilitates a much more complicated set of explanatory interactions, it also enables greater argument about the passage of time and the rate at which change takes place in a temporal register. Discussion of temporality encourages arguments about whether things are changing too slowly or too quickly, as reflected in debates about hyper-globalisation and the reactions to it (Ohmae 1999, Hirst and Thompson 2009), or 'slow movements' seeking to revert the experience of different phenomena to an amenable pace more akin to the past (Feit 2012). Not least of the potential conflicts between campaigns for the fast and the slow is the promotion of change for change's sake for the former and the risk of a lapse into melancholia for the latter. Therefore, as political subjects invoke the pace of political change as a good or bad thing, inherent risks of conflict emerge in temporal understanding that need to be revealed rather than shrouded by the problematic cover of linear notions of time.

All of this suggests that the positioning of temporal understanding at the front of the stage in addressing a wide range of political issues can help us to navigate through their contested waters. It can enhance better understanding of political problems, reveal a multiplicity of ways in which

we may act upon them, and highlight the variety of potential impacts that
particular courses of action may have. Political temporality can unsettle
established understandings and provide space for alternative readings to
flourish. It does so in full recognition of the power of temporality to
unveil new forms of disagreement or new elements of particular issues
that were not previously thought to be controversial. Therefore, while
it is in part a diachronic perspective on politics, it depicts a much more
complex picture of the then and now of diachronic analysis. In this sense,
political temporality is 'multi-chronic'. It identifies the future as a much
more active factor in political analysis and suggests that we need to pay
greater attention in politics to the 'in between' spaces that lie at junctures
of pasts, presents and futures.

If past, present and future are considered as dynamic, then no object
of analysis can be treated as a completely distinct temporal entity. Rather
the objects of politics are always in a transitional process of *becoming* as
they interact with multiple political subjects and other concrete phenomena (Connolly 2011, Bergson 1911, Deleuze and Guattari 1994). This
complexity makes political analysis a more difficult practice; one where
sometimes it is necessary to simplify to some extent to render political
action feasible. However, as useful as simplification might be as a political technique, it also opens up space for political disagreement about that
which has been simplified and why. These disputes might reject the mode
of simplification, the importance of what has been left out, the motives
of the political agents engaged in simplifying, and so forth. This makes
clear that the toolkit of temporal analysis needs to develop methodological
approaches which facilitate this contestation to ensure that debates about
the nature of particular political techniques are able to stay alive in discussions about how we act upon specific issues in grounded situations.

The concept of political temporality presents challenges for most of the
major contemporary theoretical approaches in political science as well as
many empirical methodologies of the discipline (Mearsheimer and Walt
2013). It also asks questions of methodologies of theoretical analysis that
are rarely elaborated in contemporary political thought. On the one hand,
disagreement about the past and uncertainty about the future invoke key
challenges to parsimonious analyses in analytical philosophy which often
bracket out complexities and non-linearity, but, on the other hand, they
also demand a concern for political action and the future which goes far
beyond typical critical and/or post-foundational theories in the continental
tradition. In what follows, I identify some of these methodological challenges and develop an account of a *process* of theoretical analysis that gives
greater priority to the concept of political temporality than is currently the

case in most modes of political theory. What should be clear at the outset, however, is the way in which political temporality demands attentiveness to the particular constraints that theorists face when developing contextual modes of analysis that place political issues and problems in particular practical environments where material structures, institutions and events have an impact on ways in which political theory can be operationalised.

The importance of context to political theory is a matter of some contention between, put simply, those who want to defend the importance of abstract philosophical analysis and those that argue for the benefits – and for some, the necessity – of grounded theorising taking account of material issues and socio-political constraints (Williams 2020). While the general concept of temporality can potentially be accommodated within either side of this debate, the *political* notion of temporality developed in this book is much more aligned with the model of grounded theory focused on the implications of material issues in particular contexts (Glaser and Strauss 2017). The reason for this is relatively straightforward. While a form of temporal analysis that focuses on past, present and future is perfectly consistent with abstract analytical techniques, abstract theory is much less consistent with the expressly *political* view of temporality (Gunnell 1998). Political temporality is focused on more than just the need to take account of time in constructing theoretical arguments. Rather its focus is on the need to understand the contested nature of the past including disagreements about the course of past events and their implications, as well as uncertainty and dispute over the material conditions and constraints of the future (yet retaining the future's centrality to the task of political theory). If political temporality is focused on conflict and uncertainty as well as the need for both to be prominent in the way in which theoretical debate is conducted, then this demands contextual analysis rather than abstraction. If we are to understand the 'lived experience' of time, then that demands groundedness to develop an understanding of the ways in which groups of humans come to interpret certain political phenomena as they do. That is, the way in which conflict and uncertainty over the past and future materialise in politics always takes place in contexts which trouble and sometimes invalidate abstract theory as a means of guiding political action.

The focus on context in the theory of political temporality also necessitates an engagement with debates on realism that have emerged in recent years largely within the field of normative political philosophy (B. Williams 2005, Geuss 2008, Galston 2010, Sleat 2018, Erman and Möller 2019). These debates have intersected with discussions on whether normative political theory should be ideal or non-ideal (Gilabert and Lawford-Smith 2012, Valentini 2009) in character and associated arguments about whether the driving principle guiding political theory's engagement with material problems in the 'real world' should be whether the action-guiding principles should be at least feasible in political practice. Of course, such notions of feasibility and/or whether theories are ideal or non-ideal in character demand some kind of interpretive exercise about the material conditions of the 'real world'. That is, they require degrees of qualification and subjective judgement that have not traditionally existed in abstract moral theories that have placed the construction of moral principles through philosophical argument before the concrete political environments in which these principles are then to be applied (see, for example, El Amine 2020 and Idris 2020 for critique of the ways in which the later Rawls had difficulty describing the non-Western world). Moralist theoretical approaches are difficult techniques to apply to the idea of political temporality because they rely too heavily on *fixity* of institutions and policies as well as assumptions about the beliefs, standpoints and behaviours of people in ways which temporal politics – grounded in contexts – finds hard to accommodate. Moralist approaches tend to make too many epistemological and ontological assumptions and underplay the inherently contested nature of much of what they construe as 'political facts' (Little 2015c). Therefore, realists from within the analytical tradition have argued for a less abstract model of conducting analytical philosophy which retains the normative emphasis of much of that tradition, but attempts to do so within a much more grounded methodology. That said, these realists tend to stop short of embracing ambiguity and epistemological uncertainty as basic tenets of political analysis and seldom engage with conflicting lived experiences of socio-political phenomena as key building blocks of political knowledge.

What Is the Methodology of Temporal Analysis?

Temporal Politics makes a case for an applied form of political theory driven out by analysis of actually existing problems and issues in specific grounded contexts. Alongside other recent attempts to break the shackles of the divide between analytical and continental approaches to political thought (Owen 2016, Chin 2016), it borrows from both traditions in its argumentation. The book advocates deconstructive techniques from continental traditions to explain the significance of temporality for contemporary political debates, whilst still leaving space for forms of normative argumentation about the implications of temporality and recognising that normative assumptions cannot be avoided in chosen methodologies of political research. Given the centrality of the analysis of language in many forms of continental philosophy, it can shed particular light on the emergence and development of language and discourse over the course of time in specific contexts. It can help to demonstrate how linguistic development is part and parcel of the political problems which applied political theory purports to address and, in a temporal register, how the key concepts we deploy in politics change over the course of time. Furthermore, continental approaches help us to understand the ways in which human lived experience of particular political issues is mediated through discourse.

Deconstructive techniques enable us to better understand how the terms in which we prosecute political debates over particular problems evolve and develop and, indeed, how they vary from case to case. Therefore, a continental approach to political temporality helps us to understand both the reasons why there is sometimes very deep division on key political questions, and also the *historical trajectory* that has led to concepts being understood in the way they are. These insights can help us to develop more accurate understandings of how concepts *may* develop in the future and their potential implications in practice, although such predictions are always contingent on changes in the surrounding environment. The focus on language in particular contexts also suggests that comparative political theory may be valuable for temporal political analysis insofar as it may demonstrate the very different notions of the importance of time in different regions, cultures and traditions, as well as highlighting disputes about the meaning of concepts in different situations and cases (Little 2018, 2020).

The first demand that temporal analysis makes on political theory is that it asks us to take account of the past in contemporary theorising and, in particular, in the ways in which the development of theory informs contemporary political practice. Therefore, in thinking about the ways in which political theory can help political actors – individuals, collectives, communities, pressure groups, institutions, parties, governments and international organisations – to make decisions on courses of action to address particular issues or problems, a temporal approach to politics invites us to understand the historical and ideational development of the particular phenomena that we are trying to address. This can take many forms, but typically it might suggest that we try to understand the contested historical background to particular constitutions of a given society, for example, the impact of colonialism, the formation of its class structure, its gender dynamics, its particular relationship with neighbouring countries, and so forth. In thinking through the development of the constitution of a particular society, we gain greater insight into the ontological questions of who is involved in a particular decision and what they might have at stake in the outcome. Temporal analysis of the past can also shed greater light on why particular issues and problems have emerged in a specific contemporary formation – when and how an issue became understood as a problem in a particular sense rather than another – that requires some form of action in the present or future.

Clearly, then, there is a Foucauldian dimension to temporal analysis insofar as it encourages a genealogical approach to understanding the dynamics of political issues and problems (Foucault 1977a). This amounts to more than just explaining the facts of the historical development of a particular issue, such as the behaviours of some people or problematic socio-political structures or outdated or inappropriate policies (Portschy 2020). Genealogical inquiry also focuses on *why* issues come to be seen as problematic, that is, what it is about particular behaviours or characteristics of certain peoples that come to be seen by wider society as matters which demand action. Therefore, a genealogical approach is concerned with the historical development of issues or problems and the ways in which they come to be construed as issues of socio-political concern. In particular, for Foucault, it was of course concentrated on the sometimes nebulous exercise of power and the means by which the state and its institutions came to exercise authority over specific issues. Potentially this involved them reproducing power dynamics that created problems in the process of acting to seemingly solve them. Therefore, a Foucauldian approach to 'problematisations' helps us to interpret particular political phenomena and the reasons behind their emergence in specific forms in contemporary society (Foucault 1998, Little 2012).

While Foucauldian techniques are certainly consistent with the explanatory part of temporal analysis, the key point is really that we understand the contested nature of these interpretations of the genealogy of particular issues. That is, political temporality encourages such a methodology not just for revelatory purposes concerning the reasons for why things are as they are, but also to explain the different interpretations of the pathways to the present and the importance of historical accounts to the disagreements that permeate contemporary politics. Contrary to what I have called elsewhere 'fact-based realism' (Little 2015c), these competing versions of historical explanation demonstrate the importance of particular narratives of development to the construction of problems in the present. What is important for political theorists to understand then in the concept of temporality is not just the definitive history of a particular set of circumstances but the contested narratives of that history. Genealogical investigation may be revelatory, but it is not singular; it reveals a history of multiple explanations of the emergence of specific phenomena that demand political action. That is, the historical 'facts' from which political actors may derive realist accounts of the present are usually contested in often finely granulated ways which can have very significant impacts on understandings of the present.

Therefore, the past in political temporality is not just concerned with multiple narratives of historical trajectories to the present, but also, vitally, it is focused on *the competing nature of these narratives*. There is much more at stake than just a different way of telling a particular story. The facts of the matter, the ways in which they intersect with other events around which there are multiple explanations, the motivations and characteristics of political actors, the relationships between policies and specific outcomes can not only be explained in different ways, but the act of explaining things in different ways denies, undermines, invalidates or delegitimises alternative accounts of the same phenomena. The issue is not just that representations of the past differ, but that they compete with each other. This competition is often highly political in itself as it calls into question truths that are fundamental to the self-identity of proponents of alternative narratives. This is nowhere more apparent than when 'post-conflict' societies continue to contest narratives of the past in the aftermath of conflict because social identities continue to be closely bound up with particular historical narratives of the events of the past (Little 2014).

Despite the centrality of Foucauldian approaches to the argument here, one of the shortcomings of continental philosophy *as a political theory* has been the inability or unwillingness of its advocates to extend its critical disposition towards analytical philosophy beyond pure critique. Given its theoretical framework, continental philosophy is sceptical of suggestions that it needs to move into alternative normative recommendations (with attendant institutional or policy advice) or more rigorous theories of political action and individual or collective agency. While this reluctance may be methodologically justifiable, it does generate questions around the *political relevance* of continental approaches. They can indeed furnish us with a better understanding of the nature of political problems through deconstruction of the prevailing language and discourse through which they are understood; however, they have shortcomings when it comes to recommending alternative courses of action or policy (Owen 2016). Therefore, *Temporal Politics* also turns its attention to more normative work in political theory to see whether any kind of fusion of the two approaches might prove fruitful.

While some analytical political philosophy works at a high level of abstraction, there is a tradition – often associated with ethical approaches to justice – which attempts to work towards action-guiding norms with some underpinning sense of practical relevance (Erman and Möller 2019). This work at least purports to be about the development of philosophical ideas which can provide a foundation for discussion of actions to address political problems. Much of this work is broadly Rawlsian in conception or at least in terms of the methodological approaches deployed within it. Insofar as it attempts to engage with practical social and political problems, this is to be welcomed. However, in various ways, theorists ranging from Bernard Williams to Stuart Hampshire to Raymond Geuss (Hampshire 2000, Geuss 2008) and many others in between have questioned the extent to which this work has actually been engaged in addressing 'real' political problems.

Much of this potential shortcoming of analytical political philosophy is methodological insofar as this tradition has often been engaged in studying political morality or developing an 'ethics-first' approach to the real world which does not quite manage to marry up ethical norms with the 'real world' problems they purport to address – what Owen (2016) calls the guidance problem. That is, while these approaches may be designed from some understanding of actual issues in the world (for example, discussion of border politics through the democratic boundary question), the *analysis* is often conducted in a separate theoretical register, and then transplanted back on to the problem it is supposed to address. This schism between real political problems and the analytical techniques of developing feasible answers (or at least workable courses of political action) is problematic, as we shall see below. It is also problematic that time and temporality – at least, in the terms discussed here, as central planks in political contestation – are rarely placed at the heart of these analyses. The tendency of political moralism is to denude complex problems of their complications to facilitate parsimonious descriptions of the issue at hand. This often takes the form of analagous reasoning whereby the complex context of the issues under discussion is deliberately reduced so that comparisons can be drawn between different kinds of issues through analogies.

However, what analytical political philosophy does attempt to provide – albeit with limited success – is the kind of normative guidance that is anathema to much continental political thought. While rather limited in the *practical political work* that it can do, normative political philosophy does at least attempt to think through the courses of action that can inform thinking about alternative policy options and/or institutional configurations to those that currently prevail. Thus, while analytical thought tends to be weaker at understanding structures of power and their connection to language and discourse in the process of problematisation amongst other things, it does at least recognise that political thinking needs to engage in some way with material political practices, even if its understanding of what constitutes 'the political' is questionable (Mouffe 2005). While continental approaches are strong in revealing and critiquing how these structures develop, operate and reproduce, they often steer away from or overtly reject the development and promotion of alternative political institutions or policies, as if unwilling to sully the critical philosophical exercise with the business of material politics, replete as it is with contingency and compromise.

Where does this stand-off – and the methodological issues it is predicated upon – leave us in terms of the means of approaching political temporality? Without wanting to simplify the entire field of political theory thereby reinforcing the schism between analytical and continental approaches as the defining characteristic, it is worth noting some alternative perspectives that potentially cut across the divide. For example, the critical theory tradition attempts to navigate a path between the two by utilising critique but directing it towards alternative ways of organising social and political life (see, for example, Honneth 2015). This outlook provides a critique of the dominant liberal strain within analytical thought and supplants it with alternative ideological standpoints informed, inter alia, by more radical variants of liberalism, socialism, political ecology, feminism, anarchism and so forth. However, like the continental tradition, critical theory tends to either fail to move beyond critique to develop alternative recommendations or else makes a utopian leap of faith to alternative models with no articulation of a political strategy to get from here to there. In many respects it struggles just as much as analytical and continental philosophy to really engage in material politics.

Critical theory is also prevalent in contemporary international relations scholarship. It is manifest in variants of critical constructivism which try to reimagine the international domain in ways which challenge the brand of realist thinking which is highly influential in some parts of the discipline (Drezner 2020). In a few notable and commendable contributions in international relations, time and temporality has been discussed as a significant issue (see, for example, Walker 1993, Hutchings 2013, Hom 2018, 2020, McIntosh 2015), but quite frequently the passage of time appears in international relations in the traditional linear manner (with many of the common assumptions about causality), rather than a focus on the contested nature of the pace and tempo of political change which is the defining feature of political temporality advanced here (Drezner 2020). Moreover, it is only relatively recently that the international relations canon has become more open to alternative theories such as post-colonialism which challenge the epistemological foundations on which it has been built and argue for a more relational ontology in the discipline (Barkawi and Laffey 2006).

An alternative perspective that cuts across the analytical-continental divide and sometimes knits them together is evident in the recent re-emergence of pragmatist political theory (see, for example, Chin 2018, Koopman 2009a). Taking inspiration from theorists as diverse as Dewey, Foucault, Rorty and Connolly, contemporary pragmatists reject the constructed division between the analytical and continental traditions and seek to reintroduce more methodological rigour into debates about the nature of political change. The focus on change and attendant notions of what can realistically be achieved by political action makes pragmatism deeply relevant to the theory of political temporality developed herein. Not the least of the benefits it offers is its capacity to bring theory and practice together in challenging the academic boundaries that have been established by the almost hegemonic notion of the analytical-continental divide (see, for example, Rorty's critique of analytical political philosophy, 'avant-gardism' and chauvinism; Rorty 1995: 202–3). That said, in terms of the actual substance of political action and change, pragmatism is often derivative of the other traditions it critiques. It draws from ideas developed in the various forms of political thought that it engages with and extracts from them ideas and concepts that can then be remoulded with insights garnered from other perspectives. As such, pragmatism always has an eye for *political* feasibility and seeks out or establishes meliorist compromises rather than engaging in philosophical indulgence. Pragmatism asks us to relinquish some of our academic conceits to make us think more clearly about how the world is and what is at stake in trying to change it. Moreover, for pragmatists like Dewey, the role of philosophy is to mediate the conflict between the language of the past and the pressing needs of the future (Rorty 1995: 199). It should be clear that some notion of temporality – especially the contested nature of past, present and future – *should* be fundamental to this approach.

Nowhere has the contested nature of time been more strongly argued than in a range of black and post-colonial critiques of modernity, culture and nationhood. From James Baldwin's many allusions to this issue, through Homi Bhabha (2012), to Frantz Fanon's invocation that the 'structure of the present is grounded in temporality. Every human problem cries out to be considered on the basis of time, the ideal being that the present always serves to build the future' (Fanon 1986: 14–15), we can see that the lived experience of racial prejudice, exploitation and oppression has often been expressed through a temporal lens. It is important not to generalise about this extensive panoply of thought for it has many different scales and ontological and epistemological touch points. For example, Dipesh Chakrabarty (2018, 2021) provides a sweeping discussion of the

Anthropocene with a clear global/planetary temporal distinction where the global is construed as moral-political, human-focused and shorter term, while the longer-term notion of the planetary examines the geobiological history of the planet as a system rather than just focusing on human history. Paul Gilroy, on the other hand, is much more focused on the micro-level lived experience of – and opposition to – racial oppression where the temporal dimension appears in 'the inevitability of time lags, displacements, historical deficits, and feedback loops' (Gilroy 2019: 380). Further, these insights have been combined with analyses of the lived experience of gender and sexual violence by writers such as Megan Burke (2019) who focus on phenomenological accounts of gendered subjectivities. Lastly, there are the notable attempts to move beyond past and current structures in building a politics of decolonisation and decolonial thinking (Mamdani 2020, Mignolo and Walsh 2018).

With regard to political theories of temporality in particular, these ideas have been applied most explicitly by commentators including Michael Hanchard and Charles W. Mills. Hanchard (1999) provides a critique of a singular or univocal depiction of modernity and argues instead for a focus on the *relationship* of black people and their political movements to this depiction. This relational understanding highlights African histories and their centrality to African worldviews:

> what I call racial time became one of the disjunctive temporalities of both Western and Afro-Modernity, beginning with the emergence of racial slavery. Racial time is defined as the inequalities of temporality that result from power relations between racially dominant and subordinate groups . . . [which] produce unequal temporal access to institutions, goods, services, resources, power, and knowledge, which members of both groups recognize. (Hanchard 1999: 252–3)

This passage points to not just multiple modernities, but also competing modernities. The existence of many experiences of modernity is not just a matter of recognising plurality, but of understanding the ways in which the *failure* to recognise plurality contributes to conflict. This failure plays out in the lived experience of material inequalities and simultaneously reinforces singular theories of modernity. Therefore, the recognition of plurality must move beyond the cycle of singular modernity (and the material inequalities it supports). Rather, a politics of plurality must *interrupt* the temporal cycle of modernity and racial time by drawing out its conflicts and their implications for the lived experience of modern life.

Hanchard's ideas have also been influential on the work of Mills (2014, 2020) and his critique of 'white time'. Mills (2014: 29, 31) locates the racialisation of time within a series of 'amnesias, excisions, [and] forgettings' that were exacerbated by settlers 'setting the historical chronometer at zero'. In line with Lawrie Balfour's work on Du Bois (Balfour 2011), Mills argues that philosophy and normative theory haven't engaged in debates on race and time, preferring to see the field as 'aracial and putatively atemporal'. From this critique of timelessness and abstract truth, Mills launches into an excoriating analysis of Rawls – in particular, the distance between our actual societies and Rawlsian ideal type models. He makes clear that rectifying racial injustice is a non-ideal exercise, not least because in no other country than the USA has race been so central to the very constitution of society, or, in Rawlsian terms, the basic structure (Mills 2014). And yet, even with his shift away from universal theory in *Political Liberalism* (1993), Rawls does not deal with the exclusion of black perspectives from the standard interpretation of how Western societies (the US in particular) are constituted. For Mills (2014: 39), this leaves Rawls with only 'white time', which is the process by which we see 'the limitation of justice to the distributive and synchronic'.

In his more recent work, Mills turns his attention to 'chronopolitics', which he defines as

> the multiple different ways in which power relations between groups – whether formally acknowledged in recognized systems or not – affect both the representations of the relations between these groups and the world, in their specifically temporal aspect, and the material relations of these groups to the world, in their specifically temporal dimension. (Mills 2020: 299)

The racial dimension of this phenomenon is taken up explicitly when he argues that even critical discourses of modernity such as Marxism have failed to recognise a range of much longer historical timespans from which to assess the emergence and development of the modern world and its projection into the future (a point I return to in more detail in Chapter 4). Mills (2020: 312) claims that this 'historical materialist calendar' neglects alternative temporalities around the world, leading to a form of 'white chronopolitics' which 'continues to structure our dominant understandings and normative judgments about the past and present of the contemporary world order'.

Mills's depiction of chronopolitics is vital because it points to a multiplicity of chronopolitical understandings which do not merely exist alongside each other. Rather, they generate contestation between advocates of differing perspectives. Moreover, this argument is not purely focused on the past, but instead it highlights how relationships between past and present stake 'particular claims on the future' (Mills 2020: 312). To summarise, then, black and post-colonial theories have provided sophisticated conceptualisations of time which inform the particular approach to temporal politics developed in the course of this book. Perhaps this is best summarised in Appadurai's articulation of the challenge to traditional conceptions of history: 'the worry about the new, the emergent, and the incomplete (as they are all instanced in our sense of what globalization is and does) is not only about the vulnerabilities of periodization but also about something deeper still, which is a panic about contingency' (Appadurai 2020: 3).

The final outlook that I would like to introduce to the discussion at this point is comparative political theory (CPT). CPT emerged over twenty years ago as a specific sub-field within political theory (Dallmayr 1999, Euben 2008, Parel and Keith 2003), and it has grown in significance over the last ten years (March 2009, El Amine 2016, Idris 2016, Jenco 2007, von Vacano 2015, Ackerly and Bajpai 2017, Freeden and Vincent 2013, Simon 2020, Little 2018). A range of recent contributions (Iqtidar 2016, Godrej 2011, Idris 2016, Jenco 2016, Jehangir and Little 2020, Rollo 2018) provide insights which link together the concerns of comparative political theorists and theories of temporality. The key intervention of CPT is to establish a stronger focus in political theory on non-Western texts that have been neglected in the established 'Western canon'. While many analysts are at pains to emphasise radical difference (Godrej 2009), at its more ambitious end, CPT attempts to bring Western and non-Western texts and thinkers into constructive dialogue with one another. However, at its weakest, it can merely provide a form of parallelism where such comparative dialogues do not take place and texts or thinkers are merely discussed alongside one another. While some theorists emphasise the distinction between cases within and outside the Western canon with the risk of reifying 'traditions' (Iqtidar 2016), others like Fred Dallmayr promote an unlikely normative goal of a fusion of the horizons of Western and non-Western approaches in which they can be brought together (Warren and Williams 2014).

These variations aside, comparative political theory provides important insights for the theorisation of political temporality because the examination of political ideas in different contexts – that is, not just key texts in isolation – helps to shed light on the ways in which understandings of the passage of time can vary considerably between them. Different traditions can have variable conceptions of past, present and future and their relationship with each other. Nonetheless, some of the methodological limitations of CPT can inhibit its application to contemporary political debates. In particular, following Jehangir (2019), the tendency of comparative political theorists to focus heavily on textual analysis or the work of specific thinkers can make it difficult to apply to specific issues or problems in context. That is, as it is often constructed (though not by necessity or definition), CPT does not necessarily lend itself well to grounded analysis and application in the present. This can reinforce the tendency of political theory to develop within the academy in the first instance before considering matters of application to contemporary political issues. What comparative methodologies in political theory *could* do is shed light on the different ways in which political concepts emerge and inform practice in different contexts. These comparisons can be between countries, regions and cultures or religions, for example, but they can also take place within a national context (Little 2018, 2020). When it comes to a concept like temporality, CPT can help to identify the different ways in which the passage of time is understood in different contexts and, hence, the capacity of alternative readings of temporality to inform more orthodox ways of thinking with the Western canon and vice versa.

Cases and Problems

One of the key methodological innovations of *Temporal Politics* is the attempt to not only outline but practise a form of political theory driven out by political issues and problems as they actually exist in particular contexts. As noted above, many approaches to political theory purport to be grounded in practical political problems or 'contextual' in one form or another (Goodin and Tilly 2006). However, in various ways, these traditions have been found somewhat deficient in developing theoretical methods which can appropriately respond to particular issues including their temporal dynamics. The first part of the book outlines a theory of political temporality that not only responds to but is also built up from grounded analysis of political problems in specific instances. 'Problem-based theory' is beginning to attract greater attention in contemporary political theory (Donahue and Ochoa Espejo 2016, Warren 2017) as an approach which moves beyond merely being grounded or contextual. All too often the outcomes from contextual analyses remain solely focused on informing academic debates rather than such debates refracting back towards the political issues from which they emanate. Potentially, problem-based theoretical analysis can contribute to this process of refraction, given that 'problems' are derived from the ideationally and materially contested nature of political issues which points to the difficulty of resolving them. Too often, then, even grounded or contextualised issues are discussed *in theoretical terms rather than as (potentially irresolvable) material problems*. Therefore, problem-based analysis may provide greater value in the development of more informed theoretical debates if it is accompanied by a problem-based methodological process of theorising whereby the questions that theory addresses, and the concepts it develops and deploys in so doing, reflect, respond to and feed back into the discussion of material political problems. The case in this book is that such a methodology necessitates an explicit engagement with the temporality of the phenomena that are the subjects of political analysis.

Having outlined the theory and method of *Temporal Politics* in the first part, in the second part of the book I engage with three such cases – although I contend that there could be many more – to demonstrate this problem-oriented methodology. Just as temporality itself is an inherently conflict-ridden domain, so too is the constitution of problems. Insofar as the definition of a problem requires issues, people and actions, which are mutually constitutive, it is unlikely that the terms on which a particular problem emerges will be understood universally or comprehensively. That is, different interpretations of a problem are likely features of this environment, and the elements which constitute it or form part of its context are dynamic and relational. A problem-oriented theory therefore needs to recognise and accommodate the disorderly and unpredictable set of elements that will become part of the equation when a particular issue is placed in a dynamic context. As political theorists, of course, we need to examine the ideational foundations and assumptions that relate to particular issues, but we also need to overlay this ideational framing of problems with an understanding of the material conditions which contribute to both the understanding of problems and the range of possible options that may be drawn upon to guide political action addressing them. This inherent dynamism is further complicated by placing these considerations within a temporal framing where the past as part of the causal root of a problem is contested, and the future environment as an outcome of political action is uncertain.

As we shall see in the second part of the book examining particular cases where political temporality is clearly relevant, problem-oriented political theory is envisaged here as a bottom-up approach insofar as it seeks to extrapolate ideas and develop concepts in light of the very real, material predicaments confronting political actors on the ground. It engages with problems on the foundational premise that those trying to act in response to a particular problem will have different and often competing interpretations of the problem's origins, its features, and the implications of specific actions to deal with it. There may also be contestation around the relevant parties to a problem, who is accountable for its emergence, and the responsibilities that subsequently apply to different groups of people. Therefore, problem-oriented political analysis engages with particular problems in specific settings with a view to framing theoretical questions, developing prospective answers to them, and then engaging in a process of assessing ways in which those answers can be applied to the issues in question. This differs from many forms of political theory which, insofar as they engage with material problems in their contexts at all, tend only to do so after the framing of questions and the development of prospective answers have taken place in the abstract.

All of this suggests that the methodology of problem-oriented theory goes beyond traditional approaches to methodological questions. The focus on problems in the first instance provides an alternative starting point – that is, one where the key questions to be investigated are framed in terms of the specific issues that are encountered on the ground rather than in a contextual vacuum. In keeping with the ecumenical approach to different variants of political theory outlined above, this suggests that problem-oriented analysis can supplement most of the major strands of political theorising. It implies that problem-based methodological tools are diverse and non-comprehensive and that there are multiple ways to conduct problem-based theory. However, the focus on problems requires some distinctive methodological assumptions as well as tools or strategies. One of these – in light of political temporality – is the method of tracking processes of change in the emergence and development of a problem in a specific context over the course of time and then mapping ways in which different courses of action on a problem might pan out in the future. The emphasis here is on the *process* of change over time.

The book employs three cases to demonstrate the interconnectedness of past, present and future. The first, focused on the *past*, examines the particular issue of the relationship between First Nations and the settler colonies that now override but fail to properly recognise Indigenous sovereignties. Chapter 4 depicts the way in which, in the Australian case in particular, those sovereignties are often rendered invisible or, when they are recognised, it comes in the shape of a pre-history to the modern settler colonial nation-state. As such, injustices that were perpetrated during the colonial encounter get treated as historical artefacts, rather than as ongoing, structuring factors of settler colonial societies. This fails to understand that the past penetrates the present and will continue to impact the future. In other words, the past can never be confined to the past in temporal political analysis and the category of the past is much longer for some members of the polity than others.

The second case focuses on the issue of borders and the movement of peoples, which is one of the major issues of the political *present*. The last decade has witnessed several crises in the displacement of peoples such as the exodus from Syria to neighbouring countries following the outbreak of war, and the plight of the Rohingya people in Myanmar resulting in issues such as the Andaman Sea crisis of 2015 and the current expulsion leading to mass camps in places like Cox's Bazar in Bangladesh. While these crises are notable for the way in which they enter present political discourse as an emergency, Chapter 5 demonstrates the ways in which these problems have a complex temporality characterised by disputed territories over the *longue durée*, often contested relationships within and between nation-states, and a great diversity of opinions about the future implications of increased movement of peoples around the world.

The third case is focused on issues concerned with the *future* as Chapter 6 considers contemporary debates on the problems or failings of democratic systems. The discussion will identify the ways in which these debates are usually framed around either 'declinist' narratives that focus on the inevitability of the reduced quality of democracy in the future as we move towards greater populism or the resurgence of authoritarianism on the one hand, or those which construe a romantic nostalgia for a lost 'golden age' of democracy on the other. This often manifests in melancholia for what we have lost rather than a focus on what might be attained in the future. This chapter adopts a different tack by identifying ways in which debates in democratic theory could be more future-oriented by suggesting not only different ways in which democracy could be organised in the future so as to reinvigorate democratic values and principles, but also a temporal methodology for pursuing these kinds of objectives. Here, the focus turns to the ways in which a temporal political methodology could imagine not only alternative futures but also a processive method for understanding their emergence.

The Normative Approach to Temporal Politics: A Processive Methodology

The theory of political temporality advanced here rests on a processive understanding of political action and change. That is, while change is occasionally spectacular, mostly it evolves as part of a long process of development. Even major world-altering events such as the outbreak of war or sudden violent attacks from states or sub-state organisations often need to be placed within a broader context of processive change over the course of time. Importantly, *Temporal Politics* does not envisage process in a teleological fashion – a process of progress – but rather as an ongoing, contingent and open-ended engagement of people and things that is constitutive of political life. Moreover, this is not to deny the importance of 'the event' in our conceptions of politics, but to highlight that even major events have a temporal context – a contested past, present and future which plays out differentially in human lived experience. Therefore, political change should be regarded as part of a complex network of actors and actions often pulling in different directions. Change does not take place in an orderly environment and it is not usually the case that a policy can bring about substantive change in isolation unless it is placed within a wider context of multiple initiatives related to a particular issue area. Moreover, political temporality implies that major change usually takes place over a period of time rather than being established instantaneously by the implementation of a particular policy or a singular piece of political action. More commonly, substantive change comes about through the implementation of a suite of policies or an amalgamation of activities in one or more fields that, taken together over the course of time, can be said to have brought about substantive change.

However, it is important to note that this conceptualisation of gradual political change is not processive in terms of an orderly progression from one policy to another or a pre-planned pathway from step to step towards a given end. Processes need not be considered as sequential and linear. While the eventual impact might be *incrementalist* in nature, a processive account does not refer to a kind of incrementalism where actors build change progressively step by step. Rather, in a disorderly environment, change is built through often conflicting policies where at times there is regression and backward steps from where we eventually end up. More importantly still, political temporality is of course focused on the future as well as the past. Therefore, we need to remember not only the path to where we find ourselves in a particular institutional or policy domain, but also the fact that we are in the middle of a dynamic change from where we are currently at. That is, our contemporary policy settings will be replaced by something else in the future and there is often a great degree of uncertainty about how that future politics will evolve. It is not clear to us in the present how our future policies and institutions will develop from those that we currently have, what impact other seemingly unrelated policies may have on a particular policy domain, or how to judge whether policies will be fit for purpose in the future (given the unpredictability of our future environment). In this sense, a processive approach to political change recognises path dependence in limiting political imagination, but it also leaves space for the unknown as new opportunities emerge in the future to do things differently. It could be said that this embodies an emergent epistemology whereby we know that a new but unpredictable present will offer us opportunities for action in the future.

What, then, does a *process* of problem-based theory look like? If it is clear that complex problems do not lend themselves easily to linear methodological strategies, how then can we strengthen established theoretical traditions and their methodological outlooks to better deal with political temporality? Rather than seeking to establish a completely new method for temporal analysis, I argue for a *process* of addressing problems that suggests a problem-oriented methodology can be adapted by existing theoretical approaches to add weight to their analyses of contemporary problems and increase their impact on debates in material politics.

The book contends that there are four main stages of problem-based theory which provide the key elements of a new processive methodology. First, political theorists need to investigate the nature of the problems they want to address rather than dealing with them at face value. Second, they need to understand these problems in a genealogical light to understand the ways in which a particular issue came to be construed as a specific kind of problem. Third, theorists need to formulate proposals to address problems in the specific contexts in which the problems have emerged, in recognition that, while there may be generalisable dimensions of their diagnoses and/or recommendations, the applicability of courses of action will vary from context to context. Fourth, they need to assess these proposals in light of other potential courses of action; this means a commitment to reviewing decisions and amending recommendations in light of changing contextual circumstances (Downey 2020). As such, this processive methodology for political theory is one that engages directly with practical politics. Moreover, given its relationship to temporality, *this processive theory and methodology suggests that once this method of analysis has been applied, then it can be reapplied in an ongoing cyclical fashion grappling all the time with path dependence and emergent epistemologies and ontologies.*

The processive methodology of temporal politics involves the identification of an issue that is widely construed to be a problem by a political collective (albeit in multiple conflicting ways). The process then involves the kind of genealogical analysis prevalent in Foucauldian problematisation and pragmatist approaches so that the problem is better understood in its historical context. In the next phase potential courses of action are developed in an attempt to address the problem, as is traditionally advocated within normative theories. Then, in the last step, the various potential outcomes of action-guiding theories will be reviewed in the light of engagement between political theorists and policy practitioners and the changing political context. While this is an imprecise science given the uncertainties of the future, it nonetheless would provide a richer canvas on which to make judgements and think creatively about political action than the current schism between theorists and practitioners. Too often this leaves political theorists with an answer searching for a suitable question and the risk of irrelevance, whilst policy actors may be left without sufficient ideational expertise to achieve desired outcomes. However, to be clear, the judgement of competing forms of political action will not be an objective or neutral practice; rather, it will be inflected by a range of ideological and value-laden characteristics. Therefore, judgement over the best course of action will vary according to the kinds of objectives that political practitioners want to achieve. The processive methodology of temporal politics does not provide definitive answers but a grounded approach which enables political action to facilitate the next stage of political debate focused on the cyclical review demanded by a new set of problems that emerge from any political action.

The processive account of temporal politics coupled with a problem-oriented method of political theorising eschews linearity and orderliness in our understanding of the move from political ideas to action and change. Instead, the method of temporal political analysis begins from a contested problem and moves through a series of steps that will enable a range of theoretically informed modes of political action on the problem to emerge. In this way, problem-based theory helps to structure, interpret and shape material political practices by guiding action upon them. Therefore, it is possible to interpret temporal politics as a methodological process imbued with particular normative principles, albeit not necessarily involving substantive political commitments to a particular kind of political order. Rather, the methodology invoked in temporal politics demonstrates a normative commitment to a particular way of viewing politics through the lens of contested notions of past, present and future in the way in which political theorists engage with political problems as they materialise in human experience.

2

Rethinking Time

Before going on to delineate the precise meaning of temporality and its implications for a temporal model of politics, it is important to discuss some of the important ways in which time has traditionally been understood in political philosophy. While the concept of time has been periodically prominent in the history of political philosophy, its implications for the practice of politics have not been evenly treated within this literature. In what follows I touch on the perspectives of many key thinkers on time including Aristotle, Augustine, Kant, Benjamin, Ricoeur and Bergson to demonstrate the ways in which the concept of time has been deployed in modern political discourse. It is far beyond the scope of the task in hand to deliver a systematic or comprehensive discussion of each of these thinkers. Nonetheless, by examining the ways in which they have articulated the meaning of time, it is possible to establish the foundations of contemporary understandings of political temporality.

At this juncture, it is important to note that the task in this book is to develop an explicitly political account of temporality. It strives to engage material politics and build theory based upon the challenges of dealing with practical problems. Therefore, while employing some of the resources that have emerged in debates on the nature of time in the history of political philosophy, my main concern is to ascertain their value in building a theory and method of temporal *politics* that can guide forms of action in material political settings. Methodologically, then, the issue is to understand how practical problems reveal a range of temporal concerns that inform contemporary politics rather than developing a theory of temporality in isolation from the material issues it might help to explain and address.

Temporal Debates in Political Philosophy

Many recent accounts of the concept of time in political philosophy draw inspiration from the perspectives advanced by Aristotle and Augustine. Aristotle's conception of time expressed in *Physics* is an important precursor to many of the theories that have been developed in more recent debates. Famously, he pondered the puzzles of the relationship between time and movement, in particular the distinction between 'nows' and the past and future. On the one hand Aristotle (2018: 82) suggests that the 'now is a continuity-maker for time . . . since it makes past and future time continuous'. On the other, however, he observes that 'time is both continuous by virtue of the now and divided at the now' (Aristotle 2018: 78). Therefore, Widder (2008) identifies the way in which Aristotle initially conceived of time in two differing ways.

First, Aristotle indicates that time is a *sequence* of 'nows'. On this understanding, the passage of time comprised a series of instances which sat in between the past and the future. However, this sequencing of time might not be entirely linear insofar as it contained overlaps between instances, ensuring that these 'nows' were not distinct from one another but formed a larger body of time where there was a 'continuity of things such that their extremities overlap and become a singular' (Widder 2008: 16). From this perspective, 'nows' could be understood as interruptions or punctuation marks in a much longer, overarching composition of time which amounted to more than the collection of these 'nows'. Knuuttila describes each Aristotelian 'now' as 'a duration-less boundary between the past and the future. Such "nows" or "instants" . . . are the limits between which the processes with definite temporal length take place' (2001: 110).

Knuuttila (2001: 110) further suggests that, for Aristotle, 'the parts of time are the past and the future and neither of them exists. They are divided by the present, which is the boundary between the past and the future (like a point which divides a line) and no part of time.' There is value here in considering the overlaps of time, especially given a multitude of temporal conceptions at work in any particular political issue. If temporal politics is constituted by multiple subjective accounts of the movement of time, then the constitution of 'now' and the extent to which it overlaps with conceptions of the past and understandings of the future work against objective understandings of these periods of time. However, a theory of temporal politics relinquishes the linear sequencing in this first Aristotelian sense of a series of 'nows'. For Knuuttila (2001: 111), in Aristotle's thought, 'Motion can be slower or faster, but this is not true of time. Time also has a fixed direction. The future changes into the past but not vice versa. The past and the present are necessary; the future is partially contingent.' The theory of temporal politics is a departure from this one-directional view of time, focusing instead on contingency as it impacts the past and the present as well as the future. Therefore, instead of a linear sequencing of the movement from past to present to future, temporal politics embraces the idea of overlapping 'nows', but combined with a view of complex, disjointed temporality with entire periods of elapsed time marginalised from overlapping concerns in the present and where the future overlaps with the past. This builds upon a notion of flow where overlaps include different conceptions of the past as well as relations between the past and the present, the present and the future, and the future and the past.

However, Widder (2008: 18) also points to a second dimension of the Aristotelian conception of time in which each 'now' is a 'real constitutive division' which becomes 'a kind of moving, living present that continually divides and synthesizes time's dimensions'. While the production of synthesis establishes an understanding of what constitutes each 'now', it also helps to divide each 'now' such that we are able to differentiate between them. This also gives rise to a sequential linearity in which the overlap evident in Aristotle's first depiction of time is relegated in order for us to articulate when change has taken place and distinguishes the 'now' from the past and future. For Widder (2008: 20-1) this provides 'foundational discontinuity' in which change is 'enframed by the discontinuous synthesis of time'. Widder's focus on discontinuity in Aristotle is an indicator of the former's leanings towards 'out of sync' and disruptive depictions of time in politics which pushes back against the flows and movement that characterise the theory and methodology of temporal politics developed here. While Widder is correct to point to the significance of these disjunctures rather than a smooth passage of historical time, he neglects the possibility of capturing these disruptions within a larger temporal movement. For Widder, the creation of a 'surface of sense' pulls us away from a disjunctured understanding of time. However, as we will see later in the chapter, this need not be the case; we can use both disjuncture and flow in understanding material politics and the political challenges of addressing specific problems. Indeed, the model of temporal politics invoked here attempts to bring disjuncture and flow together to understand the contingent and non-linear process of political change.

Partly this highlights the specifically political approach to temporality adopted in this book. Where Knuuttila's (2001) discussion of Aristotle focuses on an abstract metaphysical approach to time, the arguments about temporality presented here are much more phenomenological in nature.

This corresponds with Hoy's (2012) approach to temporality which does not dwell on the metaphysical issues around the reality of time but instead focuses on the lived experience of time. While the philosophical debates on Aristotle (and, later, Augustine) have often concentrated on the metaphysical debate, the highly subjective 'time of our lives' is the material issue at the heart of temporal politics (Hoy 2012: 41–2). In the spirit recommended by Paul Ricoeur (2008: 3–4), the methodology of temporal politics requires a 'phenomenology of time-consciousness' rather than a more abstract metaphysical approach to time. Therefore, while a philosophical discussion of this phenomenological approach may lead into extended discussions of Husserl and Heidegger (Hoy 2012), the point of *Temporal Politics* is to understand the nature of a politics of time that emanates from the aporetics of temporality, as Ricoeur describes the series of paradoxes that emanate from the earlier treatments of time in Aristotle and Augustine. Rather than seeking to resolve the issues that are described in Ricoeur's aporetics of temporality, this book is focused on the question of how we live with them. It understands these gaps and paradoxes as constitutive of temporal politics; they are the very fabric on which a temporal politics is played out. In other words, how do we understand the nature of politics given the gaps and paradoxes that prevail in differentiated and conflicting lived experiences of time?

It is at this point where Saint Augustine's philosophy of time becomes particularly relevant. As most commentators acknowledge, his discussion of time in *Confessions* articulates valuably with Aristotelian conceptions of time (Augustine 1963). Once again, just as there are different conceptions of time in Aristotelian thought, so too is there more than one perspective on time emerging from Augustine. Indeed, this emanates in part from Augustine's failure to provide a clear definition of time: 'if I am asked what it is and try to explain, I am baffled' (Augustine 1963: 264). At the outset of Book XI of *Confessions*, it is clear that the Lord does not exist within a human conception of time but is, instead, 'outside time in eternity' (Augustine 1963: 253). At once, then, there is a distinction between different types of time as experienced in human life and a broader cosmological notion that provides a much more significant backdrop to earthly perceptions. Augustine (1963: 254) states to his God that 'no moment of time passes except by your will'. Later, he states that

> time derives its length only from a great number of movements constantly following one another into the past, because they cannot all continue at once. But in eternity nothing moves into the past: all is present. Time, on the other hand, is never all present at once. The past is always

driven on by the future, the future always follows on the heels of the past, and both the past and the future have their beginning and their end in the eternal present. If only men's minds could be seized and held still! They would see how eternity, in which there is neither past nor future, determines both past and future time. (Augustine 1963: 262)

For Nightingale, 'contrary to what has often been maintained, Augustine does not offer any philosophical or theological definition of time in . . . the *Confessions*. [Rather] he tries to explain how we are aware of time and how its existence could be explained from the psychological point of view' (Nightingale 2011: 113). As a result, there is an imperative to distinguish between the different perspectives on time in Augustine. This has been framed in different ways – not least in the common idea of 'cosmological time' that informs many of the more metaphysical discussions of Augustine's thought on the nature of time (Bardon 2013). Of course, the primary concern for Augustine was theological: 'the birth of Christ is not simply another event in time, one more "instant" or "now". It is its fulcrum and permanent point of reference, binding every point of secular time, past and future, instantaneously, to its sacred origin and destination' (Skrimshire 2019: 74).

Nightingale's distinction between *psychic time* and *earthly time* is perhaps the most useful framing for a conception of temporal politics. She refers to 'two temporalities' in Augustine in which 'humans have bodies that are subject to earthly time and minds that distend in psychic time' (Nightingale 2011: 8–9). While psychic time refers to 'inner time consciousness', earthly time refers to the objective ageing of the body within a temporal space. The notion of psychic time is particularly valuable as it refers to the ways in which the mind is 'distended' through memory of the past and expectations for the future. This makes the human mind incapable of an objective 'grasp of the present' (Nightingale 2011: 8) because it is simultaneously embroiled in emotive responses to the past and the future. This emotive dimension highlights the fact that the mind may refer backward to memory in ways which might invoke multiple emotions such as fear and/or happiness, romantic nostalgia or melancholia, regret, trauma, forgiveness or love. Simultaneously, it may equally project to the future with emotions of fear (again), optimism, redemption, the likelihood of disappointment, negativity or the continuation of old enmities, to name but a few of the emotive dispositions which affect the psychic state of time. Augustine's perspective on psychic time therefore suggests that to 'acquire my sense of self, indeed to know myself as a self, I must engage in gathering, in rendering my past close to me. Without this closeness I could not fathom my current commitments and ends, patterns of conduct and feelings – in short, my existence as a whole' (Chowers 1999: 58).

Thus, Augustine enables us to imagine not only the distention of time that characterises the human experience of life, but also the ways in which it connects with sometimes smoothly connected and sometimes paradoxical understandings of time and temporal change amongst human beings. When this is multiplied by the interaction of many different human responses as well as the interactive nature of emotional responses, we can see that the foundation of temporal politics is a complex, contested and fluid environment. However, this earthly perception of time into past, present and future is illusory and exists only 'in the mind': the 'present of past things is the memory; the present of present things is direct perception; and the present of future things is expectation' (Augustine 1963: 269). The use of these terms in Augustine is in accordance with earthly usage, but he is clear that this perception of past, present and future is incorrect from a perspective of eternity.

The Augustinian conception of time is important to temporal politics because it also highlights the experiential basis of interpretations of the movement of time. In Nightingale's view, this highlights that humans understand and experience different temporalities through different social and cultural (and, I might add, political) lenses. This means that the experience of time is grounded in particular contexts and socio-cultural practices ensuring that interpretations of time's passage are always potentially politically contentious. Even in the case of monocultural communities, individual experiences of the passage of time will vary, thereby injecting sources of dispute into any issue with a temporal dimension:

> Augustine argues that the practice of the measurement of time is based on the fact that human consciousness functions by anticipating the future, remembering the past, and being aware of the present through perception. Through this distension of the soul (*distention animi*) we have in our memory images of things which were present and which we expect to be present. (Nightingale 2011: 112)

While Nightingale's book focuses on the 'different ways of measuring, ordering and experiencing time' (2011: 9) in relation to the cultural effects on the body of different temporalities, *Temporal Politics* focuses on the *political* implications of these diverse temporalities. It therefore concentrates on the ways in which the socio-cultural manifestations of this Augustinian conception of time have profound ramifications for the lived experience of material politics.

The foundational work of Aristotle and Augustine provides valuable insights for the conceptualisation of temporal politics, not least in emphasising the importance of phenomenological approaches to understanding how time manifests in the lived experience of politics. However, before returning to these phenomenological underpinnings in debates that have emerged over the last century and a half, it is important to identify how conceptions of time developed with the arrival of modernity. The next section focuses on the more secular accounts produced in modern societies which relinquished some of the theological assumptions in Augustinian approaches.

Modernity and Secularism

In his book *Diverging Time* (2002), David Carvounas draws on Reinhart Koselleck to develop the argument that the key change in understanding the shift from pre-modern to modern thinking on time was a gradual evolution in disposition towards the future. Where pre-modern thinking had focused on the past to teach about the present and understand trajectories into the future, the emerging modern account of temporality began to see the future as something that could be changed. It suggested that societies and peoples were not beholden to their past and could think about collective decisions that could forge a different kind of future. From a political perspective, this was a significant manoeuvre because it undermined the notion of a continuous temporality in which the future was preordained to a position whereby those punctuating 'nows' in the first Aristotelian sense were not just interjections into an established flow of time, but rather the points at which certain political actions could change the course of time. Thus, while actors could not escape their past in terms of the creation of the particular 'now' in which they found themselves, they were in a position to help change the direction in which a society was moving. For a temporal view of politics, this was a significant shift away from eschatology towards an account that placed political action and vectors of potential change in a more prominent position in deciding the course of time.

Carvounas tracks the emergence of modern thinking on time from Hobbes to Tocqueville as a way of explaining a fundamental shift in emphasis. Unshackled from the view that human societies were essentially constrained by their past, modern thinkers embraced the perspective that we are engaged in the production of the future. Potentially this was a much more optimistic stance that rejected the predestined future of pre-modern perspectives:

The arrival of modernity and the dislodging of future orientation from its reliance on past experiences, therefore, required a shift to occur in

the trend and substance of political philosophy. Subsequent and predominant trends in modern political philosophy valorized the future,
demoted the past and placed humans in the role of potential authors of
a yet-to-be-scripted future. (Carvounas 2002: 12)

Of course, this perspective, focused on the potential for progress, found
its most cogent expression in the work of Immanuel Kant. Kant's notion
of progress did not dispense with the past – after all, humans needed
somewhere to progress from as well as a progressive future – but it did
draw a clear separation between the past and the future and proffered that
the latter was not beholden to the former. Indeed, Carvounas argues that
we can see a somewhat linear conception of the past in Kant as a gradual
shift to the modern present, but a break occurs in his thinking whereby
the future is essentially constructed from thought and action in the
present.

For Eyal Chowers, however, this clear distinction between past and
future in Kantian thought is problematic insofar as it risks underplaying
the importance of memory in our conveyance of the future. He argues
that for a range of thinkers ranging from Bergson to Benjamin later in the
nineteenth and twentieth centuries, the past became important again to
highlight the ways in which the modernist project had lost sight of the
significance of memory. Chowers states 'this surge in the valorization of
memory at the turn of this century points to forgetfulness as the malaise
of the modern self' (Chowers 1999: 58). In other words, the shift from
the past to the future that accompanied modernist thought had *effectively*
dispensed with the past in the form of the importance of memory in our
interpretations of the present and the future. If pre-modern thought had
been too backward-oriented in its temporal provenance and ultimate teleology, modern thought made the opposite mistake in underplaying the past.
In both approaches, then, the inherent interconnection between the past,
present and future was lost. For key commentators at the turn of the twentieth century, a new perspective on time demanded 'criticism and rejection
of linear, progressive notions of temporality as well as to the articulation
of novel, semi-cyclical concepts of time that enabled conversation between
distant and qualitatively unique moments in history' (Chowers 1999: 58).
While for Kant the march of time had been progressive and linear (albeit
at a faster or slower pace at different times), the new approach emerging
in the early years of the twentieth century was as much about disappointment, decline and cyclical patterns as it was about progressive movement
from the past into the future. Even though Kant had couched his *political* arguments in terms of provisionality (Ellis 2005), there remained a

relentlessly progressive underpinning which was to come under a critical spotlight in the twentieth century in particular.

In both Christian and modernist thought, then, there are important shifts away from Aristotelian temporality. In the first manoeuvre, Christian thinkers like Augustine formulated a shift away from the series of 'nows' to a view of time as centred on one pivotal, all-encompassing reference point (Skrimshire 2019: 71). In the second manoeuvre, modernist political thinkers sought to unshackle the future from this singular anchorage, embracing the possibility of hope and progress towards a better secular future. However, in dispensing with the anchor of Christian theology, modernists also opened the possibility of alternative conceptions of time which did not entail such a view of progress. Indeed, whilst Enlightenment thinkers proffered a positive, rational vision of the future, they failed to account for a temporal view of politics in which the past with all its contestation and disagreements would continue to impinge on the present and future. In short, if a secular model of time meant dispensing with the certainties of Christian thought, then it also opened up the possibilities of fear, despair, hatred and disappointment amongst a range of emotive dimensions in politics which reflected contested pasts and uncertainty about the future. The loss of the anchor was not just a lifting of the burden of theological beliefs, it also opened time up to the actual experiences of human societies and the ways in which they transcended standard conceptions of past, present and future.

The negative dimensions of modern conceptions of temporal progress are prominent in Walter Benjamin's rejection of the progressive hope in modernity (Benjamin 2007). Where progressivism develops a narrative of time whereby, despite some of the horrors of the past and the fact that war, violence and bloodshed remain part of modernity, an inexorable movement towards rational betterment is under way, Benjamin suggests that this march of progress is built upon foundations of subjection and exploitation and what he terms 'catastrophe' (Chowers 1999: 66). Therefore, depictions of the past which paint a picture of movement away from such barbarism towards a more progressive, hopeful future are guilty in his eyes of forgetfulness, especially around the constitutive role that such events and processes play in the development of modern society. As Hoy makes clear, Benjamin is not suggesting that we literally 'forget' events of the past, but rather that they get rewritten into disjointed incidences in which their interconnections and their combined impact become unravelled. For Benjamin, this 'story of the progress of civilization is an ideological shambles that distorts and enervates the present. We are at the mercy of the storm, and the message is that our sense of ourselves as moving forward is an ideology that ignores the victims of history and the reality of barbarism' (Hoy 2012: 154). Similarly, Chowers (1999: 68) points to Benjamin's view that 'Humans can experience the immense richness of perspectives and truths that is potentially open for them, but moderns tend to flee from this experience, locking themselves within false, socially constructed certainties'.

The value of Benjamin's argument for temporal politics is that (often conflicting) memories of the past inflect our ways of knowing the present and our possibilities of imagining a future which is contingent and ambiguous. Rather than building on the progressive certainties of modernity, we need to comprehend the shakiness of our epistemological foundations and the unforeseen outcomes of actions in the present. As Hoy puts it in his discussion of Benjamin's engagement with Nietzsche:

> This vision of past enslavements is not the beginning of knowledge of how things could be better, although it does lead to the knowledge that universal, progressive history is untenable. There is, after all, no standpoint from which to observe the entirety of history. Universal history is written from outside or at the end of history. But we are always only ever in history, and its end is always in a future – one that will never come. (Hoy 2012: 156)

Engagement with Nietzsche also impels Nathan Widder's conception of 'time's dynamics' which he describes as 'embedding the past and memory in the present in such a way as to propel time into an always open and indeterminate future' (Widder 2008: 1). As we shall see in Chapter 7, this perspective draws us towards a Deleuzian interpretation of time which challenges 'mechanistic causality and determinism with understandings of time as a nonlinear synthesis occurring underneath the realm of consciousness' (Widder 2008: 10). But where Widder emphasises the disjunctured and out-of-sync nature of Deleuzian conceptions of time, there is an alternative but related perspective that concentrates on continuity, movement and flow. While both approaches are relevant to the notion of temporal politics (given it invokes flow as well as discontinuity), at this point in the book we turn to theories of continuity and movement, examining, in particular, the vital contribution of Henri Bergson.

Openness and Becoming: Bergson's Temporal Theory

Henri Bergson has become a central figure in contemporary debates about temporality, although he was a somewhat neglected figure in anglophone political philosophy in the second half of the twentieth century until greater attention was drawn to his ideas in the work of Gilles Deleuze (1991). Importantly, Bergson was also influential with some American pragmatists of his time, which gives an indication of the ways in which his thought can transcend categories within political theory. This pragmatic element of his thought is perhaps a product of Bergson's broader career, which was not only as a philosopher, but also as a diplomat and then working at the precursor to UNESCO. Given my contention that a temporal method of politics necessitates some engagement with the realm of human action, Bergson's turn to practical politics is certainly relevant. Like others discussed in the course of understanding the turn away from Kantian modernism, Bergson felt that Kant's philosophy was insufficiently 'open' to allow for proper understanding of temporal phenomena (Lefebvre 2013: 116). Bergsonian theory opens up a different conceptual arsenal for a model of temporal politics through the development of central ideas such as openness, duration, mobility and becoming.

The key temporal concept in Bergson's thought is duration. While precise definition of duration is somewhat elusive, it refers to the existence of multiple, interrelated elements within the same temporal domain – qualitative multiplicity – as opposed to quantitative multiplicity, which is more focused on the kinds of heterogeneity whereby different entities can co-exist, but are contrasted with one another. That is, in quantitative approaches, multiple elements are seen as distinct from one another, whereas in qualitative multiplicity, the connectedness of elements is the key factor such that distinction between them is much more difficult. As such, Bergson's approach is infused with relationality and an affective dimension. I will delve into Bergson's imagery to explain this in due course, but in more recent scholarly literature we can see some similar sentiments, albeit not always discussed in terms of Bergson himself. For example, the work of Michael Freeden (1996) on political ideology demonstrates the ways in which political concepts can be seen as ambiguous, indeterminate, inconclusive and related to one another. Similar approaches have been deployed to highlight the existence of multiple emotions, related to one another rather than clearly distinguishable, which mark societies moving out of deep political conflict (Little 2017). This notion of indeterminacy correlates with Bergson's philosophy of time which emphasises relationality and is regarded as an affirmation of openness (Lefebvre and White 2012).

Colebrook (2012: 77) echoes these sentiments on Bergson's approach when she states that 'time is composed of distinct living durations . . . and the whole is just this highly complex, highly differentiated, constantly altering, constantly creative, openness'. Similarly, she contends that the Bergsonian critique of 'mechanical chronological time' sees 'no such thing as a distinct part, sufficient and complete unto itself'. Rather, we have 'a life of fluid and dynamic interrelatedness' where everything 'exists in relation; relations are dynamic and have no ground or systemic imperative outside the ongoing creativity of living and individuating action' (Colebrook 2012: 77). This methodological disposition towards openness complements the approach of temporal politics for it rejects the over-determination and finality in which the main issues and problems in politics tend to be disclosed.

Bergson's methodology lends itself to a creative politics that can harness the indeterminacy and ambiguity which is actually characteristic of many contemporary debates and challenges, as we shall see in Part Two of this book. Importantly, Ochoa Espejo (2012: 159) contends that the Bergsonian approach in *The Two Sources of Morality and Religion* is one designed as a form of 'relief from false problems'. That is, specific issues and problems may exist in the world but their component parts – be they people, policies or institutions – and, in particular, the ways in which they interrelate are not fixed or determined. On the contrary, the significance of their interrelationality is that these intersections potentially become spaces for creativity and enterprise. In this vein, the existence of indeterminacy and ambiguity is something that might be embraced rather than ignored or targeted for better analytical precision. Following Ochoa Espejo, Power (2012: 174) contends that, for Bergson, 'the best way to refute a theory is to present an alternative hypothesis that cleaves closer to the facts under consideration or, more radically, to demonstrate that, in view of these facts, the problems that one's rival seeks to solve are entirely false'.

This approach correlates with what we might see as a pragmatic or 'realist' interpretation of Bergson's theory and method. In a way, it reflects a line of thought that would later be followed by contemporary theorists seeking to marry together elements of Foucauldian thought, realism and pragmatism (Little 2012, 2015c, Koopman 2011b). Or, as Carl Power (2012: 177) suggests, Bergson may be connected to a tradition of thought in which the human agent should be conceived as 'a being who is immediately engaged in the world and whose understanding of self and other is first and foremost expressed in practice . . . According to Bergson, the basic error of traditional moral theory is intellectualism: our lived reality is confused with the means by which we symbolize it.' For Power, this locates Bergson closer to the outlook of a range of post-structuralist theorists – contemporary and historical – who tend to privilege ethics over political morality with the former considered as more of an open form of

morality and the latter as transcendentally closed. This theoretical perspective regards 'our explicit motives and reasons for action [as] secondary
in relation to the play of largely unconscious forces that constitute us as
living beings. This involves making the body, rather than consciousness,
the model of practical philosophy.' As a result, rather than 'measuring
life against moral values that are supposed to stand over and above it,
he [Bergson] measures the value for life of different kinds of morality'
(Power 2012: 186).

This rejection of closed transcendental morality is where the practical
element of Bergson's thought comes into the equation of temporal politics.
A focus on lived experience as the central object of analysis inevitably
leads to a perspective centred on subjectivity and multiple practical considerations. For Bergson, these precede and indeed are more significant
than the attempts of philosophers to rationalise them post hoc. Power
(2012: 187) states that

> the superiority of the open over the closed is lived before it is rep-
> resented, felt before it is explicitly thought. Our moral and political
> decisions outstrip the reasons we give ourselves for making them. The
> best a philosopher can do is to invent concepts that clarify the choices
> we face, outlining the critical differences at stake.

This crucial methodological intervention is what clarifies the connection
between Bergsonian theory and the pragmatist tradition. The task for
theorists is not merely to moralise about the right course of action in
abstract analogies, nor is it to criticise and deconstruct without consideration of the ways in which lived experiences translate into fields of practical action. Following pragmatist intuitions derived in part from Bergson's
non-scholarly life (insofar as it can be separated from the scholarly) and
his explicit engagement with thinkers such as William James (James 1910,
but see also Allen 2013), the key to openness as a methodological stand-
point is to enable creativity of action when faced with political problems
and challenges. This approach can be highly cognisant of the divergences
that political problems engender: the tendency towards disjuncture, 'us'
and 'them', and the friend-enemy distinction. As a factual recognition of
the actuality of the play of politics, on the surface this is frequently the
case. However, the pragmatist inclination is always to work in the spaces in
between, the grey zone where creative opportunities lurk. Therefore, for
Bergson, it is vital not to take such divergences at face value, but instead to
recognise that 'to stop at division would wrongly imply that a purely open
or closed phenomenon exists. It does not' (Lefebvre 2012: 203).

These spaces for creativity are a part of the political condition for our model of temporal politics as well as Bergsonian methodology. This condition points to the radical incompletion of politics, be that in the space of policy design and implementation, programmes for radical social and political change, or in insurrection or revolutionary upheavals. The processive dimension of politics that will be outlined in the final chapter is one in which political action and political failure are intrinsically connected (Little 2012). Again, this correlates with Bergson's understanding of the political as a space in which 'every leap forward is followed by a fall; every revolution is betrayed to some extent by the social and political order meant to preserve its achievements; every emancipatory ideal can also serve as an instrument of oppression' (Power 2012: 190). The Bergsonian method suggests that, if all political entities are composed of misaligned 'open and closed tendencies', then the possibility of failure is immanent to all political phenomena due to the existence of 'its actual mixed reality' (Lefebvre 2012: 202).

This returns us to the concept of duration and the implications of Bergson's method for the representation of time in history. As noted by many scholars, Bergson employs rich imagery in describing duration as 'qualitative' rather than 'quantitative' multiplicity. According to Lawlor (2010), in *Time and Free Will*, Bergson points to quantitative multiplicity as a situation where the composite elements of a whole in a specific space are distinct from one another and can be enumerated:

> When we look at a flock of sheep, what we notice is that they all look alike. Thus a quantitative multiplicity is always homogeneous. But also we notice that we can enumerate the sheep, despite their homogeneity. We are able to enumerate them because each sheep is spatially separated from or juxtaposed to the others; in other words, each occupies a discernible spatial location. Therefore, quantitative multiplicities are homogeneous and spatial. (Lawlor 2010: 36)

In conceptualising duration, Bergson distinguishes this kind of multiplicity from a qualitative form which is more temporal. In quantitative multiplicity we must be able to separate and juxtapose the entities within, whereas qualitative multiplicity is where several different elements co-exist and overlap in a way that makes the components parts indistinguishable, especially as they exist in relationship with one another. This is particularly the case with the co-existence of several states of mind at once, each contributing something to each other and co-constituting what Bergson calls 'the duration'. In such qualitative multiplicities, then, the multiple factors that co-exist cannot be completely isolated from one another; indeed, their relationships with each other are part of the fabric of their existence.

Following this description, think back to the discussion of emotions in politics earlier in this section where we discussed the simultaneity of fear, hope and disappointment in post-conflict societies. The point was not just that these emotions are temporally coincidental, but that their relationship is what characterises the societies of which they are a part and their relationships help to constitute the society in which they exist. In this example, fear and hope intersect with one another such that neither can exist without the other: the positive futurity of hope is fundamentally connected to fear of a reversion to past violence. At the same time, the fear based on lived experiences of violence impels hope based not so much on a prediction of better times in the future, but rather on a turning away from the infinite regress that can only be engendered through the pursuit of something better. Simultaneously, however, both fear and hope are interrelated with disappointment given the understanding of inevitability of failure due to the radical incompletion referred to above. If we understand this scenario as one of a complex qualitative multiplicity, then these emotions cannot be identified in completion like a single sheep amongst a flock (to use Bergson's imagery). Rather the relationship between these emotions is what makes the heterogeneity of these responses qualitatively multiple – they co-exist and relate to one another in ways that mean they cannot be juxtaposed. As mentioned in Chapter 1, not only are fear and hope not opposites, they are involved in an indistinct relationship with one another (see Huber 2017 for a Kantian take on these issues).

While Bergson's concept of duration has been described as 'inexpressible', it is perhaps useful to turn to his own technique of description using rich analogies to explain the form of continuity and inter-penetration which comprises duration. One of the primary images Bergson uses is that of a tape being drawn between two spools, one of which is releasing the tape and becoming smaller, while the other winds in the tape and becomes larger. In this analogy the past is the spool which becomes larger as the tape moves and the space between the spools is the present (Barker 2012: 59). This emphasises continuity and, as many scholars have noted, there is a preservation of the past – indeed, an accumulation of the past – without it being juxtaposed with the present or the future. They are interdependent and co-constitute our world.

The significance of this analogy cannot be underplayed for it identifies explicitly the continuity of the past in the present. It makes clear that 'history is not . . . a fully elapsed duration . . . [with] its outcome . . .

stripped of any element of chance' (Jankélévitch 2012: 223). Rather, for Bergson, we can only genuinely understand the notion of duration – including its futurity as well as its past – if we introduce the element of unpredictability. Jankélévitch describes this as 'the untamed and intractable element, disturbing and exciting, the random element, in a word, that constitutes the risk of temporal being. When we do not know what tomorrow will bring, it is time to tremble and the heart beats fast' (2012: 223). Indeed, Jankélévitch points to the way in which the understanding of duration in Bergson's own work evolves from the past-focused interpretation of *Time and Free Will* in which the major point is the continuity of the past in the present and its imposition upon futurity through the accumulation of the past, to a focus on the future and becoming in his later works:

> Is not becoming, which brings about the future, a continual 'advent'? Is not becoming to become something else by a constant process of alteration? The focus of becoming—le devenir— is no longer memory—le souvenir—but the future—l'avenir. The 'survenir'— what comes up— definitively supplants the 'subvenir'—what has gone under the bridge. Becoming rediscovers its true vocation, whose name is futurition or innovation. A vocation is something we feel called by, whereas tradition is something we feel the pressure of. (Jankélévitch 2012: 238)

What is vital to remember in this conception of the future, however, is that it is not to be confused with earlier Enlightenment conceptions of progress. While change is inevitable in any future-oriented perspective, this does not mean that we should confuse Bergson's concern for the future with a progressive outlook. On the contrary, and akin to later Foucauldian approaches, Bergson is keen to point to the ways in which our understanding of problems establishes the framing around which we understand possible actions to deal with them. However, if problems were reconstituted in other ways, a different set of possible answers might emerge. Therefore, for Bergson, this highlights 'the importance of the formulation of problems in philosophy and once again he claims that because solutions are always presupposed by the very statement of the problem, the correct formulation of a problem is not just a matter of good methodology but absolutely decisive' (Marrati 2012: 306). This contrasts with many contemporary understandings of realism whereby it is supposed that scholars can simply read off from the facts what the problem is to be addressed (Little 2015c). From a Foucauldian perspective, however, it is more important to challenge the constitution of the real rather than accepting the actuality as it is depicted by so-called realists. The contestability of the real is a significant point of intersection between this perspective and Bergson:

> The category of the possible represents, in his opinion, the very para-digm of a poorly posed problem and the confusions that stem from it. In the history of philosophy, just as in everyday language, we assume that the category of the possible contains something less than that of the real or, in other words, we assume that a possibility is necessarily lesser than its real counterpart. For Bergson, however, the exact oppo-site is true: it is the possible that contains more than the real, and the question is to understand where this error comes from and what other false ideas stem from this poorly posed problem. (Marrati 2012: 306)

What we see then in Bergson's discussion of the possible is an indication of the centrality of the movement of time. Movement is not definitively positive or negative, but it is nevertheless an ineluctable part of the con-cept of duration and is vital for our understanding of temporal politics. This challenges philosophy's inability 'to give conceptual determination to existence . . . [as] a direct consequence of its desire to grasp what is eternal in time, to understand movement only as the realization of a pre-existing possibility outside of time' (Marrati 2012: 308). This condition is reflected in the limitations of diachronic philosophical analysis to move from understandings of 'past-then' and now, or now and 'future-then', to comprehend the complexity of movement in between these two temporal points. The point of temporal politics is to unsettle these distinctions. In Bergsonian analysis, it is the movement that is significant, not least because the static depiction of then or now is illusory, due to the radically incomplete nature of the status of a 'then' or a 'now'. Marrati summarises this element of duration thus:

> Time can no longer be thought of as the external framework in which events unfold but must instead be conceived as a truly active force: time is active in and of itself. When Bergson claims, 'if [time] does noth-ing, it is nothing,' he appeals to what could be described as a properly ontological pragmatism . . . The being of time is nothing apart from its specifically active power. The criticism of the category of the pos-sible is thus a necessary consequence of a theory of duration. (Marrati 2012: 309)

The final section of this chapter examines how the Bergsonian concept of duration lends itself to the notion of 'becoming' which has emerged as a significant concept in contemporary political theory (Connolly 2011, Braidotti 2013). In so doing, it will explain how a thoroughgoing theory of temporal politics necessitates thinking about the implications of becoming, insofar as it invokes a methodology that analyses the unknown, the incomplete and the unforeseen. The key point here will be to explain the connection between the concept of becoming and the practice of politics and political action.

Political Action and Becoming: A Practical Theory of the Possible?

In *The Two Sources of Morality and Religion* (1977), Bergson articulates a theory of movement and multiplicity which provided the inspiration for later work on becoming such as that of Deleuze and Guattari (discussed in Chapter 7). The key notion in this world of becoming is that of the political environment being characterised by fluidity and motion in time-space and a logic of multiplicities. This gives rise to the question of what such a fluid and dynamic environment means for political action. How do we act in such uncertain circumstances where we cannot be sure of the impact of our actions?

By way of a response to these questions Bergson (1977) outlines two different trajectories of open and closed societies. The closed society is a static community that does not accommodate change and diversity. These societies are depicted as self-centred, imprisoned within their own enclosures. The modern state is a clear expression of these kinds of communities, which are primarily concerned with self-preservation. Bergson uses the concept of the closed society to provide a criticism of *Utopia*, in which a bounded community was imagined as an ideal type of organisation. Closed societies are governed by what Roberto Esposito calls the 'immunitary paradigm': a negative protection of the self that excludes difference, relationality and a life with the other, with the stranger (Esposito 2012). These communities draw strict boundaries between inside and outside, self and other, and culture and nature. The members of the closed society, writes Bergson (1977: 266), 'hold together, caring nothing for the rest of humanity, on the alert for attack or defence, bound, in fact, to a perpetual alert readiness for a battle'.

The open society, in contrast, broadens morality well beyond the frontiers of the static system of closed communities. The open society is not determined by the boundaries of race, ethnicity, gender or even necessarily the human species. It is dynamic; it celebrates diversity and generosity.

Bergson insists that the difference between open and closed societies is not in degree, but in kind. The open society is not the opposite image of the closed community and the aim is not to expand simply the boundaries of altruism to embrace the entirety of humanity. Bergson (1977: 38) suggests that the open society is not simply the transition from 'love of country' to 'love of mankind': 'its form is not dependent on its content.' He resists the idea that we can love others in the same way we love our own kind. Bergson never seeks to replace one order with another. Rather, his interest is in the 'constitutional logic of multiplicities', the movement, the indeterminacy and plurality (Deleuze 1991: 117). Perhaps unlike other philosophers of the open society (for example, Popper 2020), Bergson's political account does not read the open society as an end, but more as a representation of a reality whereby society is in a mode of constant transformation and becoming. According to Deleuze and Guattari (1994), becoming amounts to a collective transformation of affected bodies in their encounters with one another. The process of becoming involves the transformation of the self and 'rest[s] on a nonunitary, multilayered, dynamic subject attached to multiple communities' (Braidotti 2011: 35).

As noted earlier, in Bergson's thought no society can be simply deter-mined to be 'open' or 'closed'. Instead, all societies involve a mixture of open and closed features and all are in a process of becoming where they may change in some ways that may facilitate openness and others which may involve closure. There is no singular mode of transformation from open to closed or vice versa. Indeed, it would be very difficult to assess degrees of openness or closure given the relational ontology underpin-ning this notion of becoming. Thus, the notion of 'qualitative multiplicity' implies that rather than things existing in heterogeneous juxtaposition to one another, they are in fact all in a process of overlapping relationality and co-existence whereby each element is in a process of becoming (as is each relationship between them). This is a constant process which has no finality; there is no teleological endpoint to which this inevitable move-ment is directed. According to Marrati:

the very way Bergson poses the problem of the development—the 'becoming'—of human societies depends upon his non-finalistic con-ception of time . . . But, writing at one of the darkest moments in his-tory, Bergson is also concerned with the future of these societies. What about change and newness in human history? What can we expect, or learn, from this history? Bergson's task is made even harder by the fact that he cannot rely on either a purely rationalist conception or any form of historicism. He cannot adopt either a Kantian standpoint or a Hegelian one: on his account, human history, that is, the development of societies and moral and religious forms, is caught up in the evolutionary movement of life and shares its complete lack of teleology. (Marrati 2012: 309)

The remaining question in establishing the Bergsonian foundations of the theory and method of temporal politics is to understand the implications of these insights for how we consider political action and the pursuit of specific ends in politics. There are no easy answers here, except that Bergson leaves open many possibilities as to how political actors might pursue their objectives. Not the least of these opportunities is space for creative thought and action, unbeholden to established ideologies or institutional constraints. Insofar as Bergson leaves open the potential for different norms and conceptual foundations as well as the possibility for institutional change, his model is one that leaves open many pathways for political development and change.

The absence of established teleologies informing different choices, replaced by a genuine openness to the impacts of our actions and choices, leaves open multiple policy options and institutional foundations. It also reflects an understanding that the intended impacts of actions or policy choices are not always those that transpire in a complex socio-political environment. When informed by a temporal perspective, it is never clear and agreed as to when we should judge the impact of those choices and actions, impacted as they will be by intervening factors between action and impact. This is the core of a politics of becoming. In the *longue durée*, some things may be 'successful' that were earlier deemed unsuccessful, and vice versa. Moreover, at any point in time the success or failure of particular actions will be a matter of dispute – not only is teleology unsustainable, but an agreed point of adjudication is equally unobtainable. Rather than treating this as a point of inertia, Bergsonian thought encourages us to embrace this uncertainty as an opportunity for creativity and a recognition of the potential of political action. Without providing a defined pathway, this is an invitation to pursue creative initiatives for political change. We will return to this approach in Chapter 7 when we investigate the *process* of political change and the ways in which a temporal political methodology might contribute to changing our perceptions of how politics is conducted.

3

Time and Temporality

Having outlined the philosophical foundations of debates on time in politics, in this chapter I will examine the implications of these ideas in contemporary social scientific research especially as they are applied to political practices and institutions. Implicit in this analysis will be a focus on not only objective notions of the passage of time – 'clock time' – but also, more significantly, the lived experience of time in the form of subjective understandings of pace, tempo and duration. This is a key distinction between 'time' as clock or objective time and 'temporality' which is focused on how time 'manifests itself in human existence' (Hoy 2012: viii). Given the limitations of political analyses that are often enslaved to objectivist framings of political time, we require a more thorough engagement with debates on time and temporality across the social sciences rather than narrowing the focus to political philosophy alone to understand the full import of this distinction. As Adam makes clear, the social scientific analysis of time is much more extensive than the discussion of the linear progression of life. She states that a concern with time involves a range of allied issues such as 'rhythm with variation, a dynamic structure of framing, timing, synchronization, duration, sequence, tempo and intensity' (Adam 1995: 17).

These framings are central to the idea of temporal politics given that it is an approach that focuses on the passage of time and the various disagreements that this mobility engenders in politics. As opposed to political theories which provide analysis as a snapshot, temporality concentrates on the pace and tempo of change and is centred on *the movement of time*. As Pierson (2000: 72) reminds us, we need to move from 'snapshots to moving pictures. Placing politics in time – systematically situating particular moments (including the present) in a temporal sequence of events and processes – can greatly enrich our understanding of complex social dynamics.' While the ensuing discussion will touch on many of the issues that Pierson raises – sequencing, causality, duration – it does so to identify the ways in which inherent dispute about such matters is an ineliminable characteristic of politics, rather than a mere explanatory factor which needs to be considered when constructing social scientific analyses. *Political* temporality refers to the fact that complex concepts of time give rise to contestation and that almost all instances of political disagreement involve a temporal dimension. Therefore, the concept of political temporality is concerned with the ways in which the complex concept of time manifests in political issues and, in particular, its analytical focus is the nature of temporal disagreement in political debate.

In order to explain this temporal dimension of politics, it is necessary to trace some of the conceptualisations of time that have taken place in political science before comparing them with other forms of sociological and historical analysis. The task here is to augment traditional political analyses and differentiate them from approaches with a less distinctly political flavour. On the one hand, this helps to explain what political science can learn from other disciplines in its construction of theories of time, while, on the other, it provides an opportunity to highlight what is specifically *political* about temporality. From this more socio-historical foundation of political temporality, it is possible to consider how a political conception of temporality relates to the different foci of other disciplines, such as theories of spatiality in political geography and the varying and much more subjective understandings of time and temporality that emerge from cultural studies and anthropology, for example. Having outlined a distinctively *political* model of temporality (though informed by many other disciplines), we are then in a position to articulate what temporal analysis can provide us with in understanding contemporary political debates.

Time in Political Science

Critics of political science from other disciplines have been quick to point to its shortcomings when it comes to understanding the importance of temporality and temporal change (Hassan and Purser 2007). In the first chapter, I indicated some sympathy with this view. However, it would be incorrect to suggest that political science has been entirely silent on time and temporality, although perhaps it has been slow to distinguish between them as analytical categories. Some of the most significant discussions of time (albeit with a limited conception of temporality) in political science come from the literature on public administration and the evolution of the state such as historical institutionalism (HI) (Pierson 2000, 2004) and the American Political Development (APD) approach which has become prominent in recent years (Orren and Skowronek 2004, Sheingate 2014).

Let us first turn to the HI and APD traditions to examine the ways in which they understand time in their depictions of the historical evolution of political institutions and the emergence of specific formations of the state. In these approaches, time is considered as pivotal to understanding the emergence and evolution of particular institutions and their practices. These approaches emphasise the complicated nature of the movement of time, the resilience of historical institutions, events and processes, and the evolutionary nature of political action and change. Time is important in HI and APD approaches because their focus on institutional evolution recognises that different temporal processes are at work in different institutional developments. Therefore, the temporal development of the state is not uniform but involves multiple processes of evolution and different temporal sequences at work simultaneously. Sometimes these processes will develop on different or even contradictory tracks, but at other times they will overlap and intersect with one another. This process is one that is described as 'intercurrence' in the APD literature (Orren and Skowronek 1996). It highlights the complex temporal processes involved in the development of the state and its various institutions and the multiple pressures that are simultaneously at work in any one temporal phase.

Two significant challenges for HI and APD approaches have particular resonance for the theory of political temporality. First, some critics have suggested that they are too focused on the development of institutional structures without sufficient understanding of the subjective nature of politics and the importance of individual and collective actors in the production and reproduction of institutional structures. Second, others have pointed to the difficulty of explaining changes in political structures through an approach that is so focused on the means of historical institutional reproduction. These criticisms are important for theories of political temporality because they highlight the importance of subjective experiences and understandings of time in guiding political action and the significance of political actors in acting creatively to bring about political change in moments where particular opportunities for change arrive.

In the literature, these are known as 'critical junctures' where enterprising political actors – both collective and individual – have greater opportunities for enacting forms of political change than would normally be the case. However, there are many countervailing forces, not least because not all members of a particular political community or collective are necessarily operating in the same temporal register at a given time. In fact, what constitutes a critical juncture may only be identified retrospectively as it is difficult for political actors to make sense of their possible courses of action in the moment, in an environment characterised by differing and sometimes conflicting interpretations of the constitution of the present. What will be a moment of opportunity for change for some actors will be a moment of threat demanding consolidation for others. This suggests that analysts of administrative politics need to devote more attention to subjective understandings of temporality rather than the mere passage of time. It also indicates that they may underestimate the centrality of conflicts over time given the existence of multiple subjective and objective conceptions of time at work in any given period. It is ironic that the political science discipline, especially the literature derived from public administration, underplays the expressly *political* dimension of temporality – that is, the political implications of contestation about the passage of time – when it addresses political change over the course of time.

Let us first look at historical institutionalism to understand the ways in which political scientists have discussed time in relation to the development of political institutions. The historical institutionalist approach is most commonly associated with Paul Pierson (2004), who explains the role of path dependence in the development of political institutions such that the history of institutional development is often sedimented in the composition of the previous institutional architecture. This is founded upon the tendency of particular institutions to value particular positive feedback loops whereupon there is greater receptiveness to information and processes that reinforce the existing modes of operating in a particular institution. Therefore institutions may preference positive feedback over ideas and practices which challenge the established methods of the institutional order. Positive feedback mechanisms ensure that historical developments remain influential in the present.

In emphasising the importance of different stages in sequential development, Pierson states that

> In path dependent processes, however, positive feedback means that history is 'remembered.' These processes can be highly influenced by relatively modest perturbations at early stages. 'Small' events early on may have a big impact, while 'large' events at later stages may be less consequential. To put this another way, outcomes of early events or processes in the sequence are amplified, while later events or processes are dampened. Thus, when a particular event in a sequence occurs will make a big difference. In politics, the crucial implication of path dependence arguments is that early stages in a sequence can place particular aspects of political systems onto distinct tracks, which are then reinforced through time. (Pierson 2000: 75)

Pierson makes the point that the beginning of a sequence may be much more open to multiple courses of action than later stages. This is because alternative courses of political action to those initially chosen can be closed off the further we progress down a particular pathway. What may have been possible at the beginning of a sequence reduces in probability the further we go in pursuing an alternative action. However, this insight generates methodological issues because it is often impossible to identify when a sequence begins. If we do not know when sequences begin, political actors cannot be placed at the beginning of a sequence given the pre-existing conditions in which they have to operate. Political actors, then, must intervene in processes which – perhaps unbeknownst to them – are always already under way.

Ultimately, then, subjects engaging in political action intervene in time-lines with established (though contested) histories and unknown endpoints (futures). Wherever political subjects start their analyses and whatever factors they take to be pivotal in the development of a particular political problem, they are inevitably intervening in an already established (though disputable) mesh of timelines. Given the disagreement inherent in these processes, it is difficult to identify definitive sequencing or causal trajectories. A simple example – taken up in more detail in the next chapter – is the case of a colonial state and how it conceives of historical transgressions against particular Indigenous peoples. While it might seem straightforward to begin discussion with the moment of invasion when dispossession initially took place within a particular territory, political analysts also need to recognise that any specific conquest took place within a broader colonial project with clear links to the colonial projects of other empires. Moreover, while there may be particular tactics that were applied in specific territories due to key contextual factors, the fact is that there was also much lesson-learning (through success or failure) between contexts too. Finally, in this example, there is a tendency in countries that have experienced colonialism for colonist-derived history to start at the moment of the historical encounter, rather than the much longer timescales which characterise Indigenous knowledges of history. In this example, sequencing and causality are highly contested entities and the beginning and end of particular institutional timelines are also disputable.

For political scientists, however, the process of addressing particular issues through the development of policies always necessitates intervening in a context with a history. As the example above suggests, it may well be incumbent on analysts to attempt to develop more historically informed perspectives on the issues they address. However, political scientists would do well to accept the epistemological limitations that intervention in extant trajectories entails and understand the incomplete nature of the facts and knowledges that they address. Put simply, political analysis, theory and action require a starting point, but we need to acknowledge the epistemological limitations that such starting points engender. Political scientists should recognise that, wherever they start from, there is a historical trajectory towards that point and often competing concurrent narratives about how a particular society reached the stage at which political actors intervene.

In politics, simple tales of causality should be resisted given the methodological impossibility of starting at the beginning. To be clear, political scientists need to make choices about where they start their time-lines and justify them, but they should do so whilst retaining humility about the epistemological limitations such choices place on our analyses. Furthermore, they need to resist the 'teleological fallacy' (Sewell 1996) which has characterised elements of historical sociology as if the trajectory into the future is settled and there is limited meaningful agential intervention that can redirect the course of social change from where we are now to where we will end up. Similarly, also from the perspective of historical sociology, Tilly (1988: 710) contends that

> past social relations and their residues – material, ideological, and otherwise – constrain present social relations, and consequently their residues as well . . . Such processes produce connectedness within time and space that goes beyond simple temporal and spatial autocorrelation; every existing structure stands in the place of many theoretically possible alternative structures, and its very existence affects the probabilities that the alternatives will ever come into being. In short, social processes are path-dependent. That is why history matters.

What does this mean for the arguments employed by historical institutionalists? Certainly, Pierson recognises that there may be multiple points of entry into a particular debate, but he does still use the notion of sequences in understanding the development of institutions in terms that imply a specific beginning to a particular sequence. For example, he recognises that while sequences may be *more* open at the outset than further along the sequential process, they are never completely open when all possible options for dealing with an issue are viable options:

> Path dependent arguments thus suggest that when sequences involve self-reinforcing dynamics, we can expect periods of relative (but not

total) openness, followed by periods of relative (but not total or permanent) stability. More precisely, path dependent processes involve three
distinct phases – three stages in a temporal sequence: (1) the initial
'critical' juncture, when events trigger movement toward a particular
'path' or trajectory out of two or more possible ones; (2) the period of
reproduction, in which positive feedback reinforces the trajectory ini-
tiated in phase one; and (3) the end of the path, in which new events
dislodge a long-lasting equilibrium. (Pierson 2000: 76)

The notion of sequences outlined here is important in terms of understanding the theory of historical institutionalism but lacks a sufficiently
contingent understanding of temporal dynamics for the theory of temporal
politics developed in this book. While the notion of phases outlined by
Pierson is valuable, it is rare that political development occurs on such a
linear trajectory, and even if it did, that trajectory would still be highly
contested by different political actors.

While phase one of Pierson's temporal sequence, the critical juncture,
may be clearly identifiable, quite often critical junctures will be contested
in the present. Indeed, often critical junctures may only be identifiable in
retrospect. Phase two is less controversial insofar as the reproduction of
institutions through practices and ideas that create positive feedback for
the institution are readily identifiable. However, we also need to recognise
that larger institutional entities such as the state involve multiple institutional formations which are often in conflict with one another or which
are working along different path dependencies. This suggests that the
notion of equilibrium in any institutional configuration is contestable at
any particular point in time. Phase three is problematic because it implies
a cleaner break between particular institutions or institutional logics than
is typically the case in practice. Again, breaks between different institutional logics *may* be identifiable in retrospect but they are much harder
to delineate in the present. Even in new institutional configurations, elements of the old are likely to remain as interconnections between the old
and the new reproduce. Therefore, the theory of temporal politics would
suggest that the sequential pathway from critical juncture to a rupture in
the logic is not linear and is, at best, discoverable through historical rather
than contemporary political analysis. For the theory of political temporality inspired by Bergson outlined here, there is too much overlap between
the main phases that Pierson identifies and this means that the sequence is
much messier and more complex than a 'clean' theory of HI would permit.

This is particularly the case with the concept of 'critical junctures'
which is so important to the historical institutionalism literature in terms

of explaining political change. Kathleen Thelen has argued that the idea of 'critical junctures' is too open at the beginning (in terms of why critical junctures might take place) and too deterministic at the other end when they have passed and established a path for ongoing institutional development. She highlights Pierson's argument that there are three main ways of understanding actions that may help to establish a critical juncture: 'those based on "self-reinforcing event sequences" (in which initial moves in one direction encourage further movement along the same path), on "non-reinforcing event sequences" (in which initial moves in a particular direction elicit powerful backlash effects), and on "historical conjunctures" (in which interaction effects between processes unfolding at the same time affect outcomes)' (Thelen 2000: 101). Therefore, it is important to understand that critical junctures are not self-defining moments of widely understood and consensual shifts in the governing logic of particular institutions, but rather moments where there is a particular valency in a certain set of activities, practices and beliefs which change the course of development. Thelen's account leaves more scope for an agential dimension to the possibilities of political change rather than Pierson's more institutionalist focus.

As noted above, the definitive nature of these changes is often only identifiable in retrospect because it is impossible – short of a revolution or the like – to understand the *temporal* significance of particular events in the present. Indeed, as Pierson himself points out, often it is small events that make the difference between two possible outcomes (or pathways) and minor choices between these pathways can have long-lasting implications. Put another way, it is frequently not a matter of change or no change, but of 'bounded change'. Importantly, Pierson recognises the significance of temporal dynamics such as duration in understanding the impact of actions on a particular sequence. Thus, 'we may gain some leverage on the impact of events which interrupt ongoing sequences by paying closer attention to the speed and length of positive feedback processes. Where disruptive events are relevant, we may need to think of processes not only as "too early" or "too late," but perhaps as "too short"' (Pierson 2000: 88). This takes us beyond simple notions of path dependence and political change that move in a sequence from critical juncture through consolidation to potential crisis. As Bridges (2000: 111) points out:

> It is a mistake to understand history as a series of cycles in which social and political processes 'are prone to consolidation or institutionalization' in arrangements which then 'reproduce' themselves until new conditions 'disrupt' or 'overwhelm' them. For one thing, this reading

leaves us content to recognize stability, but condemned to surprise at change. For another, although there are times when 'external' shocks reconfigure societies, change is not always provoked by outside forces. Elements of change and disruption inhere in superficially stable situations; if we cannot recognize and theorize these we settle for superficial readings of politics and society.

Therefore, following Bridges, it is vital to understand the sources of political change and the structural configurations that give rise to them within extant political institutions and the broader socio-political architecture of a given society. This does not preclude the occurrence of internal events or external pressures that can push a given society in one direction or another, but it is important to resist determinism in describing processes of structural change as if agential factors were irrelevant. Rather material things and political subjects – both individual and collective – adapt to their environments and they co-constitute and shape these contexts rather than being defined by them. This extends to institutions as well (Jervis 2000). This co-constitution and co-evolution of the subjects, institutions and material objects that comprise society also contains an important temporal dimension insofar as the development of particular societies proceeds through an interactive process between subjects, institutions and other material objects in such a way that it is difficult to identify critical junctures or turning points in the present. This makes the social scientific analysis of temporality both vital and exceptionally complex:

> One of the important tasks of social science is to try to determine what kind of feedback will characterize a given situation. Actors similarly have to make such estimates and many policy debates center not on the immediate consequences of various courses of action but rather on the political dynamics that will be set in motion and the long-term consequences that will ensue. This means that not only are timing and sequencing important in determining political outcomes, but people's beliefs about timing and sequencing . . . are part of the story. (Jervis 2000: 100)

Jervis highlights the complex interaction between the political dynamics of institutions and the ways in which those dynamics are *interpreted* by political actors. These interpretations are manifold, not least because the relevant 'political actors' are as much everyday subjects as they are political elites. Institutions, then, interact with subjects (both individual and collective) as well as other institutions. The result is a complicated network mired in agential interpretations and broader socio-political dynamics. This requires a more fluid, relational approach to change in political institutions than HI theorists like Pierson usually allow for in their sequential models.

The institutional focus of HI has been extended through the greater recognition of the agential dimension of political change in some recent debates in public administration, most notably in the American Political Development (APD) approach. In particular, some of the APD literature invokes notions of institutional development which are useful in helping us to clarify the distinction between the linear passage of time and the more subjective concept of temporality developed here. Insofar as public administration scholars reflect on the relationships between political institutions and actors and the particular structural contexts in which they interact, the distinction between time and temporality is significant. The objective passage of time enables diachronic depictions of then and now and facilitates approaches which highlight the differences and/or connections between political institutions in different periods and/or the impacts of particular administrations. Linear understandings also enable public administration scholars to identify specific impacts on institutions which can be connected with particular political actors who held office or influence at certain times or broader changes taking place simultaneously in other societies across the world. By examining changes in a comparative light, we are able to identify broader trends across regions of the world that enable us to attach labels to eras and processes such as the 'Keynesian welfare state', 'worlds of welfare capitalism', 'new public management', 'neo-liberalism' and so on. However, this demand to categorise more often than not means that these labels tend to cover up as much as they reveal about a particular polity.

The idea of political temporality developed here problematises these more timebound analyses. It suggests that there might be greater value in understanding administrative change in a more evolutionary fashion which is as much characterised by pragmatic political responses to failure as it is by clear programmes of institutional development or policy change associated with particular sets of political actors (Little 2012). This is not to say that such programmes do not have an effect, but it is to suggest that direct causality between actions and outcomes can be very difficult to identify. Political temporality suggests that the institutional environment at any given point in time is characterised by a plurality of institutions that have developed and evolved in shifting environments characterised by contradictory sets of policy objectives and inconsistent political narratives.

Importantly, where the dynamic complexities that characterise the 'temporal ecology' (Hassan and Purser 2007: 10) of a particular administrative context might often be regarded as an impediment to definitive political action and change, they might also be conceived as the spaces in which political creativity can emerge. Path dependence need not merely bind us to the past because the interaction of a complicated range of factors always generates emergent properties that deft innovators can seize upon to generate new ideas and policies (Orren and Skowronek 2004, Little 2012). This highlights the need to understand both durability and dynamism (Sheingate 2014: 462). Therefore, while the emphasis on path dependence in historical institutionalist accounts is well justified (Pierson 2004), the difficulty of extant institutions operating optimally in a highly fluid and shifting environment is both a facilitator and an inhibitor of political and institutional change, especially where creative political actors are alive to the kinds of opportunities that may emerge in these conditions. Political action on this view is as much an art as it is a science. However, it also makes it more difficult to attribute direct causality to particular actors or policies in the course of understanding political change.

One final reflection on this discussion of time in public administration is the extent to which it has taken place at the margins of debates in political theory. Indeed, it is a shortcoming of the discipline of political science that there is such a schism between theoreticians and scholars more focused on the practice of politics. While I am not interested in attaching blame one way or the other, neither side of this division is well served. However, it also points to the fact that not only are political theorists involved in contretemps about boundaries within the realms of theoretical debate (for example, the analytical-continental divide), they may also find themselves unable to impact theoretically informed debates taking place within other sub-disciplines. In the case of the theory of temporal politics, this will be addressed through the discussion of a range of cases and examples in the second part of the book. However, having identified the ways in which time is discussed in the public administration literature, in the next section we examine the ways in which political theory has discussed temporal issues. While the issue of the future is a spectral presence in political theory, it is fair to say that most of the temporal discussion in political thought has focused on the conceptualisation of history and the past.

The Politics of Time: Past, Present . . . and Future

As we saw in the previous chapter, there is a significant history to the discussion of time in political theory. For the purposes of understanding temporal argumentation in the present, however, the question we need to

address involves the implications of these historical debates for contemporary political science. The answers can be drawn out in at least two ways.
First, we can address the significance of the relationship between history
and political theory to investigate the extent to which historical knowledge
percolates into contemporary theoretical debates. Put simply, this approach
identifies the importance of understanding this disciplinary relationship if
we are to use the past to make sense of the politics of the present. Second,
we can draw upon the kinds of historical methods of commentators such as
Foucault (1998) to demonstrate why genealogical methods are appropriate
in informing contemporary political debates and policies. This historical
methodology can be married with contemporary accounts of pragmatism
(Koopman 2009a, 2011a) as a way of bridging the gap between history and
political theory. Both of these approaches provide valuable insights into
the way in which time appears in the politics of the past and the present.
However, neither devotes sufficient attention to the future and its relationship with the past or present. I examine both approaches in this section
before returning to the future in the final section of the chapter, outlining
a specifically political understanding of temporality.

History and Political Theory

The relationship between history and political philosophy has a lengthy
background but has been thrown into a sharp light by the re-emergence
of realist political theories in the last two decades and their critique of
the universalist aspirations that underpin much modernist – and particularly liberal – political thought (Floyd 2009, Floyd and Stears 2011). Floyd
and Stears recognise that there has never been a consensual understanding
amongst political philosophers on the import of history on the work that
theorists do but suggest that there are two main challenges underpinning
this issue: universalism and realism. The first of these challenges relates to
the understanding of 'political principles as timeless prescriptions, applicable and determinate in all times and in all places, and understanding
them instead as theoretical distillations of whatever moral culture it is that
we happen to find ourselves a part of' (Floyd and Stears 2011: 2–3). Not
surprisingly perhaps, the theory of political temporality articulated here
is sceptical of theories which seek out 'timeless prescriptions' as if it is
possible to establish and maintain singular defensible understandings of
particular principles in ways that are not susceptible to interpretation and
judgement in relation to specific issues and problems in particular contexts.
Indeed, in the cases outlined in the second part of the book, we can see

that defenders of universal principles are engaged in active disagreement about how best to articulate universal principles, let alone enact them.

Second, Floyd and Stears frame the debates within the realist perspective as disagreements between idealistic and pessimistic accounts. Iain Hampsher-Monk (2011), for example, makes a case for cordoning off the study of the history of political thought from the complicated realities of political practices and actions, whereas, writing from the Harvard School of realist philosophy, Sabl (2011) disputes this separation to argue for a much more open conversation about the constraints we face when learning lessons from historical realities. Melissa Lane (2011) goes further in arguing that engagement with historical constraints need not lead to conservatism and instead may invite further reflection on how to change or move those constraints. The case for engagement with historical context is made most convincingly by Honig and Stears (2011), who provide a challenge to the idealist/pessimist distinction and the different depictions – all of them partial – of what constitutes realism. Rather than abandoning the contextualisation of political theory in history and assessment of possibilities, Honig and Stears ask us to 'accept that such efforts will never overcome the complexities and dilemmas with which political philosophers are always faced. It is crucial, therefore, that political philosophy be "real", yet also vital that we recognise that this reality will always itself be contested' (Floyd and Stears 2011: 8–9). This perspective is closely aligned with the theory of political temporality outlined below.

It is clear that the conversation about the relationship between political philosophy and history has been taking place in a rigorous fashion and with a significant focus on the theoretical implications of the methodology of understanding practice. However, the focus on these debates has primarily been on the relationship between the study of the past and understandings of the present. There has been much less focus on the future and, indeed, the best that can be said is that the theorisation of the future is implicit in the work of those theorists who (1) theorise the nature of the political in general so that the only universal is a continuous presence of political disagreement, and (2) do so with an open mind as to the way in which such essential features of political life as political contestation may manifest differently in varying contexts. Thus, if there is a universal element in the very understanding of politics, it is the existence of disagreement at the heart of what we as political theorists are trying to make sense of. The recognition of this ineliminable element of politics is what makes the contextualisation of political theory in practical political issues so important in understanding the temporal development of political ideas.

Ultimately, in grappling with the challenge of how political theorists should conceive of the importance of history to their craft, Floyd argues for an approach that is contextualist (rather than abstractly universalist), optimistic (rather than idealist or pessimistic) *and* real. However, he recognises that this engenders what he calls the 'ranking problem' around different goals. Whichever particular problem (or dimension thereof) we try to address will lead to different prioritisations of potential answers. For Floyd, this requires social scientists to think about (1) the probability of achieving each political goal, (2) the amount of political capital required to at least attempt to reach each goal, and (3) the relative value of each such goal when achieved.

Floyd contends that the last of these considerations should be the stock-in-trade of political philosophers as other social scientists have more of the tools and methods to engage in the first two. However, from the perspective of a theory of temporal politics, all three are significant in grounded political analysis such that none of them can be clearly distinguished or prioritised over the others. The theory of temporal politics needs to not only address all three of the categories Floyd refers to above, but also *demonstrate the relationships between them*. Indeed, it is vital to make a case for engagement between political theorists and other social scientists to try to ensure that the intersection of these three points is properly identified and addressed in context. Floyd should not be surprised that the 'discipline' of political philosophy gets accused of 'crass universalism' or 'naïve utopianism' (2011: 210), if it is not prepared to interact with the more engaged practices and methodologies of other social science disciplines. Moreover, the focus on the relative weighting of these questions in Floyd's argument belies a normative underpinning where objectives are clear and rankable; in practice, the material positioning of political actors may be ambiguous and ranking of preferences and negotiated outcomes with opponents will depend on opportunism or pragmatism rather than reflecting the achievement of steadfast principles through a coherently rational approach to those with whom we disagree.

As the discussion of temporal debates in public administration and the discussion of unforeseen consequences in complexity theory (Little 2012) make clear, the idea that we can simply plan to achieve particular goals or weigh up attempts to do so against one another does not reflect an accurate picture of the interaction between political theory and policy making. The idea of unforeseen consequences undermines Floyd's conception of the 'relative value of each goal when achieved' as the driving methodological principle for political theorists because it highlights the problem of the absence of direct causality between action and outcome in a complex environment, as well as the possibility that actions to address one particular end may have deleterious consequences in other spheres beyond the direct domain of the particular goal pursued. This criticism notwithstanding, Floyd (2011) is correct that there are multiple questions and options in addressing his three desiderata in any political problem. The theory of political temporality suggests that they need to be augmented by recognition that whatever we do will generate unintended outcomes and unforeseen consequences in either the issue at hand or other adjacent areas requiring political action (and, therefore, generate a need for further action).

Floyd (2011) recognises the problem of trying to work through the 'relative value' of different political options especially when it comes to overarching principles or 'compound concepts' such as justice. His example is when political theorists promote particular concepts such as free speech which are insufficient in isolation to deliver broader principles like justice. As a 'compound concept' justice comprises numerous subsidiary concepts (Freeden 1996, Little 2018) which are often interlinked with one another. To act in a certain way to promote one of these concepts also raises the possibility that, in so doing, the decision-maker endangers or compromises another concept which is also of value to those pursuing a model of justice. Floyd is sceptical that these kinds of dilemmas can be navigated by purely procedural approaches. Instead, he turns to the work of Simmons (2010) to find guidance as to what to do when faced with a choice of morally permissible alternative actions:

> what really matters is whether or not we have got nearer to the achievement of perfect justice as a matter of long-term political strategy, not whether or not the current policy removes as much injustice as possible *right now*. You might, as [Simmons] admits, have to take one step backwards now in order to take two steps forward later. (Floyd 2011: 213)

Therefore, in temporal terms, Simmons's approach suggests that the goal in decision-making is to place us in a stronger position to achieve a longer-term objective. However, while Simmons thinks that this is just a transitional phase, Floyd disagrees by suggesting that the political actor is left with something of a balancing act between the immediacy of action on short-term issues and the retention of long-term objectives. For Floyd, while not necessarily wholly satisfactory, this is potentially a more useful place than painting oneself fully into the moralist or realist corners. Importantly, however, in relation to temporal strategy, I contend that this is also a potentially pragmatic basis on which to ensure that longer-term objectives can be retained *and adapted* in light of changing political circumstances which are affected by short-term decision-making. The reference to long-term strategy also provides Floyd's arguments with a future-oriented dimension that is lacking in some alternative accounts, albeit his account of the future is too locked into the idea that we can accurately predict outcomes and causality in the longer term.

What neither Floyd nor Simmons addresses is the aforementioned issue of unforeseen and unintended outcomes from our choices of political action. Moreover, neither grapples with the fact that actions taken by other political actors may mean that our intended outcomes do not eventuate or, if they do, they appear in a compromised form. Simmons is correct to say we end up in a transitional phase, but not perhaps in quite the way he understands it. After political decisions are made and policies designed and implemented, we are not necessarily in a phase closer to where our longer-term objective lies because actions and decisions taken elsewhere may have compromised our original decisions. Moreover, this is not necessarily immediate, but the temporal nature of the process means that once we have made decisions that might move us towards a longer-term objective, other actors may then intervene in ways that make that objective less likely to occur. In other words, Simmons underplays the fluidity of the political and the temporal interventions that impact on our objectives. Here perhaps Floyd is closer to the mark (although he too does not deal with the issue of unforeseen consequences of action but he does recognise uncertainty and caprice) in his depiction of a balancing act between the long and the short term. As intimated above, the key is that the retained longer-term objectives continue to inform decisions. However, in order to do so, political actors need to be adaptive to the changing trajectories of the political environment and be willing to shift short-term decisions accordingly. While it is not a zero-sum game between short-term decisions and long-term objectives, Floyd is correct in terms of temporal methodology to emphasise approximations to ideals as the real object of pursuit rather than perfect justice.

Ultimately, Floyd provides a welcome engagement with temporal arguments in his treatment of the relationship between history and political philosophy. He rightly warns against historicism and promotes a model of political theory based not on the provision of the right answers but on good judgement between competing morally justifiable options. As noted above such judgement requires decisions based on approximations to ideals rather than perfect justice, but it also requires a coherent sense of the long-term objectives that an actor is trying to achieve. The long and the short term are not incompatible although the route to the former from the latter can take multiple paths and the connection through a particular avenue may not always be clear. Most political theorists, regardless of ideological persuasion, have some understanding of actions and outcomes at the heart of their work and therefore incorporate – albeit not always explicitly – a temporal dimension. Floyd's work clarifies that progress is uncertain and that the very terrain of political theory is ambiguous and unpredictable.

This returns us to the question of what it means for a temporal politics to be realist. Extending the argument of Honig and Stears above, a realist temporal politics needs to understand and indeed embrace contingency and uncertainty about outcomes. Rather than the dominant strains of realism in international relations which imagine that a pessimistic, rational self-interest drives strategic choices made by political actors (states) within an anarchic environment, the realism of temporal politics demands that we understand our epistemological limitations and the uncertainty about outcomes that they engender. It also eschews the assumption that we can know the motivations of political actors abstracted from the context they are located within. Indeed, temporal realism works within a framework of relational ontologies which change and develop over the course of time. There is no certainty about the individual and collective actors, their preferences or their particular motivations in this account. In both ontological and epistemological terms, then, temporal political realism requires strategic calculations in conditions of uncertainty, ambiguity and indeterminacy. The nature of strategic choices in this terrain will be a matter of calculation amidst this uncertainty rather than being something that can be read off *a priori* from assumptions about the essential character of rational actors. This points to the need to engage with a different set of theoretical resources to find a model of realism that is suitable for the conditions of temporal politics, and here the engagement between genealogical approaches and pragmatism offers further guidance.

Genealogical Pragmatism

An alternative approach to questions of how to accommodate the past in contemporary political analysis has emerged in recent years through the work of theorists such as Koopman (2011a) who have brought together the historical analytical techniques of Michel Foucault (1998) with the pragmatist tradition in political thought. In an interview in 1984, Foucault states that

> It is true that my attitude isn't a result of the form of critique that claims to be a methodical examination in order to reject all possible

solutions except for the one valid one. It is more on the order of 'prob-
lematization'—which is to say, the development of a domain of acts,
practices, and thoughts that seem to me to pose problems for politics.
(Foucault 1998: 384)

While – not unusually for Foucault – this is an ambiguous statement, it
does indicate a different approach to the question of what political theory
involves than more standard accounts and it also incites methodological
queries about the ways in which we understand and investigate the political issues that we address (Bang 2014). For Foucault, 'problems' are always
constructed and their production emanates from the empirical settings of
institutions and practices in combination with the forms of language that
are embedded within them. Problematisation also elicits methodological
questions about the ways to address specifically political problems and
implies a more temporally orientated approach.

Foucauldian approaches suggest that theorists should never take problems at face value but instead they should work through a process of inter-
rogating them to find out *why* they are construed as a political problem,
how they are constructed as problems, and *how* these constructions are
embedded in the language and practices of particular institutional configurations. Problematology develops a method that suggests that there are a
number of prior questions which should precede that of 'how do we solve
this problem?'. For commentators such as Osborne, the work of problematology always has a historical element, albeit an unconventional form
of historical inquiry that challenges the very basis upon which historical
knowledge is developed (Osborne 2003). Therefore, when faced with a
number of potential pathways to the resolution of a particular problem
or issue, it is a fruitful historical method to go back to the problem itself
and unravel its particular formation. That is, what diverse solutions share
is a common grounding in a specific formulation of a problem and it is a
beneficial process of thought to unpick the pathway from sets of solutions
and the way in which a problem has been framed to its origins (Foucault
1998). This is because the framing of problems in a particular way provides
the realm of possibility for solutions; it is only through grappling with the
construction of the problem as a *problem* that we come to understand the
constraints that have been placed around the development of solutions and
the available choices over political action (Little 2012).

Like the analysts of the relationship between history and political theory discussed in the section above, however, Foucault provides us with
few answers on the issue of the future and its precise relationship to
the decisions that are made in the present. Problematisation provides us

with a methodological tool for analysis ('a critical ontology of ourselves', Foucault 1997: 132), but not one that can be deployed to decide between particular options to address a contemporary problem. Therefore, we need to delve deeper into Foucault's work to address this task of adopting and adapting the methodological techniques that he provides, while still pursuing possibilities for political action. His reflections on Kant's 'What Is Enlightenment?' (Foucault 1997, 1986) provide some insights into how a genealogist might engage in practices which could deliver a future orientation. In particular, two specific temporal aspects of Foucault's discussion of Kant provide such a platform: first, Kant's focus on 'present-ness', and, second, the depiction of Enlightenment as a break or exit from the past. On the first point, Kant provides a somewhat heroic, 'mature' conception of the philosophy of the present as one that defines 'its own present and the forms of knowledge, ignorance, illusion in terms of which it identifies its historical situation' and shifts towards a focus on what is happening today (Foucault 1986: 90). In the second step, Enlightenment is presented as a break from the past such that the modern philosopher is no longer involved in a 'longitudinal relationship to the Ancients, but rather what one might call a "sagital" relation to one's own present-ness' (Foucault 1986: 90). Through these two manoeuvres, Kant presents Enlightenment as an exit or escape from the past (Foucault 1997: 105) in a way that runs counter to the Foucauldian perspective outlined below and the temporal argument developed here.

From this foundation, we can delineate a more future-oriented dimension to Foucault's perspective. He outlines the way in which, using Kant, modernity can be construed as an attitude rather than a particular phase of history. But where, for Kant, this was focused on the possibility of a progressive future based on the absence of subjection to authority, Foucault (1997: 125) focuses instead on 'a practical critique that takes the form of a possible transgression'. Importantly, then, we find the seeds of an 'experimental' attitude which should be put to the 'test of reality, of contemporary reality, both to grasp the point where change is possible and desirable, and to determine the precise form this change should take' (Foucault 1997: 126). Therefore, while Foucault is undoubtedly reticent about promoting specific socio-political changes, he does provide insights into a disposition or ethos with which we can address contemporary issues without losing sight of their historical foundations. He describes this 'critical ontology of ourselves' as a critique that is both 'the historical analysis of the limits that are imposed on us and an experiment with the possibility of going beyond them' (Foucault 1997: 132). Moreover, it should also be noted that in his later writing on the concept of parrhesia (Foucault 2010),

Foucault did begin the work of addressing more fully the implications of his ideas for political actors, although much of this was focused on the role of the politician and the strategic task of weaving together the numerous perspectives on issues into demoi (Bang 2014).

All of this is to say that Foucauldian problematisation can be a useful technique for political theorists if it is deployed as a problem-oriented approach that encourages the unpicking of problems to enlighten political actors on the possibility of alternatives. Inevitably, then, if a problem is reconstructed on a different foundation, it will generate new modes of resolution and, in turn, this will generate a new subject to be problematised. This amounts to a *recurring* process, one of a continual cycle of genealogical critique to historical problematology, reconstruction, action and renewal through to critique once again. This takes us well beyond problematisation as a primarily philosophical exercise and it permits us to place the deconstruction and reconstruction of problems at the heart of a highly dynamic depiction of politics that is pregnant with the possibility of and the need for action. As Folkers reminds us, 'Foucault analyses problematizations and thereby reproblematizes them. He does not just insert contingency in a total structure of power and knowledge, but rather illuminates the cracks in the historical situation that are there already' (Folkers 2016: 22). The question becomes one of how we act politically on these problematisations and reproblematisations in the present and what implications these actions have for the future.

Ultimately, problematology in general and problematisation in particular do vital work in unveiling the structures of power in the ways in which political actors have used indeterminate concepts (Freeden 2013) in determinate ways to construct the problems that we have to address through political action. It suggests that theorists need to find

> a provisional ethos instead of a determinate, legislative morality, a series of problems rather than a 'theory'; and, in methodological terms, a question of problematology rather than sociology, realist history or even – at least in a legislative sense – philosophy. Problematology entails, in this context, not just the diagnosing of problems and not, certainly, the dictating of solutions; but, if anything, the multiplication of further problems such that we are constantly attuned to the tasks of an on-going ethics of the problematic as a sort of critical virtue in itself. (Osborne 2003: 14–15)

However, what problematology does not – and cannot – provide us with is a guide for political action on a collective level. That is, problematisation invites the decomposition of the problems that are established as political challenges, but with little scope for the construction of alternatives. Insofar as it is focused on action at all (and this is limited in Foucault as he sees problematisation as a matter of 'thought'), it is concerned with the role of ethics in individual conduct. However, this still leaves the political theorist interested in engaging with material politics with an important challenge. After investigating and deconstructing problems through genealogical methods, how do we engage with them collectively once they have been unpacked *and* reconstructed? How do we go beyond Foucault and use problematisation as a foundation for political action? In temporal terms, how do we move beyond the historical focus of genealogy to incorporate the future? To address these questions, I turn now to the field of pragmatism (Auxier 2002) to assess the extent to which it is able to further the theory of political temporality.

While Foucauldian problematisation leads us towards a more thorough understanding of the major issues construed as problems in political science, it is lacking in terms of its capacity to inform strategies of present or future political action. It helps us to understand the historical origins of problems and opens up the *possibility* of alternative practices to those that prevail. However, it does not – in isolation – provide sufficient grounds for a political theoretical conceptualisation of temporality. For this reason, it is necessary to augment such genealogical approaches with alternatives such as pragmatism that are more attuned to questions of political action in an uncertain and ambiguous environment. Pragmatism is a diverse category of political thought encompassing a number of approaches and perspectives including the work of Peirce, James and Dewey in the nineteenth and twentieth centuries and, more recently, Richard Rorty (Rorty 1995; see also Chin 2018, Koopman 2009a). However, it is most commonly associated with the work of John Dewey, who is renowned for his promotion of a form of 'melioristic reconstruction' (Koopman 2011b: 245) as a political strategy. Dewey was concerned with progressive improvement through informed political judgement on particular issues. In this sense, pragmatism is as much a form of political practice as it is a political philosophy.

However, in recent years, amid the growing literature on pragmatism in contemporary political theory, it has become clear that pragmatism has multiple affinities with other variants of political thought including both realism and genealogy (Chin 2016). For example, there is a growing body of literature identifying links between pragmatism and key realist philosophers such as Bernard Williams (2005) as well as genealogical thinkers such as Foucault (Auxier 2002, Koopman 2010, 2011a, Stuhr 1997). Others such as Joseph Margolis (2017) have long argued that pragmatism was a potential point of reconciliation between the analytical and continental traditions. These links are significant for pragmatists because, as Festenstein has argued, the greatest weakness of pragmatism is that it 'is often thought to view politics as primarily a matter of collective problem-solving, glossing over core political phenomena such as power and conflict which subvert the hopes for such a shared enterprise' (Festenstein 2016: 39). However, Dewey, for example, criticises 'canonical value theories' and suggests that the conflicts between them can only be resolved in practice rather than through theoretical engagement (Festenstein 2016: 43). In effect, this places the practice of politics at the methodological centre of analysis rather than political moralism.

Clearly, pragmatism places judgement in political practices ahead of 'antecedent theory'. However, the question remains as to how those acting in politics – and therefore making judgements – are to acquire the tools to decide on courses of action in the face of 'the politics of truth' (Foucault 1977b). In other words, surely pragmatists still require someone or something to develop the 'raw materials' of political choices? As most pragmatists understand, political actors do not make judgements free from their own prior ethical or ideological commitments, so this does raise the question of whether pragmatism can only function on a practical level through alignment with some or other theoretical approach that contains core normative implications. While the practice of politics is clearly engaged in the process of trying to address, ameliorate or solve problems, the options that are formulated reflect certain moral or ideological values or principles as well as particular structural socio-political interests. This condition is something that realists such as Raymond Geuss have been clear about (Geuss 2008). It is notable that in Richard Rorty's pragmatist discussion of 'Philosophy and the Future' (Rorty 1995: 203–4), he ultimately advocates a problematic cosmopolitan liberal egalitarianism which he pits against static 'cultural traditions'. The role of the philosopher in this context, he claims, is 'persuading them to be free' (Rorty 1995: 205)!

A further feature that pragmatists share with realists like Williams as well as Foucauldians is an emphasis on understanding the historical foundations of the problems that are being addressed, without being drawn into historicism. It is vital for pragmatism in practice that actors comprehend the nature of the problems they act upon so that judgement can be as informed as possible. This requires awareness of the temporality of the issue that is being addressed and the various ways in which a particular issue might have been construed in the past. Therefore, in a different time in history the nature of a problem – say, migration – would have looked somewhat different depending on a range of contextual factors and, in turn, this would have inflected the judgements that were made about one particular course of action over another. Koopman notes that, for Williams, 'it is precisely at these limits—where philosophical explanation breaks down in the face of deeply contingent complexities—that historical inquiry can kick in as useful for both explanation and understanding' (Koopman 2010: 11). This argument obviously resonates with problematisation as well insofar as Foucault sought to use genealogical investigation to reveal the nature of the choices that we face when we address problems in the present. Ultimately, while idealist, moralist theory sometimes simplifies situations to navigate philosophers through the murky waters of contextual problems, Koopman uses Williams, Foucault, Hampshire and pragmatism to suggest that complexity needs to be embraced rather than removed from our understanding of political issues.

While there may be complementarity between realism and pragmatism on the one hand and genealogy and pragmatism on the other, questions remain over whether there is a distinctive way of integrating these perspectives into a single methodological approach. Perhaps James Tully's public philosophy comes closest with his invocation of a method to help political actors to navigate this terrain (Tully 2008). It suggests that we need to redescribe 'a problematic practice, illustrating its contingency to expose the nature of the present set of limits and open up alternative manners of collectively organizing that form of cooperation' (Chin 2017: 21). Chin (2016: 218) also argues persuasively that hybridisation of these theoretical methods rather than a synthesis may be the most productive approach to these questions because 'a philosophical synthesis [is] a project which always risks reducing methods to their common denominators or rendering one framework into the other's terms'. The argument for a political theory of temporality set out below attempts to provide the kind of hybridity recommended by Chin and avoid the flattening of the differences between these approaches. It invokes elements of the contextual bent of realism, the historical problematisation of genealogy, and the practical judgement of pragmatism to explain how the theory of temporality provides a significant new perspective in contemporary politics.

Theorising Temporality *Politically*

In this final section of the chapter, I move towards an outline of a method for temporal politics that will inform the remainder of the book. This is predicated on five key facets of political temporality that should underpin the ways in which we address material problems in contemporary politics. These facets relate to some traditional distinctions in the philosophy of time such as McTaggart's distinction between A series and B series time (McTaggart 1968), but also differ in important ways that play out in specifically *political* formations. These five key dimensions of temporal politics, *taken together*, differentiate it from the generalised notion of temporality in the social sciences as well as the standard treatments of time in political philosophy:

1. The focus on the passage of time (duration, tempo, etc.) rather than 'clock' time;
2. The lived experiences and perceptions of time rather than objective notions;
3. The political disagreements engendered by contestation over political temporality;
4. The future orientation of temporal politics;
5. The ubiquity of temporal concerns in politics.

The Passage of Time

While 'clock' time is obviously important in political debate, its depiction as linear and objective is reductive of the plurality of conceptions of time. Temporality, on the other hand, is concerned with the passage of time and issues such as the tempo of change and conceptions of the duration of particular problems or entities. Duration can be used to distinguish temporality from the linear passage of time on a uniformly understood trajectory between past, present and future. Against this objective trajectory, temporality dwells on the existence of the past and the future in the present and sees the clear distinctions of objective, linear depictions of the movement of time as unreflective of the ways in which socio-political issues develop. Moreover, temporality is focused on issues such as the pace of political change – including whether it is too fast or too slow – and the manner in which these perceptions manifest in the discussion of political issues.

Lived Experiences of Time

Temporal concerns with the passage of time emanate from the subjective nature of interpretations of issues such as tempo and duration. In its rejection of a purely linear, objective approach to time, political temporality engages with the phenomenological realm of subjective lived experiences. Thus, whether political action and development is taking place at a pace that is too fast or too slow is at least partly predicated on the interpretations of those undertaking or experiencing the change. As these will vary, our experience of the passage of time is structured by the temporalities of other subjects and institutional configurations (Sharma 2014: 8). Moreover, our subjective perceptions of what is too fast or slow is often structured by the nature of developments external to ourselves. Our lived experience of time develops within this externally structured domain. Thus, perceptions of the pace of change have direct implications for how political debates are conducted on specific issues even if temporality is not obviously the subject of debate.

Contestation over Temporality

As noted at the outset, temporality is an increasingly important concept across the social sciences, but the theory of temporal *politics* focuses on the contested nature of subjective lived experiences of time. While it need not necessarily be the case amongst all people and on every issue, the subjective experience of time engenders conflict and disagreement about issues where temporality is an important dimension of our understanding of them. This is especially important when it comes to political action, where disagreement about experiences of change, how to act, and the implications of such actions over the course of time can become particularly fraught. If temporality is about lived time and how subjects experience it, then it is ripe for contestation. This is particularly the case where there are disagreements about the history of a particular situation such that the issues that political actors address are already a potential source of conflict.

The Future Orientation of Temporality

While the scholarly literature in the social sciences is paying increasing attention to the issue of temporality, political theory has been slower to take account of a model of politics that is concerned not just with the past and the present but also with the future. While everyday political debate consistently invokes the future in terms of the benefits or dangers of taking a particular course of action in the present, these discussions typically take place with a much higher degree of certainty than is warranted in complex contemporary societies. Political debates about the implications of actions for the future tend to be conducted in quite bounded and definitive terms, as if the direct causality of an action or policy in relation to outcomes has a much greater degree of certainty attached to it than is actually the case. This is because such arguments underplay the impact of decisions in other fields/policy domains, or those taken by different arms of government, civil society actors, international organisations and so forth. The theory of political temporality, however, involves the future in a different way – it puts forward a conception of *uncertain* futures – one that involves many unknown opportunities and dangers. Just as we cannot achieve consensus on the past, political temporality suggests that we cannot predict the future, even if we can identify some of the risks and potential problems. The epistemological challenge for temporal politics is how to think about political action in uncertain conditions.

The Ubiquity of Temporal Concerns in Politics

The book will examine the concept of political temporality by discussing a number of cases of issues in contemporary politics where the primary features of political temporality come into play. However, in no way should the cases examined in Part Two be thought of as exhaustive; indeed, temporal politics affects innumerable political debates and issues (albeit in myriad ways). This is best exemplified through an investigation of specific cases to demonstrate temporality's dynamics and its implications for how political theory might be conducted differently. Therefore, the cases are chosen as instances where the issues related to temporality are apparent and where the political implications of considering the debates in a temporal theoretical light is most beneficial. In light of the need to examine cases where temporality plays out differently in contemporary political issues, in the second part of the book Chapters 4 to 6 will examine, firstly, the *contestation of the past* by examining the politics of Indigenous-settler reconciliation in conflictual, settler colonial societies. The second case chapter will examine a key debate in *the present*, namely, contemporary controversies on borders and migration in a temporal light to demonstrate their relatedness to *the past and future*. The third case examined will be contemporary debates about democratic decline in a national and international context and the ways in which they do or do not invoke discussion of alternative democratic arrangements in *the future*. These three cases will illuminate the concept of political temporality in practice and in context, before we return to the question of the theory and conduct of temporal politics in the final section of the book.

Conclusion to Part One

Political temporality is becoming an increasingly significant issue in contemporary politics and it generates important challenges for political theory. It encourages theorists to think in different ways about their task by emphasising a grounded, contextual form of theoretical analysis focused on political practices and problems. It places these practices and problems in a historical framework where the past is contested – insofar as there is dispute about the dynamics of events – and, most importantly, the import of those events for subsequent political developments. However, temporal politics also examines the implications of the present for the future and suggests theorists need to think more systematically about a future that is unclear and uncertain. This implies that fresh thinking is required around political action with greater emphasis placed on contingency and the epistemological gaps informing our choices. Furthermore, temporal politics is grounded in the lived experience of human actors and, as such, engenders a view of human societies as comprising relational ontologies between individuals and collectives where epistemological uncertainty is rife. This makes disagreement and contestation much more likely to occur than not, given the variety of human experiences. It is in this realm of contested and overlapping interpretations of past, present and future that temporal politics must intervene.

PART TWO

4

Contesting the Past:
Temporality in Indigenous Politics

If temporal politics is concerned with the political ramifications of time as it is experienced by individual and collective subjects, then the discussion of temporality in the field of Indigenous politics is a particularly apposite place to begin our discussion of particular cases and contexts of temporal politics. The blunt reason for this is that, in the words of Leanne Betasamosake Simpson, 'Indigenous thought does not dissect time into past, present and future. The future is here in the form of the practices of the present, in which the past is also here influencing' (Simpson 2017: 213). Bearing these cadences in mind, then, this chapter does not seek to superimpose an inappropriate model of temporal classification upon Indigenous theory, but instead focuses on the ways in which the fact of different extant temporalities in contemporary societies is misunderstood or deliberately shrouded in settler colonial and post-colonial societies (Nichols 2020).

Whilst challenging the classifications of past, present and future is of course a central part of the theory of temporal politics expounded here, the conception of those categories is explicitly ambiguous, overlapping and non-specific. In other words, it deliberately leaves open the definition of temporal divisions and is methodologically committed to plural interpretations operating simultaneously. Moreover, the theory of temporal politics recognises that such an understanding of multiple temporal landscapes existing together is potentially a matter that may generate political conflict. The final caveat before moving forward with the argument is that the theory of temporal politics articulated here deliberately resists imposing essentialised models of Indigenous or non-Indigenous time. It recognises the multiplicity of Indigenous temporalities, while still drawing attention to some similarities between them, such as resistance to delineated, distinct categories of past, present and future. How such resistance is articulated and experienced between different First Peoples will be varied. Likewise,

I do not seek to impose uniformity on non-Indigenous communities. They too will vary according to a number of factors, such as culture and religion or between the lived experiences of recent migrants vis-à-vis longer-standing settlers, that can impact on their temporal outlooks.

The co-existence of different temporal registers is a common feature of societies that have experienced political conflicts such as civil wars, international political disputes, genocide and forms of violent colonialism. In terms of history, contested views of historical violent events and processes of political change are bound together with complex political phenomena such as truth and memory and overarching meta-objectives like societal reconciliation in a maelstrom of competing narratives and discourses. Likewise, the future is frequently highly uncertain in these conflictual and 'post-conflict' societies, not least because many of the conflicts or their long-term impacts remain unresolved in the contemporary era. Quite often, these debates involve major developments such as building new political institutions (e.g. parliaments, truth commissions and/or independent judiciaries), shifting political cultures (e.g. through attempts to develop a free press, or anti-discrimination legislation, or new religious freedoms), and sometimes changes in the very physical space of a conflictual society through the redrawing of borders or the construction of new forms of segregation to keep conflictual groups apart from one another (Little 2014). Not surprisingly, then, these societies are ripe for further contestation where often old conflicts are replayed in the contemporary era over some of these new sets of arrangements. Taking decisions in the present in these circumstances therefore overlaps with the disagreements on the past and often enshrines the past and present in new initiatives that will influence life in the future. Therefore, these societies are good cases to demonstrate the contested nature of temporal politics.

While any of these specific forms of conflict could be discussed in this chapter, I focus here on Indigenous politics in particular as an exemplar of the temporal political disjunctures which prevail in post-conflict societies. Indigenous politics – and, to be more specific, the attempts of settler colonial states to engage Indigenous communities in reconciliation processes – is a useful example because not only does it demonstrate the key aspects of the disputed past and unpredictable future of political temporality, but it also highlights the nature of conflict in temporal politics. This form of conflict is often not explicit for a variety of reasons that will be explained, and yet it goes to the heart of why temporality is such a pivotal issue in making sense of the varying ways in which the future of Indigenous politics in colonised, post-colonial and settler colonial societies can be imagined. These imagined futures are fundamental to driving forward processes of political action for change in the present as they reflect aspirations for particular policy outcomes. What becomes clear is that often the political aspirations of First Nations peoples are marginalised and sometimes completely invisible to the colonial eye (Little and McMillan 2017), thereby ensuring that ignorance of the past plays out in contemporary politics and, in turn, engenders disagreement about a future state of affairs. Once again, temporal politics in this space is neither linear nor sequential.

There is a small but growing political literature examining these dynamics. From the more traditional domains of political theory, James Tully (2008) stands out as a non-Indigenous scholar who has taken First Nations peoples and their claims to sovereignty seriously over many years. Tully's work examines the radical consequences of Indigenous sovereignties if the challenge to the settler state is followed through, and, significantly, he is insistent that these issues need to be articulated in relation to specific contextual settings rather than in the abstract. However, in recent years we have also witnessed greater attention for important First Nations authors in this space articulating radical claims that challenge many of the core assumptions of the colonial environments in which they work (Leanne Betasamosake Simpson 2017, Coulthard 2014, Audra Simpson 2014). In Australia these kinds of concerns have been articulated by prominent Aboriginal and Torres Strait Islander academics including, for example, Mary Graham, Aileen Moreton-Robinson and Irene Watson (Graham 1999, Moreton-Robinson 2015, Watson 2014a). While there was never a good reason for the relative invisibility of these voices in mainstream politics, there is certainly no excuse for their continued exclusion in contemporary debates and that should make the contested histories and disagreements about the future more transparent than ever before. While the notion of temporality has been implicit in these discussions, in the ensuing sections I try to make clear that the import of temporality has fundamental ramifications for Indigenous politics that are likely to entrench conflict for a long time to come. In line with Tully's grounded approach, the focus in this chapter is primarily directed towards Indigenous politics in the context of Australia, though where appropriate and relevant, some more general comparative observations will also be made.

Importantly, we need to reiterate the point that a theory of temporal politics deployed in relation to Indigenous political struggles is not merely locked into historicism, important though the historical experiences and processes of settler colonialism are to the politics of today. However, as Coulthard and Simpson (2016: 251) remind us, the risk in a solely historical analysis is that the temporal character of events is discussed in a way that positions dispossession as 'some historically situated event' rather than 'an ongoing practice of dispossession that never ceases to structure capitalist and colonial social relations in the present'. Moreover, as noted in the previous chapter, it is vital to avoid teleological arguments that consider the dispossession of Indigenous peoples as a necessary condition of a process of radical consciousness to be used in the establishment of radical alternatives, what Coulthard and Simpson call 'normative developmentalism'. Instead, this chapter highlights the 'temporal aberration' in connection to indigeneity as highlighted in the powerful opening to Mark Rifkin's book *Beyond Settler Time*:

> Native peoples occupy a double bind within dominant settler reckonings of time. Either they are consigned to the past, or they are inserted into a present defined on non-native terms. From this perspective, Native people(s) do not so much exist within the flow of time as erupt from it as an anomaly, one usually understood as emanating from a bygone era. (Rifkin 2017: vii)

Rifkin is clear that there is a disjuncture between settler and Indigenous temporalities and he points to the imposition of settler temporalities over those of First Nations peoples leading to 'the denial of Indigenous *temporal sovereignty*' (Rifkin 2017: 2). Importantly, and in keeping with the perspective articulated in the first part of this book, he recognises that Indigenous temporal orientations are multiple and becoming. Therefore, he is explicit that Indigenous experiences of time are not uniform and that there is no clear and absolute distinction to be drawn between 'Natives and non-natives' when it comes to temporality. Rather it is important to understand Indigenous temporalities in all their multiplicity and variation – a 'pluralization of time that facilitates Indigenous peoples' expressions of self-determination' (Rifkin 2017: 3–4). Of course, as Coulthard (2014: 60) reminds us in his discussion of an alternative ethical framework based upon 'grounded normativity', Indigenous temporalities are likely to have a much stronger spatial dimension, built upon particular kinds of ontological relationship to particular places, than non-Indigenous temporalities (though this is not to say that there cannot be different kinds of non-equivalent, non-Indigenous connections to places at all). To highlight the centrality of this relationship between time and space, it is worth citing Rifkin at greater length to identify a number of ways in which Indigenous and settler temporalities may vary:

> modes of periodization; the felt presence of ancestors; affectively consequential memories of prior dispossessions; the ongoing material

legacies of such dispossessions; knowledges arising from enduring occupancy in a particular homeland, including attunement to animal and climatic periodicities; knowledges arising from present or prior forms of mobility; the employment of generationally iterated stories as a basis for engaging with people, place, and nonhuman entities; the setting of the significance of events within a much longer timeframe (generations, centuries, or millennia); particular ceremonial periodicities; the influence and force of prophecy; and a palpable set of responsibilities to prior generations and future ones. (Rifkin 2017: 19)

With these important caveats in place and recognising the multiple ways in which a plurality of temporalities may be operative in the discussion of a specific issue at a given time, it is useful to start our analysis of how Indigenous politics informs and reveals temporal methods by looking to issues in the historical positioning of Indigenous peoples in settler colonial societies through the Australian example. The next section will focus on some of the different forms of settlement that took place in the Australian states in the nineteenth century to demonstrate the unevenness of settler colonialism before federation. From this historical foundation, I then move to a discussion of the various initiatives that have been undertaken in the last thirty years to enact some form of transformation in the relationship between Aboriginal and Torres Strait Islander peoples and the Australian state. While these efforts have been mostly inauspicious in terms of social transformation, they did culminate in the Uluru Statement from the Heart in 2017 which reflected a separate Indigenous-led consultation process. Importantly, the Uluru Statement also invoked temporal understandings which demonstrated the ways in which the past, present and future are inextricably connected. In the final section of the chapter, I return to the idea of uncertain futures and examine the way in which the underwhelming government response to the Uluru Statement reflects another missed opportunity to accelerate processes of transformation in Indigenous-settler relations in Australia. The case is made that many of the flaws in the Australian federal government's response since 2017 have been predicated on temporal misunderstandings.

Competing Conceptions of the Past

While it is commonplace in societies such as Australia for there to be symbolic identification of the importance of Indigenous-settler relations through, for example, educational programmes in schools or acknowledgements of Aboriginal and Torres Strait Islander peoples at public events, there is seldom any real depth of understanding of the significance of disjuncture between the temporal registers of Indigenous and non-Indigenous peoples. Therefore, while it is not unusual to come across references to the arrival of the First Fleet and the colonial encounter, very little attention is given to the 'pre-history' of the country over tens of thousands of years before the arrival of settlers, the formation of the colonies, and later the establishment of the federal state of Australia as we know it today (Donaldson 1996). Therefore, even in narratives of the history of Australia in which the violence and bloodshed of the colonial encounter and subsequent injustices experienced by Aboriginal and Torres Strait Islander peoples are recognised, the structure of the discussion is still predicated on knowledges and practices of the settler colonial state. This has profound implications, not least because Indigenous communities trace back their connection to land and sea for at least 60,000 years before the colonial encounter. In light of this long view of history, the last 250 years is a blink of the eye (albeit a period when so much harm has been perpetrated against Indigenous peoples and their cultures). Nevertheless, it is clear that the temporal horizons of Aboriginal and Torres Strait Islander peoples, though not uniform, are radically different from those of settlers and that most of this 'pre-history' is ignored in contemporary mainstream political discourse.

Even though acknowledgements of Indigenous peoples in public events in Australia often talk of Aboriginal peoples as the 'traditional owners' or the 'original custodians' of the land, it is still unusual to hear non-Indigenous speakers identifying that those lands (and associated sovereignties) were not ceded. In Australia, the notion of 'ownership' tends to be treated as a historical artefact, rather than recognition that the relationship between Indigenous peoples and the land is integral to indigeneity in Australia today and integral to Indigenous claims of sovereignty. A more honest and less euphemistic way of acknowledging this 'traditional ownership' or the custodial relationship would be to say that the relationship between Indigenous peoples and the land remains intact, despite the imposition of a colonial model of sovereignty against their will. Moreover, this partial history is also reflected in the recognition of local Indigenous peoples in different parts of Australia as traditional custodians, but not recognition of their differentiated status as *First Peoples* who had their sovereign status removed from them through colonisation. Instead, there is a common narrative that is alive and well in Australia today of an undifferentiated Aboriginal and Torres Strait Islander people that fails to recognise the differing claims and relations of particular First Nations peoples and their often quite divergent experiences of encounters with settlers in the varying colonies. The undifferentiated Aborigine becomes a manipulable subject of settler colonial discourse, and an atemporal subject at that.

The failure to discuss Aboriginal and Torres Strait Islander pre-colonial histories in the narration of Australia's past is also coupled with the relative invisibility of Indigenous peoples in many of the standard colonial histories. Occasionally Indigenous peoples appear as bystanders or victims in stories of the development of the Australian state, or historically as subjects when they were charged with crimes by the settler state (Little and McMillan 2017); but these representations are largely after the colonial encounter with few representations of Aboriginal history before that point. This has led to the invisibility of large parts of the Australian story. Moreover, many of the paradoxes of the form of settlement are glossed over, which in terms of political temporality is highly problematic if we are focused on the connections and flow between past, present and future. Therefore, it is important to have a clear understanding of the historic relationship between Indigenous peoples and settlers that gave rise to conflicts that the country is still incapable of addressing today, including the legal and political representation of those relationships in the Australian Constitution.

While there is considerable literature on the history of Australian colonisation (Reynolds 1981, Curthoys, Genovese and Reilly 2008), there is comparatively little attention in political science given to the particular relationships between the colonies and the Indigenous peoples within their borders, prior to Australia becoming a federation in 1901. Specifically, little is said about the structural impediments that prevented colonies from forging a meaningful relationship with Aboriginal and Torres Strait Islander peoples and the ramifications of that problematic relationship in today's politics. Importantly, the establishment of each colony enshrined the 'conflict' of colonisation in different ways so there was never a unitary or evenly applied process of colonisation. Nonetheless, the imposition of the legal doctrine of *terra nullius* – the fiction that the land was not occupied by humans when settlers arrived – made Indigenous peoples' conflict with settlers invisible, and therefore denied the reality of some of the violent interactions between the colonials and the Aboriginal peoples they encountered (Watson 2014b). Ultimately, the establishment of the colonies – and the nation of Australia that grew from their formation – was based on an incorrect mode of acquisition in terms of both international law and the internal common law, a pattern reflected in European settlement across the world (see, for example, Borrows 2015 for reflections on the application of *terra nullius* in British Columbia).

Recognition of the different experiences of the colonies prior to federation is vital to understanding the ways in which the relationships forged
between the individual colonies and Indigenous peoples affected the
relationship between the Commonwealth and Indigenous people collectively. Each colony was created in particular circumstances and therefore
some 'special' relationships were formed between the colonial powers and
Indigenous peoples. As a result, the foundation of each colony demonstrates that the legal fiction and justification for the application of English
law (the doctrine of *terra nullius*) was a source of conflict within both the
English and colonial apparatuses. The core of the conflict was the idea
that the land that was being colonised *was* occupied *but not by humans* so
that, in fact, the settlers were not engaged in colonisation. This created
the dilemma of how to recognise natives/Aborigines/Indigenous peoples
and how to treat them in light of the legal assertion that they (Indigenous
peoples) were sub-human. As we shall see, that generated many anoma-
lous and paradoxical situations. Although each colony was established in
accordance with the law at that time, examining them separately demonstrates the conflictual basis of the subsequent emergence of the nation of
Australia and clarifies why Indigenous peoples have long argued that they
never acquiesced to the sovereignty of the colonial powers. Moreover, any
long-term aspiration to have a 'reconciled' Australia must take account of
the legal and political dimensions of how 'two sides' came into existence
and, therefore, how the recognition of Indigenous peoples will continue to
generate legal and political conflicts in the future.

Even during the establishment of the first colony in New South Wales,
the British Crown had difficulties reconciling the justification of *terra nullius* with the recognition of the existence of native peoples. King George III's
instructions to Captain Phillip encouraged 'friendly relations' between the
new arrivals and Indigenous peoples through protecting their lives and
livelihoods. The New South Wales Legislative Council was formed in
1823 to advise the Governor on matters relating to law-making for the
colony, including managing relationships between the new arrivals and
Indigenous peoples. Ultimately, this involved recognition that Indigenous
peoples were more than 'sub-human' through, for example, the provision
of land grants for Aboriginal people in direct contradiction to the application of the doctrine of *terra nullius* (Reynolds 1981). However, Reynolds
also records the rather different forms of interaction in the second settlement in Van Diemen's Land on the island state now known as Tasmania in
1803 where there were many violent engagements and where charges of
genocide have been levelled against the British colonialists (Lawson 2014).
These violent exchanges further signified the paradoxical disconnection

between the law (as technically these Indigenous people were legally invisible) and the everyday politics of Indigenous-settler conflict (Reynolds 1981).

Queensland was established as a penal colony in 1824. Like the other eastern 'states', it was originally part of New South Wales before it became a separate colony in 1859. When the penal colony was established in 1824 there were large conflicts between the colony and Indigenous populations. The first Governor of Queensland, Sir George Bowen, informed the Colonial Office in England that 'the native tribes ... are far more numerous and more formidable in Queensland than in any other portion of Australia' (Ørsted-Jensen 2011: 15). This amounted to more than clear recognition of the existence of Indigenous peoples; it also indicated that the management of the relationship amounted to more than just leaving them alone. Reynolds makes clear that this led to significant frontier exchanges and violence in Queensland (Reynolds 1981). From the outset, then, it was clear that, given the larger numbers of Indigenous peoples in Queensland, any mismanagement of the relationship could lead to the very real possibility of increased violence (Rogers and Bain 2016).

The course of colonisation was different in Victoria. The first settlement was in 1834 and the capital, Melbourne, was founded in 1835 by John Batman, a free settler (Boyce 2012). Like Tasmania, the colony was regulated from New South Wales until the passing of the Australian Colonies Government Act in 1850 (UK). However, a different kind of relationship emerged between the free settlers and Indigenous peoples, not least because Batman signed a treaty with local Wurundjeri elders (Attwood 2009). Although the Batman treaty was subsequently not recognised by the British Crown, this engagement between the new arrivals and Indigenous peoples by way of treaty-making also highlights the difference between the justification for the acquisition of territory (*terra nullius*) and the reality on the ground. Again, the paradox of the establishment of the colonies vis-à-vis *terra nullius* is laid bare by the actual practices of the individuals and communities involved.

A further anomaly occurred in South Australia, which was established as a free colony rather than a penal colony. This was achieved by the enactment of the South Australia Colonisation Act in 1834 by the Parliament of Westminster. Pursuant to the statute, the colony was established by the 'Letters Patent under the Great Seal of the United Kingdom erecting and establishing the Province of South Australia' in 1836. This is significant because the Letters Patent amounted to the incorrect application of the doctrine of *terra nullius* because they recognised Aboriginal peoples as rights holders insofar as they expressly directed that a 'relationship' must be founded that respected the rights of the Indigenous peoples over their lands. This was the first time that the Crown had acknowledged the existence of Aboriginal peoples as humans and the rights of Aboriginal peoples attached to those acquired lands (Letters Patent, n.d.).

This brief overview of some of the varied patterns of colonisation in Australia demonstrates the different ways that Indigenous peoples engaged with settlers and the uneven application of the provisions of *terra nullius*. The development of public law in each colony entrenched the invisibility of Indigenous peoples who were not considered to be British subjects and remained outside of the reach of the law on some matters. Conflict emerged because the legal basis of settlement in Australia was that there was no one inhabiting it with a prior legal claim to the territory, and yet the political and legal reality was one where there was conflictual engagement with Indigenous peoples and they were managed in different ways. In temporal terms, these initial conflicts remain as ghosts in the legal system to this day. Essentially, the legal and political justifications that rendered Indigenous people invisible and denied the existence of political conflict still pertain. This affects our understanding of contemporary debates about reconciliation because it obscures the conflict between the settler state (and its people in general) and Indigenous peoples in particular.

The historical relationship between law and politics in navigating the relationship between Indigenous peoples and the colonisers has been highly complex. The positioning of Indigenous peoples inside and outside of the colonial legal system further illustrates the internal conflict within the legal system, as well as the conflict between the colonial state and the Indigenous peoples. For example, the criminal law of each colony had difficulty in articulating the legal status and relationships of Aboriginal people. Three cases in particular demonstrate inherent confusion and tension between members of the judiciary: *R v. Ballard, R v. Murrell and Bummaree*, and *R v. Bonjon*. These three cases concern the relationship between Indigenous peoples and settlers in matters of criminality (Little and McMillan 2017). This is significant because at law, only humans can be criminals. At this point, the 'jurispathic' nature of the law made the relationship between Indigenous peoples and the settlers confused. Under the criminal law, there was no jurisdiction of a court if Aboriginal people committed crimes against each other. In contrast, when there was violence between Aboriginal peoples and settlers, Aboriginal people become subjects of the Crown. The Court in *R v. Bonjon* stated that Indigenous peoples were akin to 'domestic dependent nations'. Although buried for a long time, the case of *R v. Bonjon* emerged as an important indicator of how the law and its mediation of the relationship between Indigenous peoples and the Crown was much more complicated than it first appeared.

After federation in 1901, the newly formed Commonwealth was expressly forbidden from having a relationship with Indigenous peoples. The Commonwealth only gained powers granted to it by the states. The states expressly excluded the capacity of the Commonwealth to have relationships and to develop processes, principles or doctrines that might have allowed for a particular relationship to form. At various times after federation, Aboriginal people agitated for appropriate recognition of a relationship between the new nation and Indigenous peoples. In particular, the Australian Aborigines League led by William Cooper petitioned the King and the Commonwealth and State crowns in 1937 and he also called for a 'Day of Mourning' on the 150th anniversary of settlement (AIATSIS 2013). Another example is the Aborigines Progressives Association launched by William Ferguson and Jack Patten which developed a manifesto describing the conditions of Aboriginal peoples (AIATSIS 2013). The newly created federation did not obliterate ongoing relationships between the states and the Indigenous peoples in their individual jurisdictions. However, it is easy to see that the constitutional conventions of the 1890s demanded that the states oversee the relationships that would eventuate in the removal of Indigenous peoples altogether. It was the responsibility of the states to 'smooth the pillow of the dying breed', (Goodall 1996). If the 'Aboriginal race' ceased to exist, then there was no relationship – nor conflict – to manage. This official policy and legal framework would be defined today as genocide.

In 1967, after years of Indigenous activism, the Australian Parliament agreed to a referendum to change the constitutional sections that allowed the states to discriminate against Indigenous people. This activism coincided with the evolution of the place of Indigenous peoples in Australian society and the emergence and advancement of political movements focusing on human and civil rights more generally in the world at that time. There was considerable pressure to shift power to the Commonwealth from the states. The successful referendum allowed for the alteration of the Australian Constitution in 1967, by amending section 51 (xxvi) to allow the Commonwealth to pass laws with respect to Indigenous peoples. The referendum did not alter the existing relationships of each state to Indigenous peoples though; it only placed the relationships between Indigenous peoples and the Commonwealth on a different footing (L. Behrendt 2007).

The 1967 amendment also had the effect of 're-confusing' the relationship between the law, politics and Indigenous peoples. As it was presented in the referendum debate, the vote was supposedly about the equality of Indigenous peoples within the Commonwealth. The premise of this discussion was that the granting of the status of citizenship to Indigenous people reflected a promise of non-Indigenous people and the mechanisms of the state to a new relationship with Aboriginal and Torres Strait Islander peoples. In fact, what the referendum did to the law was to remove a restriction on the Commonwealth Parliament legislating 'with respect' to Indigenous peoples. In this way, the popular debate about the 1967 referendum and the actual legal implications of the successful referendum are somewhat at odds. The 1967 referendum did not advance 'reconciliation'. Instead, it entrenched the law as the apparatus that allowed the Commonwealth to act on Indigenous peoples rather than creating a new legal relationship between them. The disjuncture between the law and politics that was manufactured through the 1967 referendum debate has necessitated the current movement for constitutional reform. Therefore, despite ongoing representations of the referendum as a major achievement, for many Indigenous peoples it actually gave rise to the issues that need to be dealt with in contemporary constitutional debates. In temporal terms, it is clear that this event was part of a very much contested past and the actual reform brought about by the 1967 referendum remains a matter of some dispute.

Of course, the foregoing discussion is cast in a very narrow timeframe in Indigenous history in Australia. The period since the colonial encounter is very much Australia's short history when compared to over 60,000 years of existence on the territory for Aboriginal and Torres Strait Islander peoples. Similar histories play out in many countries across the world, where Indigenous communities have been overwhelmed by colonial forces and different temporal logics (Iparraguirre 2016). In Australia, Donaldson (1996: 198) reminds us that not only were there particular temporalities that guided the lives of Indigenous communities before the colonial encounter, but 'Aborigines maintained their own temporal order and its priorities against this [settler] regime' including its work ethic, which was anathema to many Indigenous temporalities. Importantly, this was not just a matter of living according to parallel temporalities, but of actively resisting the work ethic that was part and parcel of colonisation: 'temporality may not be expunged when relatedness to the past and openness to the future are combined with a flexible and imaginative use of counterhegemonic temporalities' (Donaldson 1996: 203). In other words, the imposition of settler structures in the states and Federation of Australia was not met with meek acquiescence, but rather active resistance practices to ensure the longevity of temporalities that preceded invasion.

In the face of often hostile imposition of settler structures against Indigenous communities, it is worth noting the resilience and endurance of these communities (Little 2014). This is not just a matter of preserving some traditional customs, practices and modes of thinking in the face of this hostility, although that is certainly part of the story. However, it is also reflective of remarkable adaptive capacity not only to survive colonial imposition, but also to develop practices of resistance in the face of such overbearing and structurally embedded colonial opposition. Therefore, when we discuss the endurance of Indigenous cultures, we should be careful not to merely fall into the settler trap of reifying cultural practices that are seen as part of a unitary, continuous 'tradition' that reflects the authentic ways of life of all Indigenous peoples. On the contrary, as Rifkin points out, Indigenous practices are as adaptive and heterogeneous as those of any other culture and comprise a variety of practices that meld traditional, contemporary and emergent contexts. In his discussion of the significance of storytelling, he uses Merleau-Ponty to suggest that storytelling should be perceived as 'a constitutive element of perception [which] emphasizes the variability and changeability of Native experiences while also addressing the ongoing (re)construction of collective frames of reference, suggesting less the transmission of static narratives than active and ongoing dynamics of perceptual (re)orientation' (Rifkin 2017: 34). If the past is more contested than most colonial narratives permit, then what of the present? In the next section we turn to questions on Indigenous-settler relations in the present to draw out the ways in which different narratives about the past infuse contemporary debates and, in turn, the ways in which they will inflect Indigenous-settler futures.

The Temporal Politics of Transformation

If the actual events of the past are contested, there is even greater scope for disagreement about the long-term implications of this disputed history for contemporary Indigenous-settler relations. The very foundations of debates in the present about meeting Indigenous demands for constitutional recognition, treaties, new Aboriginal and Torres Strait Islander institutions to provide 'voice' to parliament, truth-telling bodies and so on are based on high degrees of ignorance from non-Indigenous people about the issues that drive contemporary Indigenous politics (Uluru Statement 2017, Little 2020). Additionally, there are many Australians for whom these demands are anathema, or where the view prevails that Australian government and society has gone far enough in meeting Indigenous demands and no further acknowledgement, let alone reparation, is required. Just as there are multiple Aboriginal and Torres Strait Islander perspectives on the best means of advancing contemporary Indigenous politics, so too is there much disagreement within non-Indigenous Australia, especially in conservative circles. This is based in part on contestation about what happened in the past on the one hand, and driven by a concern that there should be no further reflection, apology or attempt to redress the position of Aboriginal and Torres Strait Islander peoples in the present on the other.

For many Aboriginal and Torres Strait Islander people, though, there is a further temporal disjuncture. This lies in the view that the current political situation is a passing episode in a history that can be traced back over tens of thousands of years (Weir 2009) and where settlers are a somewhat recent (albeit dominant) addition to the constitution of society. In this environment, the push to 'move on' is a fundamental part of the problem. Therefore, not everyone involved in the discussion of contemporary Indigenous-settler relations is necessarily working in the same temporal register. The 'temporal ecology' of experience (Hassan and Purser 2007: 13) in Indigenous-settler relations consists of disagreement about the timescale of the issue under discussion, the pace at which change has taken place, and the urgency or otherwise of the political options confronting political actors. Not surprisingly, this is mirrored by confusion and division in Australian political circles; although this disarray is often not highlighted in narratives of bipartisanship between the two major political blocs.

In a context like Australia (and many others), this is further complicated by the intersection with forms of racial ordering to create a much more complex and fragile environment. Put simply, not all parties to the debate about Indigenous-settler relations in Australia understand the temporal dimension of the debate in the same way and this is compounded by considerable ignorance about relationships between Indigeneity and race. For example, events that some non-Indigenous people might construe as merely the past or historical issues can be very much a contemporary concern around racial politics for Aboriginal and Torres Strait Islander peoples, as was in evidence during the Black Lives Matter protests of 2020. The attempt to garner greater contemporary prominence for unresolved Indigenous-settler conflicts in the past is as much about the future understanding of Aboriginal experiences and the need for them to be retained at the heart of the self-understanding of contemporary Australia. Therefore, debates that are *solely* focused on which particular institutional configuration is needed to reconcile Indigenous and non-Indigenous peoples in Australia are wide of the mark, if they are not properly focused on the plurality of Aboriginal histories *and their contemporary resonances* in forms of racial ordering. Too much of the reconciliation effort in Australia from the early 1990s was focused on drawing a line under the past, rather than highlighting the fundamentally misrecognised nature of the problem to be addressed. Such mainstream perspectives on the need to 'move on' were inherently part of the problem in Australia and the educative part of the reconciliation process was lost amidst the premature demand to solve a problem that had not been properly understood by most non-Indigenous people.

This disjuncture in temporal registers is also evident in the urgency with which contemporary processes of change are presented in public in Australia. The passage of time is a complex issue in Aboriginal and Torres Strait Islander politics: on the one hand, we are advised by (mainly non-Indigenous) political commentators that the current window for constitutional change is a chance of a lifetime, a window for change that will close sooner rather than later. It seems that this reflects a desire to have the issue over and done with so that Australia can 'move on', regardless of sub-optimal outcomes. Aboriginal and Torres Strait Islander peoples, however, are well aware that such discourses have been prevalent since at least the 1980s, with every initiative hailed as a major breakthrough and an opportunity to finally right the wrongs of Australia's past. From early discussions of treaty in the 1980s, through the politics of reconciliation in the 1990s and into the new century (Keating 2001, Dodson 1993), the Mabo decision in 1993 (Sanders 2018, J. Behrendt 2007), the Apology to the 'Stolen Generations' in 2008 (Barta 2008), and the stop-start discussions of constitutional recognition for over a decade now, it seems that each 'critical juncture' is quickly followed by another usually invoking a different concept. The endurance demonstrated by Indigenous peoples during these 'debates' has been remarkable and there is undoubtedly a desire amongst them to steer their own process and deliver substantive change in a way that has not been the case with government-driven political processes thus far. It wears thin to be told that there is yet another urgent initiative only to see terms which do not reflect Aboriginal desires or inputs, and to be told that these proposals are urgent. These critical junctures often promise a lot, such as 'the extension of social justice' initiatives alongside land rights legislation as articulated in Prime Minister Paul Keating's infamous Redfern Park speech in 1992, but they often deliver much less (Keating 2001). However, in 2017, the Uluru Statement marked a different phase in these developments (Uluru Statement 2017, Little 2020).

Following the formal reconciliation process from the early 1990s that resulted in little substantive change in Indigenous-settler relations, the Apology to the Stolen Generations from Prime Minister Kevin Rudd in

2008 promised yet again to reset relationships between Indigenous and non-Indigenous peoples in Australia (Barta 2008). However, it quickly became clear that the Apology, while welcome, was focused on a particular kind of wrongdoing against specific victims – those who had been removed from their families as children – and was not capable of addressing the broader structural inequalities experienced by Aboriginal and Torres Strait Islander peoples in contemporary Australia and their grounding in a historical experience of conflict. While the Apology was significant, then, it could not reset broader relationships between Indigenous and non-Indigenous peoples (especially as child removals continue today). Following a hung parliament in the 2010 federal election (Crozier and Little 2012), the issue of constitutional recognition of Indigenous people as the original inhabitants of Australia, their unique relationship to the land and sea, the particular cultural traditions of different Indigenous nations, and their languages, customs and legal practices came to the fore as the Australian Labor Party (ALP) sought a deal with a small group of independent members of the House of Representatives to form a workable parliamentary majority. These circumstances were the conditions under which the idea of recognition of Aboriginal and Torres Strait Islander peoples in the Australian Constitution seemingly gained real political traction.

In the ensuing decade, however, Australia had five Prime Ministers across its two predominant parliamentary blocs and a wide range of initiatives designed to advance the case for constitutional recognition of Indigenous peoples. Despite an ostensible bipartisan approach to the issue, the process has always been open to partisan fractures, not least because the nature of the object being pursued was always opaque, the process was intermittent and ebbed and flowed according to the political circumstances of the day, and it was largely devoid of ordinary Indigenous input. Perhaps not so explicit were the different temporal registers with which governments and their initiatives were working. The former coalition Prime Minister Malcolm Turnbull (in collaboration with then ALP opposition leader Bill Shorten) formed a Referendum Council in 2015 to advance the process, including a limited Indigenous consultation exercise across the states and territories of Australia. Following this consultation process convened by prominent Indigenous leaders in Australia, many of the key participants and activists gathered at Uluru for a National Constitutional Convention to discuss the proposals for constitutional recognition and to deliver a response. The result was the Uluru Statement from the Heart which was delivered on 26 May 2017 by key Indigenous leaders and its proposals were subsequently taken up by the Referendum Council.

The terms of reference for the Referendum Council were to lead national consultations, build on the work of previous initiatives since 2010 regarding constitutional recognition, and then report to the Prime Minister on the consultations and 'options for a referendum proposal, steps for finalising a proposal, and possible timing for a referendum' (Referendum Council 2017).

The Uluru Statement made the case for three parallel forms of recognition to make the ensuing process meaningful: a truth-telling exercise to enable the articulation of Indigenous history, an agreement-making process to enable a resetting of the relationships between First Nations and the states and Federation of Australia, and the formation of a new institution or process to ensure an Indigenous voice to parliament (Uluru Statement 2017). The truth-telling and agreement-making parts of this tripartite approach would be supervised by a Makarrata Commission. Makarrata is a Yolngu word defined in the Statement as '*the coming together after a struggle*' (Little 2020). Five months after the Uluru Statement, the Turnbull government rejected the recommendation of the Referendum Council for an Indigenous voice to parliament, arguing that it would inevitably become a third chamber of the Australian Parliament and therefore would undermine Australia's parliamentary democracy (ABC 2017). This view was subsequently rejected by a number of senior legal figures in Australia (including two former Chief Justices of the High Court, Murray Gleeson and Robert French; see Appleby 2019). Once again, then, Indigenous politics in Australia and Indigenous-settler relations were left in a state of uncertainty. This uncertainty was accentuated by the fact that the Uluru Statement had been a clear statement from Aboriginal and Torres Strait Islander peoples of their relatively consensual view on the terms on which the debate should be conducted; its summary rejection by the coalition government was a slap in the face of those who had done so much to engage in the consultation process and develop the Uluru Statement – a document forged on Indigenous terms.

However, what became a little lost in this debate is that the Cabinet rejection of the proposal focused almost entirely on the 'Indigenous voice to parliament' prong of the Referendum Council's Final Report. Even though actual concrete proposals for the nature of this voice were beyond the remit of the Council, they were nonetheless rejected *tout court* by the Cabinet. However, much less was said about the other two elements of the Uluru Statement that were to come under the auspices of the Makarrata Commission, that is, the processes of truth-telling and agreement-making. The focus on the Indigenous voice to parliament has shrouded these other parts of the debate, in particular the likelihood that Makarrata – focused on the issues of truth and treaty – would be as contentious, if not more so, than the Indigenous voice proposal. Indeed, the Uluru Statement insinuates a long road ahead by indicating that 'Makarrata is the *culmination of our agenda . . .* It captures our aspirations for a fair and truthful relationship with the people of Australia and a better future for our children based on justice and self-determination' (Uluru Statement 2017, emphasis added). This implies a much longer duration than the settler imagination (or the governments deploying it) envisages.

A close examination of the Uluru Statement and subsequent supportive commentary (Appleby and Davis 2018, Appleby and McKinnon 2017) makes clear that, for Aboriginal and Torres Strait Islander peoples, there is connection and overlap between past, present and future. Indeed, the key to political action in the present to address Indigenous-settler relations is to ensure that the past is kept alive in the future. While this involves significant exercises such as institutionalising truth-telling, it also involves retaining the memories embedded in Aboriginal languages and cultures including the historical connections to the land and sea through contemporary practices. It is vital, then, for these practices to become enshrined in a vision of the future of Indigenous-settler relations. The temporal view of history invoked here is tens of thousands of years rather than merely the last 250 years since the colonial encounter. The general perspective on temporality underpinning the Uluru Statement is sophisticated (if implicit) and differs dramatically from an approach to political action in the present which is concerned with drawing a line under the past so that the problems of Indigenous-settler relations in the past and present do not tarnish the future politics of Australia. Rather Uluru invokes a sophisticated temporality that recognises that the past inevitably lives in the future, and that the current political debate, at least amongst non-Indigenous participants, seems more focused on a resolution of issues and the entire Indigenous-settler problem. In other words, it lacks the kind of temporal political perspective of the kind articulated here and in the Uluru Statement.

This temporal disjuncture has profound ramifications for debates about the way in which the Uluru recommendations for truth, treaty and voice might be operationalised. Where governments and many non-Indigenous people may engage with Indigenous affairs as matters to be resolved and put to bed, for Indigenous actors the approach to these debates is quite often focused on the need to keep alive specific political issues as well as legal, social and cultural practices as ongoing and future concerns that are fundamental to their political identity. Indeed, it is politically problematic to try to put issues to bed that have not even been properly understood thus far, especially around the longevity and significance of Aboriginal and Torres Strait Islander traditions. Therefore, Indigenous-settler relations have a fundamental temporal-spatial dimension which reflects a substantial disjuncture that will be the source of ongoing dispute and future contestation (see the words of Vine Deloria Jr cited in Coulthard 2014: 60). Any approach – institutional *or* ideational – which fails to respect the fundamentally contested nature of the issues at stake is more than likely to repeat the mistakes of the past (and present). From this perspective, fundamental disagreements about temporality are of pivotal importance in getting to the heart of the issues between Indigenous and non-Indigenous people in Australia today. As well-meaning as they might be, efforts to right wrongs, reconcile competing interests, close gaps in key social indicators, or 'recognise' Indigenous people as a means of resolving Indigenous/non-Indigenous divisions are likely to fall short of the kinds of temporal understandings required to make sense of the demands of Aboriginal and Torres Strait Islander peoples.

In the wake of the report of the Referendum Council, the progress towards treaty/agreements in Victoria and the Northern Territory, and the commitment of the ALP to pursue the recommendations of the Uluru Statement, Australia is now facing an opportunity to enact some of the most far-reaching reforms in Indigenous affairs in settler history in the country. However, yet again, the federal government (as at mid-2021) has conceded that change is unlikely to happen in the current parliament (although there have been a number of sometimes contradictory statements on this point from Prime Minister Scott Morrison and his Minister for Indigenous Australians, Ken Wyatt). At this juncture, and with an eye to the discussion of processive politics in Chapter 7, it is worth reflecting on the temporal 'process' of the last forty years of Indigenous-settler relations in Australia.

Without a doubt the political initiatives of these years have been frustratingly slow, with small advances delivering piecemeal reforms often followed by retrograde steps – think here of different Prime Ministers that have promised change, such as Bob Hawke's declaration of intent for a treaty in the 1980s, John Howard's retreat into 'practical reconciliation' in the 1990s, the discussions of constitutional recognition through the Rudd-Gillard-Abbott post-Apology years, until Turnbull's rejection of the Uluru proposals. This points to a different kind of path dependence where, despite the ebbs and flows of slow transformational processes with movement forward followed by steps back depending on the political complexions of different governments, the intent of many Aboriginal and Torres Strait Islander political activists has not shifted dramatically. Many Indigenous aspirations remain remarkably consistent and steadfast, albeit the reaction to different government initiatives may be positive or negative depending on the urgency with which activists view the process of transformation. Thus, it could be argued that there is an enduring and resilient path dependence in Indigenous politics to pursue long-term objectives, even where government initiatives fall far short of Aboriginal and Torres Strait Islander aspirations or directly contradict them. The temporal implication of this point is that these substantive objectives will recur in the future regardless of the precise form of piecemeal reform in the present.

Insofar as Australia as a whole does not yet have a treaty or treaties or an established institution designed to facilitate truth-telling (despite efforts to implement one in Victoria being well-advanced), there do seem to be opportunities to build something fit for purpose and genuinely transformative. On the other hand, there have been numerous attempts since the 1970s to form institutions that can provide an Indigenous voice, albeit frequently ignored by parliament or government. This has included institutional developments such as the Aboriginal and Torres Strait Islander Commission (ATSIC), which was abolished by the Howard government in 2005, and the National Congress of Australia's First Peoples (NCAFP or 'Congress'), which did not receive expected funding after 2013 from the Abbott, Turnbull and Morrison administrations and which went into administration in 2019 (Allam 2019). It is important, then, to identify ways in which path dependence might inflect the formation of any new institutions so that they are better equipped to deliver meaningful change for Aboriginal and Torres Strait Islander peoples. However, this requires more than an 'institutional fix'. Rather, it demands a different *ideational* trajectory that does not fall into old, stereotypical attitudes, beliefs and concepts used to interpret and account for Indigenous peoples. In other words, it demands recognition of the problems of established patterns of paternalism and/or neglect that have characterised Indigenous/non-Indigenous relations in the Australian state thus far to try to ensure that they are not replicated in any new institutions focused on truth and treaty. These problematic attitudes and beliefs have been represented by differing policies in recent times ranging from the Northern Territory Emergency Response to the Closing the Gap campaign (Anthony 2018, Macoun 2011). Most importantly of all, they require direct engagement with the Aboriginal and Torres Strait Islander peoples who are going to be impacted by them in their inception, if they are to inspire sufficient support from Australia's Indigenous communities.

Uncertain Futures

If the Uluru Statement reflects a sophisticated understanding of the temporal challenges of the relationship between past and present, what implications does the idea of uncertain futures hold for Indigenous and non-Indigenous peoples? In many respects uncertainty about the future is the biggest challenge in the space of Indigenous-settler relations insofar as Aboriginal and Torres Strait Islander peoples are pressing for political change and non-Indigenous people and Australian institutions seem very poorly equipped to deliver it. As noted above, the arguments are quite often performed on different temporal planes. Ironically, however, Indigenous peoples in general are potentially well-equipped in this political debate, given their long experience of the failing efforts of the Australian state to deliver substantive change. Although the many false dawns have been painful, the disappointment engendered by the inability of the state to match its promises with outcomes has led to a situation where Indigenous communities have taken the lead in making their own demands and establishing the grounds on which the debates about the future should take place. That is, there has been frustration at the failings not only of the Australian government but also of non-Indigenous people to understand the issues at the centre of Indigenous politics, including many of those non-Indigenous people who purport to speak for, on behalf of, or in the interests of Aboriginal and Torres Strait Islander peoples.

The message articulated at Uluru highlights the importance of Indigenous communities having responsibility for their own political existence, should a modicum of such an opportunity emerge in the post-Uluru political environment. This is not to say that Uluru was a silver bullet to rectify Indigenous/non-Indigenous relations in Australia, but it provided a clear pathway that should inform debates about future institutional design and the ideational content that needs to underpin the development of alternative political institutions. Indeed, such is their dissatisfaction with the Australian state that many Indigenous peoples in general are more than prepared to move towards much greater self-government if they are empowered to do so by a voice to the federal parliament or by First Nations institutions formed through agreements with state governments. At the same time, they are equally aware that it may well come to nought and that the settler state will once again prove to be incapable of relinquishing its hold over Australia's Indigenous peoples. Despite making some radical demands for change, there is also an innate pragmatism at work in this mindset, born of disappointment with the historical efforts of the Australian body politic to accommodate Aboriginal and Torres Strait

Islander perspectives. From a temporal perspective, this reflects a capacity to deal with whatever the future holds, be that initiatives co-designed to build new institutions for Indigenous peoples, through to yet another reversion to the modus operandi of the settler state.

However, this pragmatic approach to potentially radical change is not well understood in non-Indigenous Australia, which typically finds the challenge of uncertain futures a much more significant existential issue. Much of the reason for this resides in the unwillingness of the Australian state to recognise its historical wrongdoing and, therefore, the inability of Australia to seriously grapple with a history of violence and conflict and their long-term implications. Importantly, although non-Indigenous Australians may be ready to countenance the idea that there was violence and bloodshed in the colonial encounter, this rarely extends to a sense of personal or collective culpability amongst contemporary non-Indigenous Australians regardless of their political perspective. While all political communities have things about which they don't like to speak (Muldoon 2017), states that have actively silenced, aggressively persecuted or attempted the annihilation of other peoples have more secrets than most. These hidden histories are stories of pain and of political reality. This inability to even countenance the past, let alone take responsibility for some of the outcomes, makes non-Indigenous people particularly ill-equipped to grapple with the uncertainties of the future. Therefore, the inability to address the past in a substantive way compromises the capacity of non-Indigenous people to embrace the possibilities and challenges of the future. The demeanour of seeking out resolution as a way of putting the past behind us means that they have no position from which to understand and embrace the idea that settler colonial societies need to 'own' the wrongdoing of the past and continue to grapple with its implications for the future. It is impossible to do this if one's disposition towards the past is either denial of wrongdoing or a misguided search for resolution before the full implications of such wrongdoing have been recognised.

Recent research into the Regional Dialogues that preceded the Uluru Statement suggests similar expectations have been invested in a process of truth-telling in Australia. The hope here is that truth-telling will secure healing for the trauma of colonisation, provide greater public understanding of the 'true history' of the country, and establish a platform upon which to build a new relationship between Indigenous and non-Indigenous people (Appleby and Davis 2018). On the basis of first-hand experience of the dialogues, Appleby and Davis (2018) contend that the demand for truth in Australia is explicitly linked to the hope for political transition. Aboriginal and Torres Strait Islander peoples, they suggest, are not just looking to clarify certain historical facts or show belated respect to unrecognised victims. Rather they are calling for truth-telling as part of a political transformation in which the relationship between First Nations and the Australian state is fundamentally renegotiated (Appleby and Davis 2018: 503–4). Given experiences with a range of political initiatives over the last thirty years, it is difficult not to prepare for disappointment in the likelihood that such hopes will not be realised. However, a processive account, as outlined in the previous section, might give greater optimism that even dashed hopes can be part of a broader tapestry that delivers more substantive and radical transformation over the course of time (as frustrating as this can be when faced with urgent and long-standing issues).

Australia is not yet at the point where concrete options for institutionalising the Uluru recommendations have been discussed amongst the wider public, but there are some emergent conversations that are starting to substantiate the principles outlined at Uluru. Appleby and Davis have argued that many of the key truths that need to be articulated are localised in nature and require processes of truth-telling in community settings across Australia. However, they go further in demanding that these truths should subsequently be collated and held in a central repository. This archive could then be a space of ongoing recognition and an opportunity for public learning for a future in which these truths are kept 'alive' and visible. In other words, it would be a way to connect the past and future in a highly visible way. However, this leaves open the question of whether a process of truth-telling involves ongoing, contemporary narratives of truth based on the lived experience of Aboriginal and Torres Strait Islander peoples or whether it would only cover 'historical' events. Both options invoke a range of subsidiary questions, not least the kinds of issues that might be classified as the types of stories to be told as truths to be recognised, and to whom should these truths apply? Are there further rectificatory actions to be taken as a result of truth-telling exercises?

If the process of truth-telling is one where only 'historical' truths are to be told, then, while doing highly important work in the present, we risk confining the discussion of injustices experienced by Indigenous peoples as historical artefacts rather than matters which happen today and will continue into the future. For example, it can draw attention away from contemporary problems such as the widely disproportionate numbers of Indigenous people dying in police custody (AHRC 2020, Allam 2020). Moreover, it is also important that historical truths are not just held in an institutional format, but that they are maintained through oral traditions such as storytelling and bearing witness. Therefore, questions of witnessing become very important to the institutional form that truth-telling takes (Nagy 2020). And it is here that we can recognise a clear role for non-Indigenous as well as Indigenous peoples.

Witnessing invokes a responsibility to listen and the possibility of retelling without intervening in the truth that was told. Perhaps one of the missing features in discussions of the responsibility of non-Indigenous people is the need to listen and to continue to reiterate stories that have been witnessed by other non-Indigenous people. To be clear, the responsibilities of non-Indigenous people are not to act as spokespeople for Indigenous peoples, given that, when the opportunity arises, Indigenous peoples are more than capable of speaking for themselves. Rather, if truth-telling is to take place, then there needs to be a clear understanding of what witnessing truth means and the responsibilities such witnessing carries with it. In a sense, a commitment to witness is an act of prefacing which in some ways acknowledges the story that is to come, but it does so in a way that combines a sense of openness and closure simultaneously. Working from a Derridean foundation, Bohle (2017: 264) states that honorary witnessing 'is an anticipation of what remains to come, of opening settled narratives to public challenge, which also mediates and perhaps thereby restricts what might be said. It is an anticipation of openness that also functions as a restriction.'

The potential shortcomings from honorary witnessing are a burden that non-Indigenous people should carry rather than expecting that the onus is on Indigenous people alone to recount the truths that are told and the need to keep these truths alive in the future. In terms of her experiences as a non-Indigenous witness to the Canadian Truth and Reconciliation Commission, Nagy states that

> As witnesses, our ongoing responsibility is to the interrelationship between past, present, and future that is embedded in the temporal sovereignty of Indigenous knowledges. Witnessing is not a one-off moment but an ethical demand to make meaning over time through response-ability to the other. In so doing, we move ourselves and settler society beyond colonial modes of recognition. This process thereby nurtures the possibility in settler witnesses of active responses that disrupt or dismantle colonial structures in order to secure Indigenous futurity. (Nagy 2020: 220)

There is also an important set of questions regarding the purposes of truth-telling. While there is undoubtedly a strong demand for truth from Indigenous peoples in the context of many settler colonial societies such as Canada and Australia, there has been less focus on the reasons why the pursuit of truth is so important. To put it another way, there are questions over the different kinds of work that truth is supposed to do in these settings. By some accounts, truth should be pursued to provide a degree of catharsis for those victims where the reality of their experiences has not properly been recognised (Minow 2000). In these arguments, truth is thought to hold potential for *healing*. Other approaches are more sceptical of this notion of healing, but do believe that the act of truth-telling is an important act of acknowledgement of wrongdoing – especially wrongs per-petrated by the state – and that these misdemeanours need to be publicly recognised despite the fact that truths by themselves cannot rewrite the past to enable people to recover and move on. Rather than seeking healing, this approach is more focused on *informing* public narratives (Ignatieff 1996). Some commentators want truth for truth's sake, while others want to use it as a means of attaining justice. This justice can be delivered in many ways from public acknowledgement through to punishment of crim-inality. Even where justice is not pursued, there is a faith in the work of commentators like Appleby and Davis (2018) that truth processes can do the work of *transforming* a society blighted by historical injustices. What is becoming increasingly clear in societies that are struggling with truth like Australia is that truth is expected to do different work for differ-ent people and is advocated for a variety of reasons. Therefore, in what-ever way it is institutionalised, truth is likely to disappoint some of its strongest proponents. Moreover, the uncertainty of the future pertains to truth-telling exercises as well. Despite the best efforts that may be put into discussion, preparation and institutional design, it is very difficult to predict how the practice of truth-telling will play out in the future of a specific context of political conflict.

In the Australian case, the debate about truth-telling is also bound together with other initiatives for social transformation which have a sig-nificant temporal dimension. These include debates on treaties within and across states and territories, arguments for reparations, and the more gen-eral advocacy invoked since Uluru on how to establish an institution that provides an Indigenous voice to parliament. Treaty discussions are advanc-ing in Victoria and the Northern Territory and it is clear that some of these issues are closely entwined with truth. For example, Yawuru leader and former Northern Territory Treaty Commissioner Mick Dodson outlines the urgency of truth-telling because of the fact that many Aboriginal elders are elderly and likely to pass away if the treaty process takes as long as it did in British Columbia (Gooley 2020). Therefore, because treaties are a 'long game', Dodson insists truth cannot wait for treaties to be concluded. Indeed, whether there is a solid enough foundation for treaty without a prior truth process is a contested issue in Australian politics. Thus, we can see temporal discord in place once again – in this specific example about sequencing as well as urgency. These discussions are not merely to be taken at face value either. Instead, as Rifkin (2017: 25) reminds us:

> In the absence of a mutual frame of reference (a common background) between Natives and non-natives, non-natives engage in forms of translation, not primarily to understand Native temporalities but to insert them within settler timescapes. That process of interpellation is not acknowledged as such, and through it, Indigenous experiences appear as exception.

The case of relationships between Indigenous and non-Indigenous people in settler colonial societies is a perfect example of some of the contestation around lived experiences that underpin the notion of temporality. In terms of historical understandings, it identifies differing timescales in what is thought to constitute 'the past' and varying interpretations of the ways in which the past lives on in the present and future. Settlers must grapple with disagreements about the sequencing of events and their impacts, as well as disputed interpretations about the urgency of political change, rather than expecting their narratives to prevail. Many different commentators may highlight such urgency, but for very different reasons: for example, the need to tell truths while victims are still alive vis-à-vis the rush for a political settlement so that we can 'move on', or the desire to deal swiftly with the symbolic so that practical matters can be attended to in health, education and criminal justice without political baggage. I've indicated in this chapter that I think the last two of these approaches to 'urgency' are misguided as if relationships in settler colonial societies can ever be conducted non-politically. But, more importantly for the theoretical purposes here, it points to the degree of temporal disjuncture in settler colonial societies. While this may take a particular form in those societies, it also inflects all divided societies, post-colonies, modern multicultural, multi-ethnic and multi-faith nations, and polities with other cultural or socio-economic divisions. The basic point is that differing temporalities – part and parcel of plurality – inhibit sameness, with the corollary that it is unwise to not factor temporal multiplicity into political decision-making.

The experience of settler colonial societies makes the co-existence of temporalities all too evident. In terms which reflect Bergson's temporal methods and his conception of duration outlined in Chapter 2, Rifkin (2017: 46) states that Indigenous temporalities operate

> less as a chronological sequence than as overlapping networks of affective connection (to persons, nonhuman entities, and place) that orient one's way of moving through space and time, with story as a crucial part of that process. In this way, storying helps engender a frame of reference, such as by providing a background against which to perceive motion, change, continuity, and possible action in the world in ways that cannot be encompassed within dominant modes of settler time.

This outline of Indigenous temporalities entails a multiplicity of Indigenous perspectives on past, present and future. It resists essentialising Indigenous timescapes and insists on a plurality of Indigenous and non-Indigenous temporalities. Temporal politics resists the reduction of multiple temporalities to the prevailing understanding of 'settler time' or 'hegemonic temporality' (Iparraguirre 2016) in which the past is elapsed, the present is the now, and the future is the unknown that is yet to come. Moreover, it is not involved in the pursuit of a 'shared time' in which differences are reduced to some kind of imposed uniformity (Bastian 2013). Instead, a theory of temporal politics must recognise the non-sequential elements of multiple temporalities and the overlapping of past, present and future.

A plurality of temporalities does not mean heterogeneity in the Bergsonian sense; these timescapes are not merely to be juxtaposed with one another. Instead, the theory of temporal politics highlights their overlap, their relationships with one another, rather than their sheer distinctness. What we have seen in this chapter is the existence of multiple temporalities overlapping and conflicting with one another. In settler colonial societies, this multiplicity has been reduced to 'settler time' where diversity and plurality in temporal outlook are not reflected in public narrative, especially involving the embeddedness of present and future in the past. Moreover, we have also seen that the failure to engage temporal plurality generates further political conflict such that the issues at the heart of temporal contestation will endure and return to spaces of political argumentation in the future. In the next chapter, we augment this argument by moving on to one of the most contested issues in contemporary global politics – borders and migration – to exemplify the ways in which the politics of the present is also imbued with disputed conceptions of the past and future.

5

Locating the Present in the Past and Future: The Complex Temporality of Borders

Political issues that emanate from unresolved historical injustice are firmly ingrained in an ongoing temporal dynamic that stretches from the past through the present and into the future. Our attention in this chapter turns to a different issue of seemingly only contemporary concern – crises of borders and the displacement of peoples – to demonstrate the ways in which it is also necessary to understand the historical and future dimensions of such urgent and serious matters in contemporary politics (Cohen 2018). The key point here is that the incidence of emergencies and flashpoints in contemporary politics does not mean that these issues can be satisfactorily handled without a thorough perspective on the historical emergence of problems from the past and the ramifications for the future of the possible courses of action in the present. This chapter focuses on the operation of borders in contemporary politics and highlights the complex temporal dimensions of their operations, including how they pertain to contemporary political debates about the displacement of peoples in both a historical and a future-oriented light.

The existence of borders is a foundational assumption in much political science and international relations. They are important in delineating nation-states, their governments and institutions, their constitutions and their citizens from each other. As many borders are long-standing, they are sometimes thought of in ways which suggest that they are somehow 'natural', especially in the case of some island nations. Moreover, borders are often understood as static and stable entities that organise the spaces in which politics takes place and within which normative debates are operationalised. From this understanding, we can start to make assumptions about particular pieces of territory, the political relations that characterise them and, frequently, the people who reside there in terms of culture and identity.

However, increasingly, this rather one-dimensional reading of borders is being raised in new forms of critical border studies (Johnson et al. 2011). It is challenged by the growing body of work on borderlands (Michaelsen and Johnson 1997) influenced by disciplines such as geography (Agnew 2008, Anderson and O'Dowd 1999, Anderson 2002), sociology (Newman 2006) and anthropology (Wilson and Donnan 1998b, Donnan and Wilson 1994, Alonso 1994) which have a longer-term interest in the specific spatiality and cultures of borders and borderlands. In this chapter the focus turns to the impact of this literature on normative perspectives in political theory and, in particular, the ways in which temporal changes in borders affect the manner in which debates on migration tend to be constructed. The key objective is to examine the 'endemic liminality' (Wilson 1994: 111) of borders and the implications of rethinking borders in more contingent terms on the application of normative theories to 'real politics' (Little 2015c).

While the main focus here is on borders between nation-states and their impact on humans at the frontier, critical border studies makes equally clear that borders *within* nation-states reflect some similar dynamics and can be equally important frontiers for people who live around them and impact a wide range of groups, including those who are effectively stateless, others who are non-citizens of the land they inhabit and, indeed, other species (McNevin 2011, 2020, Ozguc 2020). The phenomenon of bordering therefore pertains to borders not only between nation-states but also within them, for example, bordering between First Nations before the formation of the modern nation-state and the phenomenon of erecting walls and fences within divided societies to keep conflictual parties apart (Brown 2010). Put simply, these issues around borderlands and the movement of people are endemic to modern political life and, thus, political theories that purport to address normative concerns about migration and the movement of people in the 'real world' need to take into account the liminal nature of the boundaries to which theory is applied.

The growing attention being given to borders in the political science literature has coincided with their renewed strength in this century, thereby contradicting the borderless world predicted by some proponents of the globalisation thesis in the 1990s (Ohmae 1999). Issues such as the emergence of new security threats and the increased visibility of political controversies around migration have increased the focus on borders as states seek to assert sovereign powers. Several governments – most obviously in the USA and the UK but also in Australia and many with less power in global politics – have sought to construct a national agenda that takes

liberal globalism to be a fundamental problem. In turn, this has created a
critical backlash with scholars highlighting problems including new forms
of biometric monitoring, the increased use of offshore or third-party bordering processes, the porosity of borders, the limits of borders as markers
of the boundaries of sovereignty, internal boundaries within nation-
states as more politically significant than peripheral borders, and so forth
(Johnson et al. 2011). Thus, the literature in critical border studies points
to a number of challenges that call into question the dominant assumption
that borders just 'are' and, more importantly still, whether they are appropriate markers of the boundaries within which legitimate political authority should be exercised over people. Essentially, critical border studies asks
us to rethink the normative basis on which borders can 'contain' actions
and policies in the 'real world'. The 'changing reality of borders' is a fact
that makes it difficult to operationalise political concepts and normative
arguments that are reliant on their settled nature (Parker and Vaughan-
Williams 2009: 583, Little and Vaughan-Williams 2017).

However, as significant as these new debates have become, it does beg
the question of what exactly is the *problem* with borders? Is it that borders
in the contemporary world are not capable of fulfilling the role that has
traditionally been ascribed to them in terms of containing threats? Is the
problem that bordering practices take place far beyond and well within
the physical frontiers of the nation-state? Is it that they inhibit mobility
and divide peoples who may share much in common? Or, perhaps more
fundamentally, are borders locking us into an unsustainable 'territorialist
epistemology' (Albert et al. 2001)? These are all important questions in
the border studies literature but, for the purposes of the book, the precise
problem of bordering that I want to examine is related to borders and temporal change. More specifically, this chapter problematises the terrain of
normative theories that grapple with complex issues such as migration but
do not recognise the contingency of borders. While critical border studies
has involved a cross-disciplinary effort to address the problems associated
with traditional conceptions of borders, a lot of the work is still concerned
with the geography and, in particular, the spatiality of border dynamics (Mountz 2011). However, commentators such as Amoore (2011) and
Parker and Vaughan-Williams (2009: 585) have started to highlight the
ambiguity of borders and, in particular, the relationship between spatiality
and temporality in this contingent condition.

The perception of borders as static, inevitable or natural is fundamentally at odds with the practice of bordering which is much more dynamic
and contingent. Of course, borders change over the course of time.

Sometimes they physically move and sometimes their fundamental character changes as time elapses. Sometimes this takes place through deliberate political action and sometimes it is much more evolutionary, incremental and even accidental. While diachronic theories attempt to understand change by examining issues at different temporal junctures, they often do so in a rather linear fashion that is not capable of digesting the disorderly manner and the uneven tempo in which change takes place in the real world and therefore the shifting political challenges that emerge as borders evolve over the course of time.

Put more simply, too many theories of change are constructed in terms of a 'then and now' mentality that is not well suited to the actual uneven and processive nature of change in the 'real world'. Thus, even where a border physically remains in the same place, its nature, its porosity, its securitisation or demilitarisation, its capacity to contain issues and people are dynamic elements that accompany its static physical nature. On the other hand, where boundaries do physically change, this has significant implications for people within the frontier but also new political relations with those on the other side of the interface. So, the fundamental issue I want to draw attention to is what I call 'complex temporality', especially the ways in which a method of temporal politics introduces elements of contingency that undermine some of the normative certainty that borders have traditionally engendered. The question becomes how to envisage the operationalisation of normative principles when the space in which these principles are played out is such an equivocal stage.

This chapter will outline the implications of complex temporality and explain why temporality and temporal change is complex rather than linear and orderly. This will lead into a discussion of the time and space of borders and identification of the ways in which spatial and temporal changes pose particular problems for the politics of bordering. From there we turn to the challenges that this changing environment might engender for political theory. In particular, the dynamic, contingent nature of bordering across the passage of time is raised as a problem for the *force* of normative argument in politics. The final section focuses on the ways in which complex temporality calls forth a notion of contingency in the politics of international borders. This recognises the centrality of borders where they exist at a given point in time for political decisions about who is in and out, but it also questions their normative power as definitive, legitimate and authoritative markers of where decisions should be taken in an environment of uneven temporal change. This is the challenge of 'time-space governance' (Sum 2000).

Complex Temporality

At the outset, it is worth outlining the meaning of 'complex temporality' so that the challenge for the theory and practice of bordering becomes clear. As highlighted in Chapter 3, temporality introduces a dynamic human, subjective and interpretive dimension around 'time as change' (Adam 2004: 24). Invoking Heraclitus, Adam (2004: 25) suggests that rather than viewing social conditions through the lens of permanence, temporality refers to the reality of perpetual change in which 'stability and rest are the illusion'. Moreover, as we have seen, much of the literature on time and temporality focuses on issues of speed – mostly the rapidity of change but also, in some of the more nuanced, ethnographic work (Longo 2017), that the acceleration of the social, political and economic world does not necessarily correlate with the changing pace of activities in everyday life (Sharma 2014: 4–6). Similarly, Coles et al. (2014: 38) contend that 'democratic possibility involves judgments not only about the past and futurity, but also about tempo, pace, or speed because these things bear (perhaps in conflicting ways) on capacities for change and for deliberation'. So, even if objective time passes in ways that could be seen to be politically uncontroversial, in practice the movement of time and the pace of change are likely to be interpreted in highly subjective ways that engender political disagreement and potentially conflict (Bastian 2013).

This establishes specific challenges for international relations scholars, given their inherent focus on spatiality and borders around primary actors (states), and these are fundamental problems that the discipline has struggled to come to terms with. As Walker (1993: 7) makes clear, definitive implications of a notion of acceleration in tempo remain elusive for international relations. This is even more the case when viewed through a lens of temporality whereby the idea of acceleration is experienced and interpreted unevenly. Thus, the argument here suggests that the problem of temporality is not so much whether change takes place at a slower or faster rate but is more focused on the *different speeds* at which change takes place *across different aspects of bordering*. For example, a border's function as an instrument of security may change more rapidly than its role as a mechanism of economic protectionism. A complex, temporal perspective highlights that political actors, ideas, processes, policies and institutions do not move at the same pace. The issue of temporality then becomes focused on the absence of synchronicity in the change that is constantly taking place in the ways that borders operate.

This understanding of temporality alludes to its complex nature. It amounts to more than the passage of time or the pace at which changes take place. Instead, it refers to the *differentiated experiential basis of the movement of time and the variety of ways in which processes of transition affect different political actors and their behaviour within a range of political institutions.* Complex temporality refers to the fact that the experience of the passage of time is neither universal nor linear. Temporal change involves contested interpretations of the nature of transition that is simultaneously backward and forward looking. Moreover, against the arguments of Büthe (2002), the differing dynamics created by multiple interacting actors and structures makes historical narratives about an orderly *sequence* of change difficult to maintain. So, complex temporality invokes processes of change that require responses to developing phenomena that are not fully comprehended as they emerge into political consciousness. Even environments, institutions and policies that have been in existence for considerable time are involved in emerging processes of development such that political actors need to be responsive to the evolution and construction of new structural conditions.

If we concur with depictions of the accelerated pace of change (Urry 2002), then the alacrity and nimbleness required to keep pace with new developments with emergent properties that have not necessarily been countenanced before is even more accentuated than mere responsiveness to ordinary change. However, as noted in Chapter 3, complexity theory also informs us about path dependence and the backward-looking nature of policy learning and our reliance on processes of change that we have already experienced. In other words, in the face of new emerging dimensions of particular problems, our tools for analysing change and our strategies for dealing with it are almost inevitably beholden to that which we already know, that is, processes of change that we think comparable in one dimension or another with the issue we are dealing with. The main point here is that we are not merely dealing with the determinate implications of temporal change; instead, the issue is that the way in which that change is interpreted by multiple actors and fed through a variety of institutional processes and policy conundrums is ambiguous.

The theory of complex temporality conveys a sense not only of differing interpretations of the pace of change, but also that there are specific political implications of these understandings of the passage of time. Importantly, the *disorderly* nature of complex temporality has important ramifications for practical political matters and material structures. The effects of uneven processes of temporal change pose fundamental challenges for how we think about the development of policies and political institutions. From the foundation of complex temporality, political change cannot merely be depicted as a linear shift between then and now.

On the contrary, different aspects of an institution or set of institutions are constantly in the process of structural transformation such that it becomes very difficult to pin down the precise implications of changes, even ones that we know are taking place. While we might masquerade in a notion of a settled political space in order to enable us to take action, the actual material environment in which actions and decisions are played out is transformative in nature. Indeed, borders are good examples of constructions that attempt to impose order on these disorderly circumstances. While ostensibly, in spatio-temporal terms, borders may appear settled or fixed at any point in time with clear boundaries for state sovereignty, they are in fact highly contingent entities undergoing processes of transformation (Walker 1993: 6–7). This is to say that, even if the territorial space of borders is unchanging over a period of time, this does not mean that the practical or symbolic meaning of the border remains the same across multiple issue areas.

The Space and Time of Borders

It is fair to say that even the critical border studies literature focuses predominantly on spatial and territorial understandings of the significance of borders rather than their temporal dimensions. Thus, while it is commonplace to recognise the shifting nature of borders across the passage of time, this tends to be done through analysis of the particular consequences of specific geopolitical formations and recognising the equivocal and sometimes unstable nature of the bordering that takes place. Even critical accounts of bordering which focus on borderlands as a particular kind of geopolitical space in which borders are frequently crossed derive their argument from the ways in which individuals and social groups behave in relation to the spaces in which they have to exist. Wilson (1994: 104–5), for example, points out that

> international borders and borderzones are liminal states (i.e., interstitial and transitional conditions of culture and community) between the ordered, structured, and unpolluted 'conditions' of nation and state. Frontiers are expected to be different and uncomfortable . . . Yet people, and communities, have developed shared cultures at and across these borders.

Given the apparent 'legitimacy' of existing nation-state regimes (especially those underpinned by democratic political structures), this is perhaps not surprising. After all, as Agnew (2008: 186) makes clear, territory is vital to the notions of popular sovereignty that continue to have considerable normative power in political analysis today. Furthermore, anthropological accounts of everyday life in borderland regions still focus on cross-border activities as a transgression against the dominant Weberian, territorial understanding of the state and its legitimacy (Wilson and Donnan 1998b: 10). Therefore, it seems clear that, even though it is widely acknowledged that borders change over time, territorial epistemology continues to dominate debates including those that are critical of these epistemological assumptions. Agnew (2008: 186) puts it bluntly when he argues that until 'political community is redefined in some way as not being co-extensive with nation-state, we will be stuck with much of the business as usual'.

Much of the contemporary work on borderlands is vital in alerting us to the contingent nature of bordering practices. This is significant in itself even if my main contention is that the temporal dimension has very specific implications for political theorising. Nonetheless, it is important to recognise that temporality is not the only source of contingency in bordering. In her analysis of contingency, Stokes points out that rather than borders providing normative force, they are in fact often experienced as highly contingent by those 'residing close to the border between jurisdictions' – 'imaginary lines separate places where economic opportunities, political regimes, legal structures, and opportunities of many sorts are vastly different' (Stokes 2007: 178). This picture is further complicated by the fact that borderlands are not just areas where states meet each other. In fact, as Anderson and O'Dowd (1999: 596) make clear, there are numerous relations that exist in border areas including relationships with other areas within their nation-state, with state institutions, with regions across the border in other states, with transnational institutional organisations and regulatory bodies, and so forth. This brings us to the significant issue that, although political discussions in various examples may be entirely focused on where a border actually sits in physical terms, perhaps the much more important issue is what is done with and around that border. In short, in a point I will return to below, the management of a border can be even more important than where it is physically situated.

First, I would like to turn to a few brief examples to illustrate equivocal dynamics around changing borders to highlight some of this contingency. No region of the world is exempt from these bordering dynamics. In Europe in the 1990s, for example, we saw not only the reunification of Germany; the split of the Czech Republic and Slovakia to create two nation-states; the much more violent repercussions of the demise of Yugoslavia with the establishment of new nation-state borders; continuing secessionist pressures in the Basque Country and, less violently, in

Catalonia; and an agreement in Northern Ireland which, arguably, shored up the border with the Republic of Ireland but made it a much less significant and de-securitised space. In a geographically small territory such as Europe, we saw a wide range of dynamics taking place simultaneously, which exposes the fallacy of arguments which suggest that borders are all becoming stronger and more securitised or weaker and less significant in the face of pressures of economic globalisation. More recently, of course, we have seen that these particular pressures were not merely symptomatic of the post-Cold War period of the 1990s. In 2014 we witnessed the violent upheaval in Ukraine alongside the Scottish referendum on independence from the United Kingdom – a matter that is seemingly unresolved. In 2016 the Brexit referendum in the UK started an ongoing process of British withdrawal from the European Union which over the last five years has resulted in a more tenuous place for Northern Ireland within the UK and a shifting dynamic as the debate ensued over the border with the Republic of Ireland (as the frontier of the European Union) (Hayward 2020).

Myriad other examples could be deployed, not least the varying dynamics around bordering in the USA depending on the physical location of the border, for example, the differing politics around the Mexican and Canadian borders and the altogether different dynamic around people arriving on boats in Florida from the islands to the south (Ackleson 2005, Konrad and Nicol 2011, Kyle and Scarcelli 2009). Likewise, we could point to the complex legal dynamics around land territory-based processes in Australia vis-à-vis maritime law and the relationship with its regional partners with whom it has maritime rather than physical, land-based territorial borders (Devetak 2004, Chambers 2011, Little and Vaughan-Williams 2017). Moreover, there are many parts of the world where the physical boundaries between nation-states mean little in practice – parts of central Asia and central Africa come to mind – where borders are highly porous and the notion of the borderland is arguably much more significant in terms of the conduct and culture of everyday life than where the lines are actually drawn between nation-states (Goodhand 2012). And, in South America, we have witnessed large flows of people from Venezuela to neighbouring countries and the emergence of similar debates to those in Europe in the wake of the Syrian conflict and displacement of people in North Africa that has led to an ongoing crisis in the Mediterranean Sea (Little and Vaughan-Williams 2017). Elsewhere the experiences of the Rohingya people expelled from Burma have led to a different set of dynamics around statelessness, with many left afloat on boats in the Andaman Sea in 2015 awaiting a state to receive them, and others cast into makeshift camps in

Cox's Bazar, Bangladesh, following their expulsion which is causing ongoing problems around support, settlement and resettlement in the region.

All of these examples, when examined in any depth, suggest that there are multiple dynamics at work in any given bordering regime and that these are highly contextual. At once this provides a challenge for political theories which often seek to formulate general principles which can be applied universally or, at least, to all societies which reflect certain characteristics, for example, constitutional democratic systems. Theories of borders suggest that such generalisation is risky because of the very specific dynamics which take place around borders and the situated nature of any particular bordering context. It is a matter of fact that bordering takes place in politics and this is unlikely to change even if certain global political initiatives might change how they function. While accepting that there may be very specific arguments about whether particular borders should exist, and recognising that considerable harm may be generated in quite arbitrary ways by the existence of particular borders, I want to argue that for political theory in a general sense, it is important that we understand what it is about the *operation* of borders over the course of temporal-spatial change that might be particularly problematic, rather than questioning whether borders should exist at all.

On the assumption that borders will be a feature of social and political life in one form or another, the more normative question becomes one of how borders are managed and how the politics around borders can cope with temporal change. This is a practical form of normativity rather than the more abstract action-guiding interpretation of norms that prevails in much analytical theory. It is grounded in material practices around borders over the *longue durée*, rather than simpler reactive responses to particular border crises in the present. In Agnew's words, this can move us beyond 'the simple obsession with borders as easily guarded land borders characteristic of much border thinking (and anti-border thinking) and towards the complexity of what borders do and how they are managed for both territorial and networked spaces' (Agnew 2008: 183–4). Moreover, on the assumption that there are fundamental flaws with understandings of borders as 'fixed', one of the key issues becomes how to deal with 'border change'. This not only refers to the redrawing of the lines where nation-state jurisdiction starts or finishes but also addresses changes in 'the symbolic meanings and/or the material functions of existing borders *in situ*' (Anderson and O'Dowd 1999: 595).

This is important because we need to comprehend the differential operation of borders. Just because they might exist objectively on a map that most people agree upon, it does not mean that they have an equal impact on those who live within them or those who live on the other side. We have already noted how those who live in borderlands may, because of their peripherality, share more in common with those on the other side of the frontier than their compatriots living at the 'core' of the bordered space. Borders do not just act on those they keep out of the governed space; they also have profound effects on those who live within them. This is why debates on migration (or constraints on it), though highly significant in themselves, should not be construed as the leitmotif of borderlands research. Many anthropologists have shown us why the study of those living on and around borders is valuable in itself given the highly specific cultural beliefs and practices that can develop in the context of bordered proximity to those alike and those different.

In itself, the movement of borders need not be a fundamental challenge for normative theorists. After all, it might merely signify an expansion or contraction of the number of people who have particular rights of citizenship or are obliged to contribute to the common good to receive the benefits of state welfare and so forth. Where the problems lie is in the linearity of this notion of border change. It assumes that the border is the boundary of the jurisdictional space and that, if it is repositioned, the jurisdiction expands or contracts in a linear fashion. However, the challenge emanates from, firstly, the erroneous understanding of how borders actually operate in the first place, secondly, a simplistic understanding of the way they might move and, thirdly, and most importantly, the desynchronised ways in which the functions of borders might shift in relation to a repositioning of the geopolitical line of demarcation. O'Dowd (2002: 114) hints at how the notion of borders as normative containers is undermined by their actual operation in practice:

> boundaries and border zones perform dual functions, as barriers or buffers on the one hand, and as gateways, bridges and zones of interaction on the other. They are manifestations of power, conquest and conflict but they are also sites of voluntary, productive and enriching exchange and identification with others. They are both enabling and disabling, standing for opportunity as well as denial, inclusion as well as exclusion, for voluntary affiliation as well as coercive power.

This suggests that borders are frequently not the normative jurisdictional containers of life for those who reside around them. Borders have varying levels of porosity and this changes over time. The Irish border is an example of one that was crossed both legally and illegally even when it was heavily securitised during the Troubles, and which has been the focus of concerted action by government authorities on either side (encouraged by the European Union) to increase traffic and movement (of particular kinds) in these areas before and after the 1998 Agreement (McCall 2011). The fact that this particular border will change again following Brexit is reflective of the fact of the shifting dynamics of borders.

However, different people have different attitudes to borders. Some will cross frequently because there are various social or economic incentives to doing so, whereas others will prefer to stay within their jurisdiction on one side of the line or the other, perhaps for cultural reasons. Therefore, borders may have a physical location, but what that means to individuals and communities varies widely. Moreover, governments on either side or both may decrease or increase the impervious nature of borders depending on the specific political context. In this sense, it is difficult to make generalisable normative comment about any individual border, let alone do so about borders and borderlands en masse.

All of this suggests that we need to be careful in the political theorisation of borders because, despite their physical situatedness at any given point in time, they are far from static and inert. What matters more is to understand their porous nature and the ways in which the degree of porosity reflects particular choices of governments and those that seek to work with or against them. As Newman (2006: 172) suggests, the 'management of the border regime determines the relative ease or difficulty with which borders are crossed, or alternately the extent to which the border still constitutes a barrier to movement of people, goods and ideas'. Significantly, the ways in which borders affect movement depend on the category of thing which is being moved. The obvious and most frequently cited example is relative openness to movement of (legal) goods set against the constraints placed on the movement of people. As Agnew (2008: 185) points out, cross-border exchanges are not just about issues of identity and security; borders are also about economic functions, as cheap labour on one side 'facilitates cheaper products for more affluent consumers on the other'. For this reason, political analysts need to differentiate between a variety of forms of border transactions and crossings and locate theories of temporal movement within this framework. As we shall see in the next section, this demands a focus on *borders as processes* governing sometimes quite contingent social and political forces rather than determined boundaries of jurisdictional order.

The Normative Force of Borders

Normative argument has not had a strong profile in the border studies literature especially in light of the growth of critical border studies in recent years. Not surprisingly, critical border studies is adept at mounting critique and highlighting a number of valid reasons why assumptions that borders have inherent normative force are incorrect and counteracted by examining the experiential cases of living in borderlands. This literature is important in helping to specify in precise terms why the normative *force* of borders is somewhat different from how we imagine in traditional notions of bordering. Here the work of Étienne Balibar (2002: 78–84) is prominent in highlighting three important aspects of borders as they actually exist in the world: that they are over-determined, polysemic, and characterised by heterogeneity. These three dimensions of bordering are significant because they undermine the normative assumptions associated with the 'forced simplicity' of the very notion of the border. Thus, the border is not just an institution in itself but 'a condition of possibility of a whole host of institutions' (Balibar 2002: 83).

While recognising the shortcomings of borders (including their sometimes violent impact on those around them or trying to cross them), it is also important to identify that not only have they helped in establishing boundaries for the rule of law, but they have also enabled the pursuit of (bounded) human betterment by creating elements of social solidarity within borders that have led to the formation of welfare states, income redistribution, formal political equality and so on (Agnew 2008: 179). Of course, this justification of bordering can be a double-edged sword: it can lead to stronger protection of borders to safeguard various privileges, it can lead to measures which seek to prevent outsiders from gaining access to social benefits, and it can draw attention from forms of global interdependence such as the relationships between consumption in wealthy parts of the world and supply chains which help to reinforce the subservient position of the weak (Macdonald 2014). So, it is clear that bordering certainly has *normative impacts*, even if borders as objects of normative theories of justice are much more complex phenomena.

Much of the normative work that refers to borders is focused on whether or not they are the appropriate vessels that should contain the conditions of possibility for things like democratic rights and social justice. For example, theorists such as Miller (2012), Nine (2008) and Christiano (2006) argue in differing ways for conceptions of justice that continue to emphasise the importance of the nation-state (and its borders) in the formation of democratic arguments for distributive justice. Others, such as Beitz (1979), Held (1995) and Bohman (2007), have argued that such justice is better conceived in more cosmopolitan terms where state borders are understood as arbitrary or incapable of providing a means of comprehending the ways in which the factors which require action to ensure justice cannot be dealt with effectively within a lens solely focused on the nation-state. In this sense borders are an impediment to efforts to realise the global foundations of arguments for justice or democracy.

A third group including Carens (2013), Meilaender (1999), Seglow (2005) and Abizadeh (2008) focuses more specifically on questions of borders as the means of enforcing restrictions on migration and the normative foundations on which we might discriminate between different groups of people in the process of movement from one part of the world to another. Of course, all three groups are dealing with significant issues in themselves, but the temporal complexity and contingency of borders is not always explicit in the literature with a resulting neglect of the ways in which this affects the conditions of possibility of normative debates. Allen Buchanan puts this pointedly in arguing that political theorists have tended to avoid these questions by working on the basis of two potentially fallacious assumptions: first, that political communities and geographical boundaries of political units are congruent and, second, that bordered political units exist in perpetuity (Buchanan 2003: 231).

As we have seen from looking at other literatures in anthropology, geography and sociology (as well as critical border studies) in this chapter, these assumptions are erroneous. That being the case, the question remains as to how to conduct political theory in the contingent and equivocal circumstances that characterise borders. Buchanan only takes us so far in this quest because he remains focused on the ethical bases upon which boundaries are established and how they might change through, for example, secession (see also Patten 2014, Kymlicka 1998, Lehning 1998). The focus remains on the making and unmaking of boundaries rather than the contingent basis on which they actually operate in practice. However, it is also the case that the critiques established in critical border studies often resist discussion of action-guiding normative questions. One exception to this is Agnew, who argues that we need to 're-frame the discussion in terms of the impacts that borders have; what they do both for and to people. From this perspective, we can both recognise the necessary roles of borders and the barriers to improving welfare that they create' (Agnew 2008: 187).

Using the work of Dora Kostakopoulou, Agnew suggests following a model of 'civic registration' whereby adherence to democratic rule where an individual resides (based on some presumably fairly minimal residency requirement) and the absence of a serious criminal record would be all that would be required to participate. This, he contends, would move us away from nationalist claims and territorial epistemologies. While this brief example is suitably cosmopolitan, it also brings to light normative claims of attachment to land – and the attendant territorial claims that are generated – in Indigenous politics around the world. While a model of borders that is responsive to the movement of people needs to accommodate those who move (by choice or by coercion), it should also facilitate the claims of those with no intention of moving because of a (frequently sub-national) connection with the land. This conundrum captures the problem with the territorial epistemology invoked through borders. Normative theories of justice and policies dealing with the movement of people cannot only be concerned with when people cross national borders (either being forced, voluntarily or somewhere in between). They also need to provide guidance on questions of how, for example, to recognise the claims of attachment to specific pieces of land of other groups such as Indigenous peoples and, even more problematically, how to capture the patterns of movement of those like nomads who potentially feel attachment to land but want to transcend borders without necessarily deep attachment to one particular territorial space bounded by established borders. In this sense, political theory should provide recommendations based on relational ontologies including not only human relationships, but also specific relationships between humans and their environments and non-humans (Little and Ozguc 2022).

There are no clear-cut answers to this problem, but a step in the right direction may be to develop perspectives around challenges to this territorialist epistemology. One example of this kind of approach is the literature around the 'fuzziness' of borders (Christiansen et al. 2000, Koenig-Archibugi 2012). While most of this literature is still bound up with territorial thinking in one way or another, it opens up vistas in which a political agenda around contingent borders might begin to emerge. In the case of Christiansen et al., the expansion of the European Union (EU) creates fuzziness about where its boundaries start and finish as it seeks to create conditions in which countries can travel through processes of accession. The case studies here were in the Mediterranean and the Baltic states. Accession processes inevitably involve the EU intervening in domestic politics from the outside because states seeking to join the EU have to meet specific conditions of compliance. Accession therefore involves fuzziness because the *process* involves a transition over time so that the right structural conditions are generated which permit new states to become members of the EU. Territorial epistemology remains in place in this analysis because it focuses on the incapacity of existing nation-state structures to contain issues. Moreover, the change that takes place in joining the EU is not regarded as a fundamental problem with borders but as more of a transitional stage that is invoked by processes of joining the European Union. Nonetheless it points to the ease with which the borders of existing nation-states can be penetrated by other states or transnational organisations (both public and private). Moreover, as the case of Northern Ireland during the British government's Brexit process makes clear, similar issues of fuzziness can emerge when trying to leave the EU as may be the case during accession processes for new members.

In the case of Koenig-Archibugi we see a more normative, philosophical argument about the conditions under which those affected by decisions taken in a particular nation-state become eligible for representation in the decision-making institutions of that nation-state. Employing the 'all-affected principle' (Goodin 2007), Koenig-Archibugi suggests that nation-state borders are not equipped to contain the democratic claims that affected individuals may want to make about the deleterious impact of particular decisions upon them. Thus, he makes the case for a set of seats in parliamentary institutions to be set aside for those who may be affected by particular nation-states, but who reside beyond their borders. The argument here, in line with some of the earlier commentary in this chapter, is that borders do not and cannot contain the potential impacts of political decision-making. While Koenig-Archibugi's argument may lean towards a problematic reliance on representation in nation-state-based institutions as a way of dealing with this issue, it takes seriously the case that the impact of activities and policies that cross borders is problematic in democratic terms where we might expect people to have some kind of say over the issues that affect them. Thus, the idea of fuzzy borders, while not attuned to the sociological issues of everyday life in borderlands, does at least flag the limits of using borders as a way of simplifying normative analysis by imagining that the politics and society of the nation-state can be self-contained.

While Christiansen et al. (2000) and Koenig-Archibugi (2012) might help us descriptively and normatively respectively in terms of dealing with the changes in borders over time and across different issues, they are less well equipped to help with the contingency that emanates from notions of contested temporality. Thus, we need to be clear that there is more to the notion of fuzziness than a mere aberration from what we consider the norm of borders. Koenig-Archibugi (2012) is clear on this: it is not as if we are dealing with a transitional aberration that will be resolved over the course of time as new nation-state or regional boundaries are constructed. Fuzzy borders means more than just that borders aren't always where we think they are. Christiansen et al. propose the notion of a 'near-abroad' but this is clearly still driven by a territorialist epistemology in that it focuses on whether the territorial space of the work of borders is conducted at close proximity or not. Koenig-Archibugi on the other hand challenges this territorialist model by highlighting that affectedness transcends borders, a view that correlates closely with the broader study of borderlands. His answer, however, is to return to representation in national democratic legislatures by those affected rather than to imagine new democratic bodies which might be capable of transcending border distinctions.

Therefore, while the work on fuzzy borders is an advance on the dominant territorialist epistemology that characterises border debates in political science and international relations, there remains a specific problem that these analyses of fuzziness do not address. This is the *unevenness of bordering across different issue areas* and the fact that different functional areas within border jurisdictions work at different speeds and effectiveness to one another. Put simply, the power of the jurisdiction of borders is uneven across different issue areas. This highlights the key point of temporality in relation to bordering and border change. The problem is not so much that borders change but more the temporality of change. That is, the different areas of jurisdiction that borders are thought to encapsulate actually evolve at different paces, so border change is never synchronous between different areas. Thus, for example, one might find that immigration policies on either side of a border are inconsistent with each other whereas trade policies are relatively consistent. The key point, then, is that borders are not monolithic – they do various things and they do them unevenly and at different speeds. Therefore, *the issue becomes how to grapple with border change and border processes that are involved in temporal change across different issue areas at varying paces.*

Towards Time-Space Governance

The challenge for political theory is not only that borders are fuzzy, and that they move over the course of time, but, more significantly in practical terms, that the speed of change is variable. Thus, while some aspects of bordering may be highly efficient (in the terms in which borders are conceived), simultaneously others may not. In this sense, the 'time-space governance' (Sum 2000) of borders involves normative challenges that are not clearly defined. For example, in examining changing borders, should we be focusing on norms of sovereignty or norms of migration or norms of justice that transcend wherever borders lie? Given that we cannot be sure where borders will be located, the closed or open nature of those borders, or how they will vary across different functional areas, the challenge lies in how to encapsulate this contingency in the justification of where borders do actually lie at a given point in time and how they should operate. Ultimately, borders are not going to disappear so theories and practices of migration, for example, need to take account of their existence and, simultaneously, the fact that they do not actually operate in a definitive, sovereign fashion.

While we could argue that borders should just continue to function in traditional ways depending on where they are established, this is harder to justify when we take on the uneven efficacy of borders in different functional areas. So, in dealing with changing borders, it is not just a normative matter of transferring their functions to an expanded or contracted group of people accordingly. This traditional approach cannot resolve the fact that borders do different kinds of work simultaneously depending on their varying forms of organisation across functional areas. Border effects may be draconian and punitive when it comes to unskilled labour migration, but relatively open around the movement of goods. However, at other times governments may encourage cheap labour migration where there is an economic need but a less than willing domestic labour force. Ultimately, it is impossible to know precisely what is going to happen to borders in the future beyond knowing from the past that they will change in either character or form or both.

The question becomes how to frame a contingent model of politics around borders that encapsulates both temporal and spatial change. The challenge for normative argument is to recognise that action-guiding theories either have to be able to transcend spatial and temporal change (without descending into decontextualised abstraction) or need to be amendable in light of temporal and spatial change. Both are substantive problems for theories which purport to be generalisable, as is often the case with normative theories. When placed in the light of the differing ways in which borders operate across different jurisdictions and functional areas, the challenge becomes even more significant. Time-space governance requires a situated approach to particular problems that recognises the difficulty of applying transcendent theories. This implies revisable forms of normativity that can respond to the changing nature of political problems over the course of temporal as well as spatial development.

This approach to 'time-space governance' would require normative thinking to engage with the particular spaces in which issues emerge and the historical trajectory that brought them to where they are now. Importantly, the historical learning should not be regarded as a definitive predictor of the issues that might emerge in the future – a form of path dependence – but it would require greater cognisance of the issues and conflicts which had given rise to the particular border formations which currently exist. Therefore, in trying to understand the ways in which borders might shift in the future, normative thinkers would at least be equipped with detailed knowledge of the emergence of particular borders and potentially might develop greater understanding of how and why they may operate in different ways across a variety of functional policy areas.

In terms of migration, for example, it may be necessary to overlay universal legal protections for refugees with specific institutions or agreements between bordering countries in recognition of the particular dynamics that undermine sovereign borders between those countries. In some cases, this might be bilateral in recognition of the effects of a particular frontier in separating peoples, or it may take the form of regional approaches to the migration of people. Moreover, as we have seen, bordering does not only take place through physical frontiers so there may be 'special' relationships which herald specific responsibilities between countries which are far apart due, for example, to a shared colonial history or legacies of war. It is vital then to situate migration within 'real world' scenarios to reflect the ways in which the movement of people across time and space reconstitutes sovereign borders (and the political institutions that rely on notions of popular sovereignty for legitimacy). Normative theories involving migration and borders are never solely matters of justice and/or individual rights; they also concern the constitution and reconstitution of political collectivities over time which, as Whitt (2014) contends, are actually fundamental to the legitimacy of democratic institutions. In terms of migration and temporal change in borders, then, a key normative principle must be the capacity to revise the constitution of the sovereign body due to new claims to inclusion. In turn, new claims to inclusion may undermine the legitimacy previously conferred in an earlier form of an institution.

Time-space governance would also require political actors to engage with emergent changes in borders and to consider how particular actions/policies might operate in reconfigured border arrangements. This is not to say that we should expect scholars to predict accurately a range of complex, dynamic factors that could change bordering arrangements, but I think we should expect greater attention to the ways in which changes in border configurations *could* affect particular normative arrangements. This dimension of time-space governance implies a *situated* approach to questions of justice and migration. Here, the nature of political change becomes pertinent because, in most circumstances, we are unlikely to witness simple shifts through particular policies such that we get a linear change in processes from one normative good to another. Instead, it is much more likely that these kinds of changes will take place over time in a processive fashion (see the next chapter, and Little and Macdonald 2013) whereby we see the incremental development of a particular normative idea across a range of overlapping and sometimes conflicting processes and institutions that contribute to the governance of particular issue areas. Taken together, these could form some kind of narrative of an emerging set of processes which correlate with a particular normative good, but they also reflect a diverse and contingent set of political actions across different issues and in response to a divergent set of political pressures and processes.

In managing migration, time-space governance institutions must look forwards as well as backwards in assessing the impact of contemporary actions. In particular, these institutions need to consider the migration that may come about in the future and how it relates to actions and policies in the present. Thus, they must take into account the particular responsibilities that contemporary policies may generate in terms of the movement or displacement of people in the future and provide a means of contesting the impacts of bordering in the present. Put simply, the contingency and arbitrariness of bordering necessitates transnational institutions that facilitate contestation over inclusion/participation in decision-making bodies and recognition that membership (and hence the constitution) of these institutions will change over the course of time (Whitt 2014).

There is a growing awareness that borders are not just a spatial problem in contemporary politics but also that there are particular temporal dynamics that need to be accounted for in the work that borders perform (Parker and Vaughan-Williams 2009). However, while the contingent nature of borders is widely understood in critical border studies, it is much less prominent in debates in normative political theory. In effect, there are separate conversations going on that reflect the analytical-continental divide. The first critical discussion gives us the tools to understand the uncertain and contingent nature of borders and the fact that they frequently do not operate internally or externally in the ways that are traditionally envisaged. The second normative debate focuses on issues such as whether nation-state borders are appropriate boundaries to contain debates about rights, justice, equality and so forth. A gap has emerged between these two debates that makes it very difficult to comprehend how we are to understand political action in a bordered world but where those borders are temporally as well as spatially dynamic. In short, how do we understand political action in a terrain where we know not only that the bordered space will change over the course of time, but also that, in the course of that temporal-spatial transition, different functional areas of the border will be more or less efficient than one another in fulfilling traditional bordering objectives. Moreover, this will pertain to whatever borders we are in a transition towards in the future. Put simply, how do we understand normative political thought and action in an environment where borders are so indeterminate and contingent across *time* as well as space?

There are no simple answers to this question, but this chapter suggests that we need to move to a discussion of how to govern borders with a view to temporal as well as spatial change if normative theories are to be applicable to existent and future border debates. There are a number of implications of this shift to a focus on time-space governance. First, it may undermine the traditional focus on borders as the firm delineators of the Weberian nation-state. Second, by opening up contingent border spaces across time, it makes clear that there is a plurality of actors in this political space, and the complexity here is not just a matter of their multiplicity, but also that their actions are often at cross purposes to one another. Thus, border spaces and debates are domains of inherent political conflict. Third, we need to recognise that the actors in the time-space governance of borders are not settled. As borders change in terms of both geographical location and functional operations, new actors will emerge with a stake in the debates and processes that are taking place. Fourth, time-space governance debates should make clearer that processes of bordering are often just as acute within nation-states as they are on the periphery. The bottom line in all of this is that time-space governance should become a more specific focus of normative argument but that this requires engagement with the fact that governance processes need to transform across changing temporal and spatial dimensions rather than governance being a settled, orderly, bounded domain with defined actors and contained issues.

Ultimately, none of the points in my argument need preclude normativity, but the focus on time-space governance and the contingency it invokes does suggest a degree of modesty is required in normative prescription. Thus, just as is the case with critical border studies, we should not expect normative theorists to have the answers to a very complex set of temporal-spatial dynamics. What I do offer here is a set of parameters that I believe should influence the ways in which theoretical debates are conducted such that they have purchase in the discussion of 'real world' problems. These are grounded in the contention that normative theories need to take seriously the constraints and opportunities for political action in the light of spatial and temporal dynamics and that any form of political change towards particular normative objectives is unlikely to be direct or sequential. This suggests that normative recommendations need to be produced through forms of grounded theoretical reflection attuned to the specific contextual circumstances of the present.

Complex temporality points to the challenges of the interaction of temporal dynamics with spatiality and I have proposed a notion of processive change as the appropriate understanding of political transitions. What processive change and complex temporality engender, however, is a sense of change as simultaneously orderly and disorderly over time and across different overlapping and sometimes conflicting institutions and processes. This correlates with some of the analysis from critical border studies but, I contend, also provides a basis for normative thinking around 'real world' challenges such as the impact of bordering on migration. The fundamental issue is how political theory stands up to spatio-temporal analysis and thus whether normative theories of migration can incorporate the demands of time-space governance in their analysis of bordering. This time-space governance requires a temporal ethos, based – as it needs to be – on not only the specific circumstances of the present, but also the ways in which that present relates to the past and the future in complex ways.

6
Uncertain Futures:
The Temporality of Democracy

Debate over the theory and practice of democracy is one of the most temporally dynamic topics in modern politics, with contention over the history of democratic practices, the contemporary challenges to democracy and the implications of these challenges for democratic ideas and institutions in the future. Even when discussion of democracy is not explicitly related to time, much political science literature, especially comparative research, invokes a distinct temporal dimension which suggests that particular eras can be associated with a golden age of democracy or a wave of democratisation or, indeed, as some contemporary political science literature suggests, a decline, retreat, threat to or crisis in democracy (Foa and Mounk 2016, Diamond and Plattner 2016, van Beek 2019, Kurlantzick 2013).

The foreboding crisis of democracy evinced in some of the contemporary political science literature is evidenced by identifying a particular set of primarily *institutional* variables as constitutive of democracy – including such things as voting, parliaments, the rule of law, a free press, for example – and then measuring the existence or strength of these features of democracy across and between different societies at different times. This enables prognostications of the current era as one of weakening democracy vis-à-vis the originary standards of constitutional democracies following earlier 'waves' of democratisation. The 'other' of these processes is authoritarianism or autocracy, and the strengthening or waning of one in a particular time period is often thought to correspond with the opposite process in the 'other'. Hence, there is a grand historical sweep in much of what contemporary political science has to say about democracy – a concern with the present that manifests itself in particular liberal forms of constitutional democracy – that belies much of the variety of democracy over time and, we can assume, in the future. A significant problem in these debates is the focus on the workings of institutions or the impact of populist politicians, and much less emphasis on the conceptual or ideational foundations of democracy or their constitution through their collectives; that is, the demoi or peoples that democratic institutions serve.

The history of democracy (Dunn 2019) is nothing if not dynamic with multiple institutional formations over time inspired by a wide variety of conceptual developments. In this chapter, those temporal elements of our understanding of democracy will be scrutinised to provide an alternative to depictions of democracy as moving in a singular way. The chapter will present a more contextual and nuanced understanding of democracy based on the multiplicity of its constitutive parts. Therefore, it is important to unpack democratic concepts and to understand the multiplicity of ways – both within and beyond *liberal* democracy – that they can be operationalised in democratic practices. This will make clear that democratic concepts and practices are sometimes prevalent in ostensibly non-democratic settings, and that democratic societies can involve some seemingly non-democratic features.

The point then is that the existence of democracy is a matter of degree and it can vary quite substantially over the course of time within a given society. It is quite possible therefore that a society might simultaneously be becoming more and less democratic at the same time as changes occur in different parts of a democratic system. A further cautionary note is that, despite the aggregative nature of much comparative political science and the interesting data that it can generate, a different approach to democracy impelled by temporal methodology would paint a more dynamic and fluid conceptualisation of democracy itself. Such an approach would recognise both plurality and fluidity in the constitutions of the people with consequential effects on the way in which democratic practices and institutions can be imagined. In terms of temporal methodology, this means relinquishing an understanding of the democratic collective as a fixed entity. This methodology should reflect both the absence of a smooth developmental historical narrative about democracy and the implications of its becoming. Democracy is not a static entity, the existence of which can just be read off from institutional facts. Rather democratic systems are better viewed through theories that reflect contingency and openness (Overwijk 2020). In light of this, and leaving aside some of the nuanced debates on his work on the relationship between democracy and autoimmunity (see Evans 2016, Thomson 2005), the ensuing discussion is developed in the 'spirit' of Derrida's 'democracy to come', where democracy is understood as an 'indeterminate' and 'indecidable' concept (Derrida 2005: 25) that 'exceeds the juridico-political sphere, and, yet, is bound up with it' (Derrida 2005: 35).

Therefore, rather than measuring democracy by the existence of sufficient constitutional democratic institutions, it is useful to return to
the foundational elements of democracy – the origins of the term in the
Ancient Greek combination of 'demos' and 'kratos'. Traditionally, these
ideas have been translated into the definition of democracy as 'rule by the
people'. As has been well documented, however, the scale of modern societies meant that liberal democracy came to focus more on representative
rather than participatory forms of 'rule by the people', and the original
Greek model was criticised for several significant exclusions on who was
permitted to participate (for example, women). Additionally, just in the
last thirty years we have seen many attempts to articulate alternative forms
of participation as a way of moving away from a solely representative focus
(Dryzek 2010) and attempts to reconsider what we understand by representation (Saward 2010).

The emergence of deliberative democracy has provided a powerful challenge to aggregative notions of representation, focused on differing forms
of more direct involvement in decision-making such as town hall meetings,
sortition, deliberative polls, participatory budgeting and many other institutional innovations. Whether one sympathises with such approaches or
not, they are significant challenges for democratic practice in their attempts
to address the shortcomings of the dominant liberal, constitutional forms
of representative democracy. Therefore, even within societies with long-
established democratic traditions, there is considerable debate as to how
to become more democratic and encourage ordinary citizens to participate
in decision-making. Often, this involves ways of re-engaging publics that
have become dissatisfied with political systems due to the shortcomings of
democratic institutions, the decisions or policies that they generate, or the
political elites who make those decisions. The 'rule of the people' is once
again under the microscope as democracy's capacity to deliver legitimate
and widely supported outcomes becomes more widely questioned, alongside its institutional shortcomings in maintaining democratic values. These
questions pervade the explosion of literature on populism in recent years
(Tormey 2014, Moffitt 2016, Brubaker 2017, Revelli 2019).

The temporal perspective on democracy not only challenges the institutional basis of contemporary understandings of democracy, but also raises
questions about the definition of the constitutive democratic body: the
'people'. This is because a temporal view emphasises the shifting nature
of the body politic rather than relying on a fixed, bounded demos within
the nation-state, as is often the case within democratic theory and practice.
In the previous chapter we saw that the idea of the nation-state as a fixed
entity enclosed by definitive borders was a problematic conception from a

temporal political perspective, given the propensity of borders to shift or be permeated in various ways. Following from that insight, if the boundary containing the people is not as definitive or impermeable as imagined in most of the writing on the topic in political science, then the people themselves are not a coherent and unchanging entity. This is the case even without a temporal dimension. For example, there are a range of insider/outsider dynamics in any society with some people accorded full political rights which do not pertain to others like non-citizens.

However, in an era of heightened migration, both legal and 'illegal', the idea of a definitive 'people' is hard to sustain. This is especially the case when a temporal understanding is introduced. Viewed over spans of time, the composition of demoi will change considerably and the changes in borders, and the functions they serve, will further impact on the question of the constitutive body of a democratic society. Significantly, where the previous chapter alluded to the claims that may be made due to historical relationships between different countries, a temporal notion of democracy not only needs to account for the relationship between the past and the present, it also needs to contemplate the relationship between the present and the future (Ware 2020). Such a temporal perspective is unusual in political science, although there are some notable exceptions in discussions of children (Nakata 2015) and inter-generational justice vis-à-vis ecological politics (Schuppert 2011) for example. The question, then, for the analysis of democracy in light of political temporality is how to develop a vision of democracy that is not purely focused on the present conditions of politics or the historical development of key institutions. The challenge instead is to develop a forward-looking dimension that can accommodate forthcoming changes to the demos and the possibility that a different kind of kratos may be required to ensure that future demoi can be said to be 'ruling' appropriately.

While the institutional manifestation of democracy is highly significant, it is vital that we do not lose sight of the key underpinning concepts that these institutions are considered to put into practice: *political equality* and *popular sovereignty* (Beetham 1999). While certain *processes* – often those associated with the liberal democratic state – prevail in the democratic literature in political science, emphasising these *processes* risks denuding the conceptual vocabulary of what democracy is supposed to entail. On this view, processes are not ends in themselves, but only means by which key democratic values may be strengthened. While political equality and popular sovereignty can be realised in different ways, losing sight of these basic conceptual building blocks of democracy risks a reduction of democracy to solely liberal democratic institutional processes such as elections, voting and the separation of powers. Emphasising these institutions at a level of generality creates its own problems by drawing attention away from the different rationalities and outcomes that underpin, for example, different voting systems, federal regimes vis-à-vis unitary states, and the case for consociational systems in divided societies compared to simple majoritarian politics. The point here is not that democratic societies generate systems and practices appropriate for their own conditions (though that is often the case). Rather, from a temporal perspective, democratic societies are changing entities such that institutions and practices that were once deemed appropriate for a given society may no longer be the most appropriate means of ensuring political equality and popular sovereignty or the 'rule of the people'.

As discussed in Chapter 3, established institutions can lead to path dependence whereby old institutions remain resilient, despite the fact that the social conditions which engendered their historical legitimacy may no longer prevail. In such conditions, a particular form of an institution may outlive its usefulness, or it may be in need of substantial reform. Therefore, the focus on institutions as the historical foundations of constitutional democracy (à la Habermas), rather than the demos, leads Bonnie Honig to ask: 'In what sense can they [people] be said to be politically free if they understand themselves to be bound to a progressive temporality in and out of which constitutional democracy in its full unconflicted expression is required to unfold?' (Honig 2001: 795).

Therefore, in bringing a temporal perspective to bear on democratic politics, we need to take account of the historical development of democratic institutions and systems, the contemporary operation of these bodies and challenges to them in the current context, and their future development so that they remain fit for purpose in years to come. This kind of analysis requires a temporal perspective that takes us beyond orthodox understandings of democracy and whether countries have it or not through the existence of a set of particular institutions. Importantly, it is quite possible to have some particular institutions such as elections or presidential systems without fulfilling some other key criteria that democratic theorists might advocate such as a free press or deliberative fora. Moreover, there is increasing debate as to the scale of democracy and whether it is sufficient to only analyse it on the level of the nation-state. Instead, democracy can be viewed and promoted at the local, regional, international or global levels, which makes path-dependent conceptions that democracy should be evaluated at the nation-state level unreflective of some of the prevailing sentiments in contemporary democratic theory.

A Temporal Conception of Democratic Institutions: Beyond Democratic Finality

From its inception, but particularly in the post-Enlightenment period, the major challenge to democracy has been the nature of its own justification and its connection to a notionally bounded space. In the previous chapter, the permeable and changing nature of borders was outlined and, with that, the changing and dynamic character of the demos. Even if borders remain in the same geographical space, the people within that space – all actual or potential members of the demos – change over time. This fact, in itself, is a challenge to the border of the nation-state as the 'container' of democracy. Moreover, the impact of the actions by a state on people living beyond its borders has brought questions around whether affectedness should be introduced as a criterion for our understanding of democracy (Goodin 2007). Affectedness suggests a more fluid and transient conception of membership of demoi, and provides a basis for questioning the *finality* of democratic boundaries. All of these debates recognising the 'boundary problem' of democracy have become a staple of contemporary political philosophy (see, for example, Song 2012, Cabrera 2014). Nevertheless, while there are obvious temporal dimensions in these debates, neither the concept of temporality nor a specific temporal methodology features strongly.

An exception can be found in a recent contribution by Paulina Ochoa Espejo (2012), who uses Bergsonian insights to critique the finality of the boundary problem. Describing Bergson's method as 'relief from false problems', Ochoa Espejo (2012: 159) approaches the 'problem of the people' as a 'problem of self-reference that arises because the demos seems to be both cause and consequence of the democratic process'. On the contrary, she tries to show how the 'democratic people is an ongoing process that evolves under the aegis of a self-creative drive derived from the lived experience of time and the indeterminacy of nature' (2012: 159). Because Bergson's work enables us to see the creative potential in incompletion, there is therefore a vista whereby relinquishing the idea of a fixed sovereign democratic body enables us to imagine democracy in a much more productive fashion. Rather than getting drawn into the paradoxes of the democratic boundary question, there is in fact an alternative way to embrace the absence of finality and

abandon the idea of the sovereign people understood as a community of free and equal individuals joining together on the basis of rational consensus. It requires, instead, that we conceive the people as primarily held together by habits and rules. It is, in this view, a closed society that may transform itself when opened up by an aspiration toward universality. Hence there is no need to explain democratic legitimacy by appeal to a legislating popular will, and there is no regress of original contracts or circularity between citizens and institutions. (Ochoa Espejo 2012: 169)

In this regard the construction of the democratic boundary question around the idea of a notional social contract established between people within an already bounded political community in which they are pre-constituted as the demos is itself a socio-political construction. Similarly, Honig questions the ways in which the possibility of considering alternative democratic formations for the future is foreclosed by an imaginary which relies on ideas such as Habermas's co-originality of democracy and law. When Habermas construes this as the foundation for a democratic future 'he turns that future into a ground. Its character as a future is undone by progress' guarantee. The agency of the present generation . . . is now in the service of a set of forces quite beyond itself' (Honig 2001: 797).

For Ochoa Espejo, the discussion of the democratic boundary problem is a Bergsonian 'false problem' generated by the inability to see the dynamic, changing nature of the demoi which constitute democratic entities. Instead of imagining a bounded political community, we would do better to

conceive the people as an entity capable of change and invention . . . In this view a democratic people can be – at least at times – compatible with indetermination. This trait allows democracy to give up the requirement of a people founded by a social contract without giving up the principle of popular self-rule. So rather than propose a society constructed on the grounds of a specific moral or religious doctrine, democratic theory can conceive of a democratic people – an open people, or better, an opening people – by appeal to the notion of creative freedom. (Ochoa Espejo 2012: 172)

In general, democratic theory has not been well-equipped in dealing with this kind of thinking about the temporal nature of its constitutive body, although authors such as Markell (2003) and Ochoa Espejo (2020) have raised substantive challenges to the view that justice, trust or community necessitates boundedness within borders. The idea of a *fluid* self-constituting democratic body is at odds with conceptions which rely upon a specific bounded space in which democratic principles must be operationalised, as is the idea that the membership of such a constitutive body can be fluid and in need of redefinition over the course of time (even if that is actually what is often practised in democratic settings). But, for Ochoa Espejo, it is precisely the case that the demos has never been precisely defined and bounded in the way in which the democratic imaginary tends to work. Therefore

> the people emerges from an entity that was not yet the fully formed people, even if in retrospect we can see that crucial elements of the people already existed. This retrospective vision allows us to explain how, in a way, the people is indeed a product of democratic processes and aspirations. In sum, given that the opening people is never fully formed, it can solve the vicious circle of self-foundation. This same move can also help solve the infinite regress of foundations because an opening people does not require an original agreement to legitimize the state in order to sustain the requirement of freedom and equality. (Ochoa Espejo 2012: 172)

Thus far, the focus has been on the way in which political theory has become entangled in the democratic boundary problem with regard to claims of how constitutional democracy is deemed legitimate, given that, by and large, the demos did not establish its own boundaries. And, even if a demos was able to self-constitute, the legitimacy of such a move would be highly questionable. In this case, we can see that democratic theory has been heavily focused on the question of 'who are the people?' and 'what authority do they have to constitute themselves?'. In a temporal light these are very difficult questions to answer given the shifts in the constitution of any people over the course of time and the consequent fluid claims to authority. That said, a temporal conception of democracy also needs to extend questions around finality to more than the constitutive body, but also to the institutions charged with ensuring the rule of the people, and the realisation of *the key conceptual foundations of political equality and popular sovereignty*. This ethos is reflected by Honig in her discussion of rights:

> Rights are not dead instruments, they are live practices. But they must be kept animate. The failure to keep them alive by continuing to use them, recraft them, and fight for them even (paradoxically) after they have been entrenched undoes the very power that we give them and they give us. Dead rights require live futures – promisingly and dangerously unscripted futures – if they are to come back to life. (Honig 2001: 800)

Either through the longevity of originary institutions or through their formal guarantee in the constitutional arrangements of a given society, particular institutions are emblematic of the specific characteristics of democracy in any polity. While we often categorise these institutional configurations via umbrella terms such as the 'Westminster system', 'federalism' or 'consociational democracy', each amalgamation of institutions brought together to institutionalise a particular democratic model varies according to the specific context. But even where the particularities of institutional arrangements under these categories are understood to be contextually specific, usually they will be thought of in timeless terms as if there is no contingency in the specific arrangements at a given point in time. The fact that British or American or Indian democracy operates in a specific way and may have done so for extended periods of time does not entail treating these systems as if they are not subject to contingency. Challenges to political systems from radical constitutional reform to revolution, changes to the social context that sweep across the world like, for example, pandemics, political leaders losing touch with the socio-cultural movements of their own societies and so on mean that democratic systems are in continual evolution (especially if we conceive democracy as amounting to more than a particular type of parliamentary or voting system). Long periods of seemingly minute change do not mean that evolution is not necessary in democratic systems and many of the major challenges they may face will derive from the inability or unwillingness of governments to change in more minor ways in the face of changing global circumstances.

The contemporary world abounds with these challenges, whereby established democratic systems are undermined by problems that they seem incapable of managing, from global health challenges like pandemics to critical social movements like Black Lives Matter to the interminable wrangling over Brexit (Ware 2020). This calls into question democratic futures if democratic systems are no longer seen to be capable of delivering on the promises of their historical origins, or they are seemingly ripe for capture by populists, some of whom, at least, do not appear to have great faith in either democratic systems or democratic practices. Moreover, as Ware (2020: 816) points out, these pressures become more acute when conflicts over political interests are combined with conflicts over social identities. All of this creates an environment in which the future of democracy is increasingly brought into question. This is a temporal challenge too for it speaks to a 'golden age' of democracy in the past depending on the particular context in question and a troubled present in which the core institutions do not deliver on their promises to enshrine political equality or where it is hard to make a case for decisions on the grounds of popular sovereignty. At least two sets of temporal questions emerge in this scenario:

1. What are the values and/or principles of democracy that we want to retain? How should we protect the historical legacies of democracies in the face of contemporary shortcomings? What are the dangers of failing to defend democracy against those who seek to undermine its foundations?
2. How could democracy be different? How could democratic values be better enshrined in different institutional configurations? Must we be beholden to how democracy once was, or should we be seeking to innovate to create new institutions that deliver on the promises of democracy in the contemporary global environment?

The first set of questions above places the future in a historical and contemporary light. These questions are genealogical insofar as they invite consideration of what it is about democracy that political theorists and actors have become so invested in. They ask us to consider what it is about democracy that we value so much and to consider the historical legacies that have been bequeathed to those of us who live in some variant of a democratic system. Clearly, historical study of democracy (Dunn 2019) will show us how democracies evolved over the course of their development and that at times the maintenance of the principles that underpin the concept of democracy required refinements or constitutional amendments through to much more radical and revolutionary change. This historical treatment of democracy emphasises the dynamism of democratic systems. They did not emerge at once and they are not monolithic. Therefore, if the contemporary era is one in which democracy is faced with substantive challenges that threaten the very existence of democratic orders, we need to revisit the core concepts underpinning these systems to rediscover and, if necessary, redefine the values and principles that are worth cherishing and defending. What is it then that we might want to retain as we move into an uncertain future?

The second set of questions builds on these assessments of values to consider the ways in which key principles can be configured in political institutions and democratic practices. The temporal register invites us to build from a historical appreciation of certain concepts that led to particular institutional architectures in the past, to grapple with the question of whether that institutional configuration is the best means of maintaining those values in the present, and then to anticipate the ways in which there might be different institutions and processes that can maintain those values in the future. Of course, this last step is speculative and invites con-jecture about how best to marry democratic values with an uncertain world that we cannot definitively envisage. Yet, this is precisely the temporal challenge of democracy, to speculate, to take risks and to permit failures, the last of which requires us to recalibrate our democratic imaginations on an ongoing basis (Little 2012). It demands of us an understanding that we will disagree about the best means of maintaining democratic values – after all, some approaches will be more protective of historical interpretations than others – and that our evaluation of future democratic practices will not be consensual. Nonetheless, I contend that such a dynamic approach can invigorate democratic thinking and enable a freeing of the mind from historical interpretations, while still retaining space for appreciation of the knowledge that we have acquired and practices that we may not want to relinquish. In the Derridean approach of Fred Evans (2016: 311) this 'dem-ocratic promise' is articulated as the 'creative interplay of hybrid voices . . . forming society's agonistic body and shaping its space and time'.

In part, this temporal approach to democratic futures enables a freeing of the mind from inherited institutional structures. While the latter may have considerable value and, for reasons of path dependence if nothing else, encapsulate political resilience, they need not be the starting point for political theorists. Instead, theorists can turn to values, concepts or princi-ples as the building blocks of politics which in turn invoke particular types of institutions or policies. But, without these conceptual foundations, we are left to build castles of sand that do not have robust claims as their political grounding. All too often when democracy is invoked in popular political discourse (including within formal democratic institutions), it is an appeal to institutions first and foremost, with concepts or values as sec-ondary considerations. A temporal methodology would reverse that order, putting institutions at the service of our values and principles, as well as the concepts which give political shape to these aspirations. This would provide the foundations upon which a discussion of appropriate institu-tions and processes can take place.

The likelihood is that any reconfigured democratic institution would bear some resemblance to previously established models, but this is not to say that important changes would not ensue in any given democracy. This could be a shift in the form of representation through electoral reform away from simple plurality systems to forms of proportional represen-tation to the implementation of new deliberative fora and so on. Federal systems could become more or less centralised with shifts through consti-tutional reform. However, this process of returning to first principles could also be the opportunity for entirely new democratic entities to be created.

This could take many forms but could include the establishment of new bodies for hitherto excluded First Nations peoples, consultation mechanisms with affected peoples beyond the boundaries of the nation-state, pre-emptive measures to provide voice to people living on low-lying islands facing climate change, new supra-national organisations to tackle problems that cannot be resolved through nation-state policies, and so forth. Thus, debates on new forms of democracy will vary from polity to polity and involve a fusion of established democratic practices, alongside amended versions of those practices, or the creation of entirely new bodies or practices to meet current and emerging political problems in the future (Evans 2016: 312). In a fluid environment where there is little certainty about the challenges in the future and much disagreement about these challenges and their implications, it is sensible to think about democracy as a shifting amalgamation of ideas and practices that relate to core goals and values, rather than as an entrenched set of institutions created in different historical circumstances or those which appear to be the most suited to our current environment.

The lack of theoretical engagement with potential futures of democracy is also evident in many of the discussions of the current malaise of democracy and the literature on democratisation. Typically, these debates have been centrally focused on institutions, not least because, given the debates are often conducted within comparative politics, it is much easier to compare institutions across different contexts than it is to compare political ideas. While the latter, comparative political thought, is a predominantly interpretive exercise, the comparison of institutions – often their basic existence more than their quality – lends itself much more readily to quantification and those are the tools of the trade of comparative political science (see Simon 2020). The production of various datasets, often using survey methodology, showing that democracy is in decline across the world or that authoritarian regimes are increasing in sheer number or challenging extant democratic societies, provides a valuable resource for political scientists, but there are three problems with this data and these methods from a temporal politics perspective.

First of all, one of the primary benefits of these comparative studies is that they provide longitudinal data that enables analysis over the course of time. However, where temporal politics is focused on the flow of change over time and the interpretation of that flow in the lived experiences of people, comparative political science provides a series of snapshots derived from methods such as regular surveys of academic experts. Therefore, despite the longitudinal nature of these studies, they are more static than might appear at first and do not engage in a qualitative or interpretive

manner with substantive contextual issues that may impact on the performance of different democracies at various points in time.

Second, most of these comparative datasets focus on the existence of a
range of democratic institutions rather than the – admittedly more difficult – task of understanding the status of concepts, values or principles in
different societies given their ambiguity and contestability. For example,
to say that country x has become less democratic because institution y has
been abolished says little about the ideational context and the fact that
the demos, the constitutive body of any democracy, may be as committed,
or even more so, to particular values or principles that inspire democracy.
The measurement of institutions may tell us a lot about elite politics,
leadership and regimes, but it does not shed a lot of light on the people
that constitute a particular society or their beliefs. Even if a society is not
a democracy, this does not mean that the people within that society do not
believe in principles that correlate with democratic values like equality or
the need for justification from 'the people' – however that is manifested,
democratic or otherwise – as the foundation of society. In short, measuring institutions – usually those prevalent in Western liberal variants
of democracy – tells us something, but it also misses a large part of the
democratic puzzle.

Third, the focus on institutions (and the variations between them) in
the comparative political science literature neglects the importance of the
lived experience of the institutions in question – a key dimension of temporal politics. The institutions that comprise liberal democracies are not
always experienced in the same way by individuals or collectives and can
operate in quite divergent ways in different societal contexts. Therefore,
the existence of particular kinds of institutions is a somewhat blunt instrument for considering the future of democracy; arguably what matters more
is their capacity and propensity for change and responsiveness to different
collective actors rather than their sheer existence. Moreover, as the comparative political science literature makes clear, the existence of a particular
institution at a specific point in time is not an indicator of the longevity
of that institution, especially in environments where political leaders can
enact quite sweeping changes which affect the way an institution works
or if it exists at all. Of course, constitutional arrangements can safeguard
against cursory change, but they cannot necessarily guarantee how an
institution works in practice. This is where lived experience becomes so
important for temporality, but it is largely absent from the comparative
political science literature.

Ultimately, the comparative political science approach to democracy
and its struggles in recent years takes the basic institutional features of

extant liberal democracies as its building blocks and, while acknowledging the differences between different variants of democracy, uses these
institutions as its model for comparative assessment. There is little in this
literature about the experience of democracy, about the ways in which
different groups of people live in democracies in differential ways, or
about the ways in which these democracies might be redesigned so that
there is a more meaningful engagement between the people who constitute
them (and those outside the democratic boundaries of a particular polity)
to improve on the values and principles that democracy is founded upon.
While, historically, particular institutions might be seen to have served
their purpose, this is not to say that longevity or path dependence is a
sufficient condition for institutions that protects them from other ways
of conducting democratic relationships. What is lacking, once again, is a
sense of a liberated democratic imaginary that is not shackled by already
existing models of democratic organisation. While it is important to deal
with the shortcomings of some of these institutions, they should not be
regarded as definitional of the possibilities of democratic organisation. In
the next section, I examine one debate on an alternative model – recent
debates on global democracy – as a thought experiment in what democracy
in the future could look like.

Performing the Demos: Towards a Processive Theory of Global Democracy

The theory of global democracy has become a prominent feature of
debates in international political theory in recent years (Miller 2009,
2010, Goodin 2010). Much of this debate has been driven by the emergence of cosmopolitan arguments developed around the need to move
beyond the limited capacity of nation-states to provide adequate democratic representation of the needs or interests of their citizens. This
approach develops a positive account of the benefits that might accrue
from rethinking global democratic structures towards an acknowledgement of the need for multi-level governance institutions that reflect the
complex and shifting terrain of the contemporary world (Archibugi et al.
2011, Held 1995, Koenig-Archibugi 2011, Macdonald 2008, Zürn 2004).
Against these arguments, a range of critics from international relations
and political theory in particular have argued that the development of
global democracy is not possible based on the structures and power relations of global politics (Christiano 2006, Dahl 1989, Miller 2010). In this
vein, much of the debate has bifurcated between 'possibilist' advocacy
and 'impossibilist' critique.

The emergence of arguments for cosmopolitanism and the identification of the potential for greater democratisation on a global level have generated a spirited debate on the nature of global democratic institutions (Held 1995). Daniele Archibugi (2008), for example, considers different institutional formations for the architecture of cosmopolitan democracy with a particular focus on the constitutional structure. In advocating a union of states, Archibugi focuses his attention on how a cosmopolitan institutional model would differ from federal and confederal arrangements. David Held identifies a number of governance challenges in the contemporary international environment ranging from global warming to a variety of inequalities in less developed parts of the world that necessitate a rethinking of the institutions designed to facilitate transparency, effectiveness and accountability on a global level (Held 2007). And, taking these issues to a different level, Raffaele Marchetti (2011) outlines a case for 'cosmo-federalism' which goes beyond the advocacy of global governance models to make the case for democratic structures built around the concept of a global polity. While all of these accounts have made valuable contributions to the debate on cosmopolitan democracy, their focus has largely been on the institutional structures that would enable democracy to operate on a global level. That is, they concentrate on the kratos – the institutional architecture – of global democracy with less attention directed towards the constitution of the demos which the kratos is normally expected to serve in democratic theory. Arguably, then, there is a need for a more specific focus on the features of the sovereign body – the demos – and awareness of the ways in which how we constitute the demos has profound implications for how we consider the design of the kratos.

From the perspective of temporal politics and with a view to transcending the analytical-continental divide in political theory, these debates have tended to drift into analytical discussions of feasibility and, in particular, an overly institutional assessment of whether alternative global accounts of democracy are feasible. However, some more recent contributions have sought to shift the focus of the debate on to the characteristics of the sovereign people – the demos or demoi – and what is required of them to perform their role in a global democratic order. For example, List and Koenig-Archibugi (2010) try to develop a more 'performative' and 'agential' approach to the constitution of the demos. While this shift is welcome, there are three main objections derived from the model of temporal politics developed here. Firstly, proponents of global democracy need to avoid ideal type models of democracy as the defining institutions through which they make sense of the performativity of the global demos. Secondly, there is a tendency in the work of many theorists of global democracy to limit their imagination to familiar, state-based models of democratic institutions and inherited depictions of democratic agency, representation, majoritarianism and so forth. Thirdly, advocates of a performative approach to global democracy need to address a wider range of theories of performativity than is currently the case, including post-structuralist theories alongside their more familiar analytical territory.

The performative shift in global democracy debates is significant because it redirects attention to the characteristics of the demos as an agent rather than the institutional form of the kratos. It is designed to move the discussion beyond possibilist/impossibilist exchanges on the likelihood of meaningful institutions emerging in a global democratic system (Goodin 2010, Bohman 2007, Miller 2009, Buchanan and Keohane 2006) towards a focus on the capacity of particular groups of people to behave in a fashion required to qualify as a demos, that is, to perform in a manner that might be expected of a sovereign body of people in a democratic system. The novelty of this approach lies in its deepening of the definition of democracy to move beyond the questions of who 'the people' are or the precise institutional architecture of an inclusive global democratic order. While these remain significant questions, the performative approach moves further than the basic compositional question of who is in and out to draw greater attention to the particular qualities or capacities of a group of people to whom democratic structures will apply. As we shall see, however, this has drawn List and Koenig-Archibugi (2010), in particular, into a somewhat 'functionalist' position where the composition of the sovereign body is defined by the capacity to comply with the demands of a narrow range of extant institutional mechanisms.

List and Koenig-Archibugi identify two particular requisite performative qualities of the demos or demoi that would be the sovereign body or bodies in a new global political architecture. These include the capacity for *internal cohesion* whereby there must be a potential for sufficient meta-agreement between political actors to frame the space within which finer-grain policy decisions could be made (List and Koenig-Archibugi 2010: 95). Internal cohesion also needs to be coupled with *external coherence* whereby individuals need to demonstrate 'coherent collective attitudes (particularly, preferences) on the issues on which collective decisions are needed, where these attitudes are defined by a suitable democratic criterion' (List and Koenig-Archibugi 2010: 94).

However, it is not clear whether these are genuinely performative matters, or indeed the extent to which they can or should be separated from the compositional paradigm that has traditionally characterised global democracy debates. Indeed, it could be argued that they are intrinsically linked because the way in which we construe the composition of the demos will have a fundamental bearing on its performative capacity in particular democratic institutions (Saward 2006). Similarly, the way in which we argue for certain performative requirements of a sovereign body will have a direct impact on the way in which we might imagine its composition; for example, it will have a greater or lesser similarity to the demos of the nation-state. The issue then is not that we should circumvent the compositional argument by focusing on performativity, but rather that we understand the ways in which the compositional and performative questions are deeply intertwined. In the case of List and Koenig-Archibugi, the arguments for internal cohesion and external coherence appear to be driven much more by the need for demoi that merely enable institutions to function properly rather than a more substantive notion of democratic performativity.

Quite legitimately, democratic actors may want to undermine and unravel the construction of democratic institutions in favour of different or better ones. Similarly, in extant nation-states a key capacity of democratic actors must be to hold democratic institutions to account and argue for change and development of institutions or their replacement if necessary. In short, democracies need to have a degree of flexibility and a capacity for change in the face of the shifting terrain in which they operate (nationally or globally). In this sense, the demos cannot be defined solely in terms of its functional utility and the kratos needs to be responsive to the shifting nature of the demos to which it relates and from which it draws its power. In terms of practical feasibility, then, a theory of global democracy needs to encapsulate the ways in which a system of political institutions (a kratos) can be established which reflects potentially *different* understandings of the demos than those which have underpinned the development of existing ideal-typical nation-state democracies.

This is a trap that List and Koenig-Archibugi fall into in eschewing the likelihood of deriving lessons from divided democratic societies because, they contend, in these hard cases the forms of democracy that are developed are too distinct from ideal-typical nation-state democracies to provide a foundation for thinking about global democracy. Whereas in the ideal-type performativity is understood to be about guiding 'collective decision-making' and facilitating 'coordinated action', divided societies often employ models such as consociationalism in which cleavages are actually accentuated. Given the difficulties of enacting democracy on a global level, however, perhaps it is precisely these hard cases where democracy has been constructed in the face of serious divisions that provide the most useful examples for those interested in global democratic structures (Little and Macdonald 2013). The lessons that might be learned from looking at democratic experiments in divided societies are precisely that democratic mechanisms can be built to a greater or lesser extent in very inhospitable contexts. There is a significant danger in the way in which List and Koenig-Archibugi develop their conception of the global demos that they build a model that is not only defined in terms of institutional functionality, but also relies upon a problematically consensual understanding of the social conditions in which democracies must operate. As we have seen in earlier chapters, a notion of temporal politics grounded in lived experience recognises the importance of contention over democratic systems rather than wishing such disputes away.

In summary of this first objection to List and Koenig-Archibugi, then, even in approaches to global democracy where compositional questions are placed on one side, the theorisation of the ideal performative nature of a global demos is related to compositional membership criteria and the ways in which those criteria will affect the behaviours and practices of those who are deemed to be members. These issues are not distinct from one another insofar as the question of composition is likely to be the source of considerable dispute and hence continued disagreement *within* the confines of the defined composition. The key question of who decides the constitution of the sovereign body remains paramount but that moment of decision – highly significant as it is – is not the end of the story of contesting the make-up of any democratic order. The compositional question remains vital to ongoing arguments about global democracy especially in circumstances where that composition is based around criteria such as affectedness (Näsström 2011). Certainly, compositional decisions on inclusion need to be made to establish any democratic structure and the grounds for making those decisions need to be articulated, but those decisions are never 'final' in a contingent and fluid democratic space (Shapiro and Bedi 2009). Democracies exist within a complex environment of shifting identities and boundaries, changing territorial claims, and turbulent dynamics of social order and power (Rosenau 1990, 1997). In this scenario democracies need to be responsive to change rather than hidebound by prior decisions about composition, functionality or particular forms of conduct.

The second major problem with the performative turn in global democracy is that List and Koenig-Archibugi remain locked within a statist paradigm in their imagination of political alternatives. Their model is reliant on notions of representation and majoritarianism that emanate from state-based understandings of democratic institutions and they seek to justify their understanding of the demos on the idea of settled and relatively consensual groups of people living within established state boundaries.

Meta-agreement becomes the decisive factor through which they assess whether a collection of individuals displays sufficient performative cohesion to be regarded as a demos. While this might be analytically plausible, the language of this argument is heavily loaded. They talk of the differences between 'destructive' and 'benign' kinds of pluralism as if these judgements are not matters of political interpretation and disagreement. It is not a definitive empirical matter to decide whether a group can address an issue within 'some shared cognitive or normative space' (List and Koenig-Archibugi 2010: 95–6), especially if such a space does not pre-exist the judgement about this capacity.

Even if the demand is only for meta-agreement as a *precursor* to qualification as a demos rather than as a substantive outcome of political action, this threatens the democratic basis upon which a sovereign body is understood and constituted. Compositional arguments at least do not attempt to police acceptable democratic viewpoints in such an overt manner. List and Koenig-Archibugi find themselves locked into this problem precisely because they remain too wedded to the need for particular institutional structures based on a familiar nation-state-based paradigm. What results is a reconfiguration of the statist model in global terms which would most likely reproduce many of the problems of representative democracy that theories of global democracy could be expected to challenge given the inadequacy of majoritarian, representative practices for many minority groups in existing nation-states (Fraser 2008). In temporal terms, then, perhaps, rather than viewing global democracy as an alternative system to existing nation-state democracies (though, ironically, based on the same systemic underpinnings), a processive theory of global democracy informed by political temporality would be more focused on redressing some of the imbalances of existing constitutional democratic regimes by entwining and overlaying them with procedures and institutions with a broader, transnational remit.

Furthermore, normative, institutional models of global democracy sometimes rely on somewhat constrained interpretations of political representation as their means of imagining the relationship between the demos and the kratos. Follesdal, for example, argues that one of the key dimensions of democratic legitimacy is representation, by which he means 'control by elected, party-based, democratically accountable representatives over governing functions' (Follesdal 2011: 100, 101). However, there is no reason why theories of global democracy should rely so heavily on these kinds of presuppositions about the nature of democratic representation. Theorists from a number of perspectives have challenged these kinds of assumptions. For example, Andrew Rehfeld has developed a parsimonious theory to show why representation is a complex and not necessarily democratic phenomenon pointing to the many non-democratic representatives operating in contemporary global politics (Rehfeld 2006, 2009, 2011).

Others such as Michael Saward (2010) have welcomed the efforts of theorists such as Held, Goodin and Eckersley to broaden the scope of definitions of who might need to be represented, but he suggests that they still remain locked into a 'narrow, legislature-constituency focus' (Saward 2006: 298). Indeed, Saward suggests that a more performative theory of representation would be one in which we concentrate on the actual *claims* being made in the name of representation rather than the more traditional focus on *forms* of representation. This invokes a much more contested and subjective understanding of representation than theories which focus on particular institutional configurations in which more settled understandings of democratic representation are based. Saward challenges the fetishisation of this version of representation in contemporary political theory and argues for a performative approach in which representatives, audiences, subjects and institutions are all being performed upon and within in the act of claims to be representative. Thus institutions 'condition the styles of representative claims . . . [but] those institutions are themselves "performed" or enacted. They are pieces of crucial institutional and constitutional culture' (Saward 2006: 311). The point then is not to do away with thinking about institutions in assessing democratic performativity but to understand that institutions are part of the performative democratic culture. Models of democracy are as much the subject of democratic performativity as individual political actors or collective groups.

Indeed, one rationale for the advocacy of forms of global democracy may be precisely because established forms of democracy (including majoritarian principles) have proved incapable of providing sufficient democratic recognition for specific minorities with demands that are not adequately recognised through existing democratic institutional arrangements. Given the fact that many minorities in different societies perceive that they can never be in the majority (insofar as power relations can marginalise groups, preventing them from ever becoming part of a cycle of majority preferences), it is difficult to justify the resort to a notion of cycles of periodic majoritarian influence (as in classical pluralism) to those who are less influential in the structured conditions of global politics in which arguments for global democracy must make their case. List and Koenig-Archibugi are too quick to resort to the established justifications of actually existing democracies in nation-states rather than looking for newer arguments that might embolden their pursuit of a justification of global democracy.

This points to the need to engage with a broader literature than that which has been the traditional focus of theorists of global democracy.

The theory of performativity espoused by List and Koenig-Archibugi is firmly lodged in the analytical mindset which has dominated the literature on global democracy. While that literature has provided admirable analytical clarity in highlighting some of the key issues at stake in global democracy debates, it has unnecessarily narrowed the horizons of the democratic imaginary to the extent that in some accounts deliberative democrats are construed as political radicals (Miller 2009, 2010). In fact, in the case of Habermas (1994) and Rawls (1993) at least, the performative element of democracy is often reduced to the requirements of procedural mechanisms that enable forms of relatively consensual decision-making to take place rather than viewing democratic performativity as part of a vibrant, contestatory concept which may *challenge* the operation of democratic institutions. So, there appears to be an unnecessary foreclosure of the debate over global democracy which has blinded some of its advocates to the benefits that could accrue from a wider exposure to alternative theoretical accounts of what democratic performativity might look like.

Unlike Miller's depiction of deliberative democracy as radical, it could be argued that some of the most influential deliberative democrats focus too heavily on the demands of institutional mechanisms and mores such as reasonableness to police democratic performativity. Iris Marion Young, on the other hand, suggests that performativity in a democratic society does not necessarily entail that the acts which are performed must be compliant with the institutional prerequisites that a particular system demands (Young 2000). Ultimately, a procedural approach which is too focused on functional prerequisites can marginalise contentious viewpoints and oppositional practices, especially those which are critical of the prevailing democratic institutions (Rancière 2010). This is particularly important for theories of global democracy because part of their advocates' rationale is the inadequacy of existing institutional configurations in the face of a range of global problems (Held 2007).

A Temporal Perspective on Performativity?

Unlike the analytical tradition (and the perceptions of what is and isn't radical within it), there is another literature on democracy and performativity associated with the idea of radical democracy that emanates from an alternative post-structuralist methodological approach (Little and Lloyd 2009). These radical democrats tend to be concerned with the contest of ideas, identities, interests and disputes about action and policies in a non-normative sense. Thus, for radical democrats influenced by post-structuralism, it is not the fact that there are differences and disagreement about substantive goals alone that is of interest (that is, a plurality containing values that are more or less incommensurable), but rather that there is a system which enables the articulation of these arguments where they differ from the dominant viewpoint and facilitates challenges to the democratic system where it is held to be unresponsive to alternative arguments. From this perspective, arguments about the appropriate nature of democracy are simultaneously compositional and performative and to reduce it to one or the other is problematic. For radical democrats, what matters is the conflict of ideas and the conditions in which they can be expressed rather than focusing on the institutional infrastructure alone (Little and Lloyd 2009). Thus, the precise mechanisms of democratic institutions are less important for post-structuralist radical democrats than the opportunity to articulate disagreement with those institutions as a legitimate form of political expression.

How might greater engagement between analytical and post-structuralist theorists around the concept of performativity help in the development of a processive theory of global democracy? In Judith Butler's theory of performativity much of the focus is on the way in which individuals develop subjective perceptions of agency and the bearing this has on political action. This construction of agency takes place within a context of preconceived, naturalised notions of what a particular actor reflecting a specific source of identity should be and do, which in turn gets reflected in a range of social structures and cultural practices. While Butler's work has been enormously influential in the post-structuralist literature and there is widespread debate about her work (Lloyd 1999, Carver and Chambers 2008, Chambers and Carver 2008, Little 2010), I focus in particular here on two elements of her theory of performativity (Butler 1999). The first is her theory of the contested nature of the multiple elements that contribute to individual identity construction, and the second is the centrality of the idea of transgression in her interpretation of how personal identity can feed into notions of political action.

Butler's politics of identity is grounded in the idea of a deeply complex relationship between social structure and individual agency which has profound implications for how we interpret political action and the relationship between performativity and democracy. Unlike List and Koenig-Archibugi, for example, Butler's conception of performativity is frequently not remotely functional in institutional terms – indeed, performativity is often construed as a transgressive act that undermines accepted norms and structures that guide political action. Thus, to act in a democratic sense is not purely functional to the democratic system. Performing in a democracy can be progressive, regressive or transgressive in terms of the optimal operation of democratic institutions and, as we shall see, this means that a processive theory of global democracy needs to be much more flexible in understanding democratic performativity.

For Butler, individual identity often motivates political action but there is a multiplicity of sometimes contradictory contributory factors in the composition of identity. Indeed, each of these sources of identity exists within a particular structured set of meanings in any given society. On this account, performing as an agent of an identity does not entail a definitive set of actions but depends instead on what that identity means to an actor, how it relates to other sources of identity, and how that particular identity formation relates to broader social expectations of what performing as a member of an identity might mean. This construal of performativity suggests that the decisions actors make are socially and culturally constrained insofar as political choices take place within pre-structured environments. Performing may therefore involve an acceptance and repetition of pre-structured roles but alternatively it may subvert or seek to change established conceptions of social roles. As with Butler's example of gender, democratic performativity framed around the functional demands of democratic institutions would be 'produced as a ritualized repetition of conventions' (Butler 1995: 175).

A simply functional understanding of performativity in global democracy defined by the repetition of actions according to the requirements of political institutions would amount to little more than 'the mundane and ritualized form of their legitimation' (Butler 1988: 526). For this reason, a processive theory of performativity in global democracy cannot merely seek progress through meeting the functional requirements of the system – performing democratic roles must also have the scope for challenging the operation of democratic institutions. Moreover, from a temporal perspective, the definition of democratic performativity cannot rely on historical understandings of what democracy entails; rather, it needs a more open account that understands democracy as part of a future-oriented process of becoming (as explained in Chapter 7).

As far as theorising the possibility of a global demos or demoi is concerned, this suggests that what it means to perform as a member of that body may take on many different guises and be variously interpreted between a variety of social actors and groups with divergent preferences and ideas. There is a lack of this agential dimension in the theory of performativity developed by List and Koenig-Archibugi. Performative functionality in their argument is defined in terms of the ways in which agents can be collectively organised to serve particular institutional ends rather than agents deciding how to conduct themselves within the structured environment of institutional norms. Butler on the other hand envisages performativity as a way of potentially subverting dominant interpretations of appropriate action rather than mere compliance with particular institutional demands. Quite simply, for Butler, to perform can mean to challenge and confound functional expectations.

What then are the implications of Butler's understanding of performativity for how we might conceptualise theories of global democracy for the future? Certainly, it implies the need for a capacity to challenge prevalent democratic processes. It hints at performativity as a way of initiating processes of further democratic reform within a given polity rather than as a way of understanding how a body of people can coalesce with the functional demands of that system. In order to fully comprehend the implications of this alternative theorising of performativity for global democracy, we need to apply performativity in terms of a complex theory of democracy which in turn offers a different perspective on how global democratic performativity might be construed. Indeed, a more dynamic, complex and contestatory conception of democracy lends itself to a more processive account of global democracy. The point here is that a different and less institutionally specific model of democracy will have fundamental ramifications for how we might go about the consideration of what a global democratic architecture might look like.

This position builds on William Connolly's theory of 'a world of becoming' (Connolly 2011) and recent developments in complexity theory (Kauffman 2008, Prigogine 1997, Urry 2002, Cilliers 1998, Geyer and Rihani 2010, Cairney 2012, Little 2012) to rethink the emergence of forms of global democracy in a more gradual and processive light. This approach suggests that democratic societies are blends of orderly and disorderly elements in terms of both the behaviour of democratic actors and the environment in which they act. As a result, to perform in a democratic society is to act not in a settled, defined space but instead in one comprising competing interpretations of thoughts and actions. The ontological fluidity at the heart of this view of contemporary societies entails that a dynamic model of democracy must always be understood as 'becoming' in terms of the appropriate configuration of institutions and systems to match a complex social order. In this light, global democracy cannot be imagined as a settled order of institutions and actors but, on the contrary, it should be conceived as part of an ongoing process of institutional reform and renewal reflective of the shifting dynamics of the composite institutions and actors.

A potentially more vibrant conception of democratic performativity would be one whereby democratic agents could behave in ways which unsettle, disrupt, challenge and undermine the established institutional order as well as act according to the prescriptive institutional demands of a model of global democracy. Instead of imagining democratic institutions and processes in ideal-typical fashion, we need to pay greater attention to the shades of grey that pertain to the practical application of any theory of democracy. In practice, democracies rarely reach the high normative aspirations that underpin their theoretical justification (Little 2008, Little and Macdonald 2013). Perhaps, then, it is more useful to focus on how global institutions can be democratised to a greater or lesser extent and to consider a processive account focused on the gradual development of more democratic structures on a global level rather than become too deeply embroiled in discussion about the conditions of possibility for an idealised institutional model. While I contend that this can be advanced by addressing some post-structuralist insights, it is also important to recognise that that body of work has little to say on how this kind of conceptualisation might translate into a model of global democracy or its attainability. In the remainder of the chapter, I take some initial steps in bringing these approaches together to provide a sufficiently dynamic conception of democracy and to make the theory of performativity operational in terms of conceiving democracy at a global level. I contend that a processive account offers the best means of advancing a theory of global democracy and working out how it might be operationalised in political practice.

In the work of Rancière (2010), democracy is identified as more of a mode of facilitating disagreement and fluidity than it is a system of institutional specificity and functional stability. Democracy is not a settled entity in Rancière's eyes but instead a space of dissensus whereby, to exist in a properly democratic fashion, there must be capacity for actors to challenge democratic institutions (and for those institutions to be changed). This would suggest that performing as a demos is not just about shoring up certain institutions or meeting their functional requirements. As such, in Rancière's theory of democracy, the ontological make-up of a demos could not, by definition, involve commitment to a meta-consensus. Democracy is understood as a means through which political actors can contest the boundaries of the political and challenge the ways in which institutional mechanisms perform their role within democratic systems (Little 2007). Rancière regards definitive attempts to ring-fence the polity, police the conduct of the demos and define democracy in purely institutional terms as 'hatred of democracy' (Rancière 2006). His theory implies that we need to imagine a model of political action within global democratic processes that can be *either institutionally functional or critical of the operation of democratic institutions.*

Rancière's dissensual conceptualisation of democracy implies that there are multiple perspectives and arguments informing political decision-making and that democratic agents often act at cross purposes to promote different interests and achieve varied goals. This ontological fact entails that political action in democratic societies by some actors will often be interpreted to be failing (Freeden 2009a, 2009b, Little 2012). On this foundation what would be the key elements of a processive theory of global democracy? For a start it must not fall into the traps that bind the argument of List and Koenig-Archibugi: firstly, it cannot take its *raison d'être* from the functional requirements of extant systems; secondly, it must not define institutional functionality through a state-based imaginary; and, thirdly, it must recognise that performativity in a global democracy cannot be construed in purely progressive terms. An additional but highly significant factor that we need to bear in mind is the complex nature of the environment in which such ideas will need to be operationalised. It is not sufficient to imagine an alternative model of global democracy without addressing the structural constraints which might stand in the way of its realisation. So, following Connolly (2011: 27), this calls for a more dynamic conception of democracy as a complex and fluid system which is characterised by competing claims and dissensus and which is never institutionally fixed or settled.

What might this perspective entail for a theory of global democracy? Certainly, it suggests that 'democracy' is not something that we ever definitively attain through the establishment of a particular set of political institutions. Rather it is better thought of as an emergent entity permanently in a state of development into new institutional formations and conceptual configurations. The process of democratisation is not a linear, one-directional, progressive movement of political improvement, but a complex, interactive engagement between an assemblage of numerous social, cultural, political and economic systems impelled by a multiplicity of logics which may enhance or disrupt democratic principles. Conflict and disagreement are vital to the kind of model outlined here because they contribute to a 'generative ethos' (Connolly 2011: 80) in which the quality of democracy can always be potentially improved. This suggests that the process of democratisation is always incomplete, and it thereby invokes the requisite of critical capacity and the necessity of the potential for democratic change. Democracy will of course be organised around certain institutions and procedures, but it is vital that these must provide opportunities for political change rather than merely becoming vessels to contain conflict.

Specifically, then, it is important to explain the implications of this general understanding of 'democracy as becoming' for the more particular theory of global democracy. The shift towards performativity is a useful step in complementing compositional questions of who is in and out in framing global democracy in terms of meaningful political action. But the major contention here is that advocates of global democracy need to relinquish attempts to define democracy in terms of functional requirements of a demos or the construction of fully fledged models of what global democracy must look like in compositional, institutional or performative terms. Instead, we need a shift towards understanding global democracy as an emergent entity which may be evident in a multiplicity of nascent democratic processes across a wide range of sectors. While the next chapter will discuss 'becoming' in more detail, suffice to say at this point that it involves a specific temporal dimension which emphasises an open disposition to the future. This disposition provides a space for political creativity and the benefits of reimagining tried and tested institutions and practices, rather than being beholden to them.

The processive model of global democracy sketched here relies on five main characteristics. Firstly, it is conceived as an emergent and evolving entity (Goodin 2010). According to this approach, it is not particularly useful to highlight fully formed institutional blueprints of what global democracy would look like with no clear sense of how to move from existing institutional democratic formations towards a new model. This gives little strategic guidance for political action and the ways in which we might move towards greater democratisation on a global level. Given the likelihood of falling short of ideal types, there needs to be some means of guiding action which *improves democratic processes* on a global level rather than judging processes solely on whether they are part of a preordained definitive model of global democracy. As Goodin makes clear, the historical development of existing forms of state-based democracy did not occur instantaneously in any particular case. On the contrary, existing systems have developed through many formations that have emanated from policy changes, institutional reforms, constitutional amendments and so forth. There is little reason to imagine that global democracy should develop along different lines and that is why a processive model focuses on the gradual implementation of democratising initiatives and the evolution of democratic institutions vis-à-vis other institutions in a complex amalgam of political, social and legal systems that operate on multiple levels.

The second dimension of a processive model of global democracy is that it is more concerned with processes designed to advance key democratic principles than those which are focused on the development of a particular institutional architecture. For this reason, a processive theory does not imagine the replacement of nation-state democracy with some new all-encompassing global entity such as a model of global federalism (Marchetti 2011). Instead, it concentrates on ways in which existing forms of national and global governance can be supplemented and improved upon by alternative modes of democratic engagement (K. Macdonald 2011). These modes of democratic engagement may sit beneath, alongside, within, between or above existing nation-state-based democratic structures in what is likely to be a complex, multi-level set of institutions which may complement each other but, at other times, may be at odds. Importantly, then, from a processive perspective, a global democratic institutional structure is not just developed on a single global scale but is understood to be multi-level in nature. Therefore, a processive theory of global democracy needs to be recognised as trans-scalar (Scholte 2014) with institutions making contributions to the overall democratic architecture on national and sub-national strata as well as on the transnational and international levels.

Thirdly, the participants in a processive theory of global democracy cannot merely be imagined as individual actors in the way that representative models of constitutional democracy construe voters and constituents. Given the potentially complex, multi-layered nature of global democracy, a processive model need not solely be reliant on elected institutions as the source of political representation and, as such, need not imagine participants in global democratic practices in quite the same way. This has clear implications for performativity in a global democratic setting. Obviously, it invokes a model of institutional pluralism with multiple venues for the articulation of a range of political arguments, but the performative corollary is that a range of different practices can contribute to the constitution of democratic processes at the global level. This will continue to involve standard state-based practices such as voting in elections, but performing a democratic role may also mean activities such as working for charities and non-governmental organisations to highlight inequalities that are not being addressed by state-based democratic institutions, or raising awareness of the affectedness of groups of people who are not party to the democratic structures through which the decisions that affect them are being taken. Thus, while direct representation by political parties is a significant dimension of the amalgamation of institutions that might comprise global democracy, individuals and groups can also be involved through a range of non-elected organisations that operate in a variety of different institutional structures to influence political decision-making. Quite simply, in a processive model of global democracy, democratic representation is not only based on electoral legitimation.

The fourth characteristic of an emerging processive theory is that it concentrates on a range of practices which are not necessarily focused on democracy as a determinate institutional system (Little and Macdonald 2013). The argument suggests that democratising processes can be taking place wherever there are efforts to enhance popular sovereignty and political equality over a variety of areas (for example, specific trade practices, the production of goods and so forth). Again, this has important ramifications for how we understand performativity, insofar as to perform democratically is to invoke particular rationalities focused on the key conceptual underpinning of democracy, rather than a narrower range of institutionally functional practices. Here we see the re-emergence of the basic principles around which democracy has been historically advocated rather than a focus on the institutional mechanisms in which they have been translated into the practice of constitutional democracy in nation-states. While these principles clearly inform many representative democratic practices, the institutions of representative democracy are not the only spaces in which the goals of political equality and popular sovereignty can be pursued (Beetham 1999). In temporal terms, the privileging of democratic values over established institutions facilitates opportunities for creative thinking about what institutional structures might best meet these core democratic principles in the future.

Finally, it is important to remember that it will not always be immediately obvious whether particular acts or practices that are undertaken in the name of democracy will make a positive contribution to global democracy in the longer run. Performing global democracy involves the pursuit of objectives beyond the functional requirements of formal political institutions. Familiar democratic practices will remain part of this complex mix, but global democracy also needs to be understood in terms of practices which will subvert, challenge and sometimes undermine orthodox representative institutions where they are perceived to be failing to operate in ways which are complementary with the basic objectives of political equality and popular sovereignty. This brings an element of subjective judgement into the global democratic equation as it will not always be definitively clear whether a particular act or policy ultimately enhances core democratic principles. Some activities undertaken in the name of democracy may be progressive, but others will be regressive when viewed in the longer run. Moreover, where there are perceived inadequacies in the operation of democratic institutions, then there may be grounds for transgression against the demands of a particular democratic institution. Quite simply, democratic performativity involves activities which have core democratic principles as their rationale. For advocates of global democracy, while these may often be institutionally functional in the way List and Koenig-Archibugi imagine, at other times they may not and we must be careful not to regard activities and practices which shore up institutional systems as the only ones which can claim democratic legitimacy in the global domain.

Temporality and Democracy: Towards a Processive Approach

Whether concerned with the idea of global democracy or not, the example above is designed to demonstrate the ways in which debates about the future in temporal politics must be related to the past and present but not shackled by them. For global democrats, this implies that they need to develop a more nuanced account of the implications of performativity to understand the potential of alternative democratic structures and practices. This account should be one in which political action in a democracy is always understood as part of the dynamic development of the system and that this can quite often be regressive rather than progressive. By this account, democracy is an entity in which neither the demos nor the kratos is fixed and settled. From this perspective, what becomes paramount is not whether a set of institutions definitively qualify as a democracy or not, or whether a group of people definitively qualify as a demos or not. On the contrary, democratic action is that which can be understood as activities or policies designed to enhance the *democratic quality* of a set of institutions or the governance of a particular field, that is, activities which are designed to enhance the core democratic objectives of political equality and popular sovereignty. A processive theory of global democracy should recognise that the pursuit of these objectives can take many different forms and therefore it need not be institutionally prescriptive. Instead, there is greater value in highlighting the ways in which a range of different practices might contribute to a global ordering that is more rather than less democratic in terms of the organising principles that underpin the institutional architecture (Little and Macdonald 2013).

A processive model does not try to understand global democracy in terms of a single, definitive institutional configuration. Instead, it is understood as a system of multi-level, overlapping processes that interact with each other in a complex fashion and which involve a diverse range of practices. A processive theory of global democracy may be about seeking normative improvements in terms of core democratic objectives of political equality and popular sovereignty for various groups who are not well-served by existing democratic systems (for example, the global poor; Fraser 2008), but that is not to say that it should be imagined solely as a process of political improvement. The performance of global democracy would take place in a complex and sometimes fractious environment in which it would be wise to expect regressive as well as progressive developments. In a processive model, the capacity to challenge prevailing institutions in the name of democracy is pivotal even when it is unclear what the precise outcomes of such challenges may be.

There is no reason why this processive model of global democracy must necessarily follow established state-based democratic paradigms or orthodox models of representation. Defining performativity in terms of the functional requirements of systems based on such state-based paradigms is something of a blind alley. Seeking to construct new global democratic processes (alongside sub-national processes) through institutional innovation and broader notions of performativity is fraught with risk and the likelihood is that such initiatives will often fail to deliver substantive democratic improvements, but that does not mean that processes of global democracy are not worth pursuing. Rather than seeking to replicate existing structures on a global scale, there might be greater utility in examining alternative policy frameworks based on uncertainty about the future and the outcomes of contemporary action. For example, these might include the wider use of mechanisms to assess policies through sunset clauses in policy agreements and other means of facilitating the contestation of decisions that are taken where we are unsure of their impacts on communities of people. The much wider usage of review processes might enable policies and institutions to move with the times and facilitate a much greater openness in our understanding of political development. After all, if the point of democracy is to advance levels of political equality and achieve a greater degree of popular control, then there is much work to be done. The pursuit of those democratic values is better construed as a *process of becoming* through the development of new democratic processes than it is through the construction of fully fledged but unrealisable democratic models that merely provide ammunition for those with less democratic objectives for global politics in mind. Indeed, a processive model of democracy may not only need to think of the becoming of democracy, but also of the ways in which such a model needs to consider issues such as climate change or the ways in which we think about non-humans in the imagination of the democratic community (Little and Ozguc 2022; from a more liberal, analytical perspective, see also Donaldson and Kymlicka 2011).

With this in mind, it is worth returning to the idea of process in the final section, in particular the relationship between multiplicity, process and becoming. Through charting time and process in debates in public policy, we return to process philosophy in the work of Alfred North Whitehead and Gilles Deleuze, before reflecting finally on how process philosophy influences temporal politics and the ways in which such an approach casts new light on the method of temporal politics as understood through the cases discussed in the second part of the book.

PART THREE

7

From Process Philosophy to Temporal Politics

The last three chapters have used examples from significant debates – relationships between settler colonial states and First Peoples, regimes of bordering and migration control, the 'decline' of democratic governance systems and future states of democracy – to demonstrate the ways in which temporality is a constant and often divisive element of many highly important issues in contemporary politics. In different ways, these cases have exemplified some of the primary contestations around political temporality such as the ways in which we account for the past (or fail to do so), make sense of competing temporal registers in contemporary policy domains, and/or disagree about the socio-political ramifications of our actions on the future. In this chapter, the focus shifts away from specific instances where temporal disputes are played out and returns to a more general theoretical and methodological account of temporal politics and the way in which it is manifest in contemporary politics. Thus, while I return to the cases chosen to exemplify political temporality later in this chapter, the main purpose is to move from the specific to the general in order to build from below a theoretical account of the ways in which political actors need to take greater account of temporality in how they imagine policy problems and work out ways to act on them. While it may be too grandiose to suggest that this is a new method for political analysis, it does provide scope for a different mindset or disposition towards political questions – one which tries to bridge the analytical-continental divide in political philosophy as well as provide a much stronger connection between political theory and public policy or administration.

The primary way of explaining temporal methods in this chapter is through an engagement with process philosophy which, I contend, provides a foundation for the incorporation of temporal concerns into how we think about politics. However, initially, it is also vital to return to some recent literature in the field of public policy to identify the way in which discussion of the policy process could be enhanced by a more thorough interaction with some of the literature in contemporary political theory. It is worth reiterating at this point that some of the most instructive work on the relationship between politics and time has come in the sub-discipline of policy studies, and its connections to discussions in political theory are well worth further investigation. As we shall see, some of this involves earlier scholars of public administration such as Mary Parker Follett who explicitly engaged with notions of process. However, first of all I shall turn to one of the most influential works in the recent public policy literature that focuses explicitly on time, Christopher Pollitt's *Time, Management, Policy* (2008). This book is primarily focused on bringing the past back into public policy debates to provide a historical dimension to analysis of the policy process which, he contends, has become too concerned with the present and the future.

Pollitt, one of the most distinguished public policy scholars of the last thirty years, argues that policy analysis requires discussion of the past so that we can best understand the knowledge, skills and practices which inform the development and implementation of public policy today. This implies that too much of the policy literature is concerned with ahistorical understandings of the pressing policy concerns of the day. For Pollitt, this is a flawed approach in that it tends to neglect the lessons that can be learned by studying practices of the past. The case for temporal politics made in this book of course resonates with Pollitt's claim insofar as I propose a method whereby historical analysis is of central importance. However, Pollitt's argument implies that past, present and future are to some extent extricable from one another and that the primary missing element in public policy analysis is the historical dimension. As we shall see, for a temporal method focused on the processive element of politics, there needs to be more of an emphasis on the interconnected process that brings past, present and future together rather than focusing on them as clearly distinguishable categories. Pollitt's contention that 'time matters' and that 'the past persists' are valuable insights from a public policy perspective, but he also needs to pay greater attention to the future, even if it is difficult to predict and direct causality is often questionable.

While Pollitt's neglect of the future and its relation to the past and present is problematic, his advocacy for historical understanding is vital for policy makers (Pollitt 2008: 161–7). He outlines numerous reasons for historical awareness including the risk that ignorance of the past can lead policy makers to adopt unrealistic or grandiose visions of what is achievable on a given issue as they may not understand the relevant constraints. Knowledge of the past also helps to shore up new or old policies through

greater understanding of earlier methods, while also enabling policy entrepreneurs to understand when there are genuine windows of opportunity
for change. Indeed, even when there is a process of major policy change,
there need not be destruction of all that went before, so historical knowledge can help policy makers to maintain elements of the past that retain
value for new policy settings. Finally, Pollitt makes the pertinent point
that political actors will often draw on historical narratives or analogies
(sometimes incorrectly) and that historical knowledge can help in rebut-
ting some of these erroneous or ill-informed narratives about the past.
These kinds of arguments are now fairly commonplace within the public
policy literature, especially those focused on agenda setting and the use of
the multiple streams framework to understand policy processes (Ackrill
et al. 2013, Cairney and Zahariadis 2016, Kingdon 1995).

Quite rightly, Pollitt is careful to disaggregate political institutions
when discussing the impact of temporality, not least because not all
policy-focused entities are working to the same kinds of ends or within
similar timescales. For example, he differentiates between the import of
time on policy institutions which are 'procedural' (such as in forestry)
where the outcomes are mainly long-term, 'coping' (such as in community mental health) where the outcomes are not readily observable, and
'production organisations' (such as authorities producing driving licences)
where the activities are easily observable, calculable and timebound (Pollitt
2008: 140). This is an important reminder that temporality has an impact
on all sorts of political institutions, but quite often in highly differentiated ways. What constitutes the appropriate tempo and duration of activities within these spaces will vary considerably, and there may also be
highly divergent forms of contestation about how to act politically when
the temporal horizons of these institutions are so varied. It also makes it
hard to make definitive judgements on the success or failure of particular
policy initiatives.

In developing his case, Pollitt makes use of John Kingdon's influential
work on policy flows highlighting that political problems, policy agendas
designed to address them, and political actors developing and implement-
ing policies are not static and predetermined. In this fluid environment,
as we discussed in Chapter 3 around the American Political Development
approach, spaces are created in which policy entrepreneurs can work to
open up and seize windows of opportunity. These windows may be problem windows, policy windows or political windows (or some combination
thereof), but they provide opportunities in which entrepreneurs can enact
important decisions with the capacity to alter political or policy paradigms
(Kingdon 1995). This scenario is complicated by the fact that some of these

windows are quite short but predictable, whereas others are of unknown duration and quite unexpected. Using Kingdon, Pollitt argues that the policy entrepreneur needs to be ready to capitalise on a variety of opportunities and be capable of judging when a particular policy domain is cyclical and when it is moving in an arrow-like and evolutionary pathway. Indeed, they must also be capable of recognising when a hitherto evolutionary policy agenda is becoming more cyclical in nature. The point here is that these policy domains in which policy entrepreneurs must operate are fluid rather than static spaces.

Therefore, in developing a typology of policy processes and their contexts, Pollitt (2008: 134–41) differentiates between four different kinds of arrangement. These are firstly when 'processes simply take a long time'. Not surprisingly, this is quite commonplace in many policy domains and policy windows within such processes may only be open for a relatively short time. This means that policy actors need to be ready to act when openings occur and they must have some flexibility in policy settings to be able to act upon an opening and adapt and implement a policy at short notice. The second situation is when there are 'contexts in which temporal sequence is crucial to outcome'. Here the windows for opportunity may also be quite short because the policy sequence may progress before a new direction can be established and implemented. In this scenario, it may need another entire policy cycle before the opportunity re-emerges, although any policy failure in this process can be foreseen as the point at which an alternative direction can be enacted in the next policy cycle.

The third of Pollitt's policy scenarios describes 'contexts in which cycling or alternation are typical'. Here, given the inherent predictability in this kind of policy cycle, there may be greater opportunities for entrepreneurs to intervene at certain points to diverge from a particular policy agenda. However, as his description implies, this predictability also facilitates a return to older agendas if the cycle remains predictable. Pollitt describes his fourth dimension as 'time tactics'. This refers to the work of policy entrepreneurs in gradually getting their foot in the door of a policy domain rather than attempting to enact some kind of 'big bang' with a radical policy agenda. The tactical dimension of such an approach is to gradually introduce policy change through, for example, enacting more attractive parts of a policy agenda first to avoid kneejerk oppositional responses. Time tactics also require astute awareness of both policy sequences and the temporality of crises so that alternatives can be presented with a suitable degree of urgency and a strong sense of timeliness.

In response to these environments that policy makers will face, Pollitt (2008: 143–5) advocates the adoption of a 'time toolkit' to provide the requisite capacity and flexibility to adapt to changing circumstances. He emphasises the importance of duration and understanding the pace of change, although he refers to time in the singular here rather than highlighting the importance of the policy maker being able to understand competing perspectives on the duration of a particular policy issue. Pollitt also emphasises the significance of choices made in a policy environment in terms of path dependence. Thus, when faced with a fork in the road of a particular policy field, it is vital to recognise that decisions will set an agenda for ensuing decisions: it will establish an arrow along a particular path and either eradicate or limit the utility of other policy options. Therefore, choosing one path or another will establish a set of parameters that opens some windows of opportunity and closes others by releasing time's arrow in a particular direction.

However, the policy maker also requires patience and awareness that policies need to be interrogated and reviewed once enacted; that is, that there is a cycle and there will be opportunities to recalibrate and turn to alternative policies if necessary. As such, policy makers need to keep their focus on the causal mechanisms that might contribute to the production and/or maintenance of particular policy agendas, to ensure that, despite cycles of review and assessment, the overall direction of a policy agenda remains on course. All the time, however, Pollitt contends that policy makers must stay attuned to 'multiple times', in recognition of the range of changing temporal perspectives that have a bearing on perceptions of the policy process. While this corresponds to some extent with the model of temporal politics developed in this book (insofar as it acknowledges a multiplicity of temporal perceptions), it does still imply a greater degree of certainty about the elements of a policy domain and their respective trajectories than is probably warranted in complex environments. The shortcoming, then, is that Pollitt does not do enough with the concept of 'multiple times'. In part, this reflects his somewhat one-dimensional conception of the past, which is mostly depicted as an established entity from which we learn, rather than a dynamic and disputed set of interpretations that have a continued bearing on the present and will project into the future.

Ultimately, Pollitt provides a valiant attempt to integrate a more sophisticated conceptualisation of time into his discussion of public policy making. He provides numerous valuable insights into the policy process and makes a strong case for the use of a more retrospective outlook in policy debates to move the focus a little more from the present and future (actions and outcomes). Nonetheless, the temporal states of past, present and future do appear somewhat static in his approach and the connection between them is not clearly articulated. The past, present and future are presented as rather fixed and settled periods of time, instead of being conceived as overlapping spaces of dispute and upheaval. As such, Pollitt presents a persuasive case for a rethinking of time in public policy and administration without grasping the full complexity of temporality and its implications for a method of conducting temporal politics:

> we can make things much easier for ourselves if we actively learn to live with the past, and with the way many of the important actions we take now may carry both consequences and requirements which stretch far into the future. In short, we can recognize the reality of long linkages over time, and adapt our policies and institutions to allow for them, or we can blunder forwards without either rearview mirrors or forward vision. (Pollitt 2008: 181)

Therefore, in the mainstream public policy literature, temporality tends to be expressed as part of a fairly standard trajectory between established stages of past, present and future. While trajectories become established through particular policy arrows and forks in the road where key decisions are taken, opportunities for policy innovations still persist through windows of opportunity where there are changes in the wider context or through processes of review in policy cycles. Both policy arrows and policy cycles have a form of linearity about them – fairly obvious and sequential in the case of time's arrow, but also implicit in the policy cycle insofar as there is an assumption of an overall direction within which policy is developed, implemented, analysed and reviewed within an overarching framework that establishes a particular direction.

Whether the current public policy literature on time invokes policy arrows and/or policy cycles as the metaphor to explain the nature of public policy making, there appears to be an implicitly processive notion of time and politics. This is reminiscent of an older tradition in public administration associated with the work of early-twentieth-century organisational theorist Mary Parker Follett (Follett 1951), and her role in connecting public administration with forms of process philosophy (which will be discussed in the following section; see also Holland 2011). Follett introduced the concept of interweaving to help to explain how public administration was best served through a model of collaboration between policy actors and a synthesis of perspectives to produce generative power. Ultimately, Follett's vision was a progressive one in which conflicting perspectives generated a positive environment of problem-solving in which disputes were overcome through rational engagement. As we shall see, this contrasts with more recent trends in process philosophy where syntheses are often construed as disjunctured rather than progressive, but it does point to an understanding of the processive nature of policy making alongside the importance of time. Like process philosophy's emphasis on becoming, Follett's interweaving is a relational theory that concentrates on productive engagement across conflict to enable a positive synthesis. It is an inherently participatory understanding of the policy process:

> This ontology's embrace of difference enables us to transform our understanding of conflict as a social problem into conflict as an opportunity for a self-organizing, constructive, unifying, harmonizing, synthesizing process that generates shared power and progress. In fact, this ontological shift is perhaps the key differentiation with liberal philosophy – rather than assuming conflict is a problem for social order, it is seen as creating the opportunity for individual and social progress. (Stout and Staton 2011: 285)

While Stout and Staton are correct to draw out the progressive dimension of Follett's model of process, it is less convincing to attach such a stance to others more centrally involved in process philosophy, as we will see in relation to Whitehead's perspective in the next section. Importantly, Follett provides a relational, processive theory where humans are all involved in acts of social production and reproduction, but unfortunately her argument is bereft of a conceptualisation of the dynamics of power, inequality or social division – a problem compounded by Stout and Staten who also fail to draw attention to the absence of a notion of power as a constraint in her work. Thus, they state that 'participation is, therefore, not an option – it simply is. Everything and everyone are related in *mutual influence* with the eternal objects and actual entities that precede and surround them' (Stout and Staton 2011: 279, emphasis added). While this is a good indication of the centrality of relationality to Follett's outlook, it underplays the impact of inequalities of power on the nature of the relationships between humans and, therefore, the inequalities that are reflected in the ways in which society is built and reproduced (as well as the ways in which public policies are developed and implemented). Therefore, as we shall see, while both Follett and Whitehead emphasise the relational nature of sociopolitical processes, Whitehead has a more substantive notion of power at work in his thought, thereby leaving more space open for processes to be regressive as well as progressive. Therefore, for Whitehead, 'power is integral to the process of concrescence, to existence and to our analyses of the world, not as some kind of "add-on", human derivation or construction, but as an integral element of how things really are' (Halewood 2011: 33).

Ultimately, the connection between Follett and Whitehead may be stronger in terms of the establishment of a somewhat pragmatic political ethos that emerges from engagement between the notions of becoming and interweaving in public policy/administration approaches and process philosophy. Both approaches are prepared to relinquish some of the certainty that tends to feature in liberal, rational theories of politics and policy making, and neither seems particularly attracted to substantive, normative commitments. That said, the progressivism of Follett does suggest a weddedness to some variant of liberalism, although it seems that the idea of achieving improvement is just as important to her as any substantive normative commitments themselves. However, for the purposes of establishing a theory of temporal politics, we need a more thorough engagement with the ideas of uncertainty and becoming as they seem vital to a clear understanding of how we consider the future in politics. This requires us to shift analysis from theories of public policy making to a more substantive engagement with process philosophy.

Process Philosophy: From Whitehead to Deleuze

Process philosophy is a broad church with a number of influential thinkers covering a range of ideological, methodological and theological perspectives. For the purposes of the argument here, I will focus primarily on the ideas constructed by perhaps the most significant process philosopher, Alfred North Whitehead, and the more recent but widely read contribution from Gilles Deleuze. At its simplest, process philosophy regards the world as dynamic rather than static and avoids representing entities as essential or determined, whether material objects or ontologies. Rather subjects and objects exist in relation to one another and, while there may be temporary stability in things as we engage with them in human life, this stability is transient and fluid. Stability is only a temporary state.

Where most approaches to philosophy imply and build from a set of static conditions based on assumptions about human beings or the world in which they exist, process philosophy is concerned with flows and becoming. In terms of temporality, more standard philosophical models – especially those associated with analytical methods – prefer the more parsimonious use of snapshots of human existence even if they recognise that each snapshot is part of some kind of moving sequence. Frequently, we are asked to make some assumptions about people and their motives or to bracket out contextual complexity, in order to draw out normative analytical principles which can then be used to inform particular decisions. However, of course, all too often these analytical methods take place at some remove from actual decision-making processes and have limited utility for those engaged in making decisions on the ground (where untidy, contextual details tend to compromise whatever ethical recommendations analytical theories develop). However, for process philosophy, this understanding of snapshots, sequences and causality underplays the relational and interactive dimensions of entities within each snapshot and the multiplicity of ways in which each entity is becoming. This refracts on the nature of the sequence itself such that a series of snapshots in a progressive sequence misrepresents the multiple ways in which snapshots may be moving and the indirect kinds of causality they engender. The challenge of process philosophy to dominant, purportedly substance-based paradigms in Western metaphysics is therefore a methodological issue (Seibt 2003).

Although there is a long history to process philosophy going back to Heraclitus, Alfred North Whitehead is the paradigmatic figure in the modern formation of process theories. The key element in Whitehead's thought is his belief in a 'nonessentialist ontology' (Halewood 2005: 58) which, coupled with his emphasis on the interrelations between human subjectivity and nature, provides the basis for his version of process philosophy. Building from Whitehead's *Process and Reality* and citing Deleuze and Guattari's *What Is Philosophy?*, Halewood (2005: 62) comments that it is 'the act of being thrown from the past into the future that constitutes being: the being of becoming. This will entail that at the human level, subjectivity is not so much a question of what something or someone is, but what they are becoming and, concomitantly, what they are "ceasing to be".'

For our purposes, this 'extensive continuum' points to a complex of relationships which, in temporal terms, extend infinitely. This runs contrary to teleological approaches and questions Enlightenment notions of progression, given the continuing and ongoing relationship between the present and the past. While process philosophy is concerned with movement and flow into the future, it does not imply that such becoming is one-directional. As Halewood (2005: 66) explains, this complicates the idea of a clear distinction between subject and object:

An actual entity's being lasts only as long as its becoming. When it has become it dies; insofar as it is no longer becoming, it no longer has any being. But this does not mean that it disappears: on the contrary, it then becomes an element in the potential creation of new entities, it is established as an element that new becomings may use as the data for their own becoming. In this way it passes from being a subject to being an object; 'thus subject and object are relative terms.' It is in this latter sense that an actual entity acquires objective immortality and as such constitutes an element within the extensive continuum.

Within this extensive continuum, then, lies the space for becoming of subjects – while it is extensive and potentially infinite in the actual world human subjects encounter, the range of potentiality is limited by the types of relationships that have been formed between different objects.

The idea of extensive continuum relates to two different ways in which Whitehead understands the concept of process: the internal/microscopic and the external/macroscopic. As Randall C. Morris (1991: 24) explains, the former is best understood through the corollary concept of 'concrescence' which refers to 'the means by which the many components of an actual occasion achieve a complex unity'. On the completion of each occasion, the process moves on, with each occasion providing data that can be part of the next stage of development. The completion of microscopic processes of concrescence provides the components for wider macroscopic processes. This connects with the second understanding of process whereby what we know as the past contributes to the present in the creation of a new occasion comprising a complex set of relations between various hitherto completed occasions. This relational process is the part that effects transitions from one stage of a process to another through complex interactions. Herein lies a space of potential creativity. Morris states that, for Whitehead, while 'the past influences and limits the freedom of subsequent occasions, the final determination of each concrescence lies with the creativity of the subject itself. The past actual world both "limits and supplies" . . . it determines the range of possibilities open for realization by the subject' (Morris 1991: 33). Similarly, Halewood (2011: 33) contends that in Whitehead's approach 'each item of existence . . . is the combination of elements, of prehensions that were previously diverse, into a novel unity through the process of concrescence'. At this point, it may be useful to unpack the key terms *prehension* and *concrescence* carefully to clarify their implications for temporal politics.

Prehension, Concrescence and Creativity

Prehension is one of the most important concepts in Whitehead's philosophical armoury. He states that 'Actual entities involve each other by

reason of their prehensions of each other' (1978: 20). One of the best definitions of this concept is provided by Sherburne (2004: 7–8):

> 'Prehension' is cut off from the word *apprehension.* 'Apprehension'
> refers to the fully conscious grasping of something; the attenuated
> version of that word, that is, 'prehension,' refers, for Whitehead, to
> the primitive, unconscious, primordial, attenuated way that, way down
> at the bottom of the scale of organic and then inorganic being, one
> actual occasion takes account of another. The becoming of an actual
> entity is its process of prehending the actual entities in its immediate
> past, in what Whitehead labels its actual world, and then harmonizing
> these prehensions into the unity of being which that concrescing actual
> entity becomes. It is helpful to note that the word concrescence means
> a growing together of the prehensions that constitute the actual entity
> which is in the process of becoming.

For Whitehead, then, every new occasion is a provisional combination of
hitherto extant phenomena into a new whole or 'occasion'. As all of these
extant phenomena were themselves formed through relations, they can
never be fully apprehended in a new occasion, but only prehended. For
Whitehead, that which endures is never 'given' but instead is achieved as
a provisional consistency, and it is through processes of prehension that
such consistencies are maintained (Roberts 2014: 976). Similarly, Morris
(1991: 26) describes the role of prehension as follows:

> An actual entity . . . is a unifying process that includes past actual enti-
> ties as data . . . Prehension is a technical term chosen by Whitehead to
> refer to the way in which an actual occasion can include, as part of its
> own essence, other entities without implying either consciousness or
> representative perception . . . An actual entity is essentially a 'concres-
> cence of prehensions'.

Entities then are both formed through relations to other entities and radically incomplete insofar as they continue to relate to other entities as they
become. Once processes of becoming are complete, that is, when there is
no more relational development, these entities become mere data to be
used in further relational processes by other entities. Unlike the process of
progressive participation and collaboration in Follett, however, processes
of prehension do not have a definitive direction except that they keep
relating to other entities as becoming continues. As Roberts (2014: 977)
makes clear, 'Processes diverge such that dissonance and resonance, discord

and harmony, are both expressions of reality's creative advance. Expressed and elaborated through prehensions, the whole is always in the making: it is incomplete.'

Channelling the work of Sandra Rosenthal, Neville (2004: 25) elaborates on this point by discussing prehension in an explicitly temporal sense:

> Time's arrow is defined by the order of prehension. Anything that can be prehended is in the past of the prehender, anything that can prehend an occasion is in the future of that occasion, and all the things that neither can be prehended by an occasion nor can prehend it are simultaneous with it. Thus, there is a sharp discontinuity between fully definite prehendable occasions and emergent prehending occasions, and a total indeterminateness of temporal relation among occasions where no order of prehending-prehended exists.

This passage makes clear where process philosophers take their leave from progressive but pragmatic public administration scholars. Whereas pragmatists tend to focus on continuity and gradual incremental change, process philosophers take a more nuanced view in which entities in the present are incomplete and still in processes of becoming. While this becoming can move them in progressive directions, it can also lead to less productive forms of change. This is unpredictable because the becoming of any entity is connected to the relations between it and other entities. As Neville (2004: 27) argues, the

> deep tragic element in passing time is that so many things are distorted when harmonized in the present or lost altogether when that harmony fails. The pragmatic idiom fails to catch that metaphysical tragedy. The process intuition of 'the coming together of,' which sometimes does not come together, or does so at an oppressive price, is far better.

This is the key distinction between a pragmatist mode of thought in which entities 'emerge out of' an engagement across difference and a process philosophy approach that concentrates on the 'coming together of' entities without any preconceived notion of what that coming together might produce.

It is at this point that Whitehead's conception of concrescence comes into play because it unsettles the kind of linear progressivism of Enlightenment liberalism. In an environment characterised by unpredictable relationships, becoming and uncertainty, the outcomes of these connections between entities and attempts to prehend earlier entities make notions of direct causality difficult to stipulate and a transactional model of politics much more contingent. As Roberts (2014: 979) tells us:

> Whitehead develops the difficult concept of concrescence as a way of disrupting the assumption of a universe entirely reducible to linear causality. Rather than being fully determined by the past, Whitehead suggests, the present involves the coming together or 'concrescence' of occasions whose particular form of togetherness was, until that very moment, rigorously unthinkable.

The idea of concrescence is fundamental to Whitehead's thought because it emphasises the 'coming together' of entities in not entirely predictable ways. Processes, then, do not progress on established pathways towards predetermined ends, but flow with, across and against different currents and counter-currents, interjections, deflections and reversals. While some paths may be more predictable than others, across the passage of time, no concrescent process is immune to unforeseen interventions. The absence of any kind of 'underlying permanence' is part and parcel of the 'vertiginous and unsettling implications of a rigorously processual ontology' (Roberts 2014: 979). In a challenge to theories asserting non-processual materiality in any subject or object, Roberts asserts that 'A prehensive materiality never simply "is": it happens . . . [M]ateriality involves processes of concrescence that are infected with moments of real creativity, or in Whitehead's terms, an ingression of subjectivity' (Roberts 2014: 979).

This brings us to the last of Whitehead's concepts that has a particular bearing on how we theorise temporal politics, namely, creativity. As noted in numerous sources (for example, Halewood 2011), Whitehead actually coined the term 'creativity' to refer to the need to respond to the conditions of uncertainty and becoming that he identifies in the notions of prehension and concrescence. Rather than merely accepting the limited epistemological basis for making definitive claims about anything, Whitehead encourages us to move beyond mere critique in engaging with the processes of human life. The absence of conceptual certainty does not mean we can do away with thinking about politics; indeed, for Whitehead, it makes the task of conceptual creativity all the more important (Roberts 2014: 981). For Halewood (2011: 36), the concept of creativity plays a key role in the formulation of 'an account of the process and potentiality of the world which avoids resorting to fixed conceptions of subjects and objects'.

Instead of a banal and one-dimensional progressive understanding of creativity, Whitehead's conception identifies characteristics including 'heterogeneity, relativity, concreteness, process, becoming and mundanity' (Halewood 2011: 26). Therefore, creativity in Whitehead's philosophy refers to the multiple potentialities that lie inherent to relationships between entities, and the fact that the coming together of these interrelationships is not predetermined. Rather concrescence is emergent as we cannot tell which related entities will engage with each other and how. This leaves spaces for creative human action, but within a range of possibilities that are not entirely within our perception or control. Of course, this always leaves openings for unforeseen consequences in the engagement of potentiality and facticity – as always, Whitehead is not thinking in purely abstract terms. There are always entities in the world which affect the process of becoming; these processes are always an engagement between material entities and ideas. It is in the realm of ideas that the greatest opportunities for creativity lie.

The most prominent incarnation of process philosophy in contemporary theory can be identified in the early work of Gilles Deleuze (1994; see also Patton 2000). There are, of course, strong similarities between Whitehead and aspects of Deleuze's philosophy (Robinson 2009). For example, Halewood (2005: 73) states that

Whitehead and Deleuze manage to establish a nonessentialist ontology by insisting upon the reality of both the extensive continuum (or the virtual) and the actuality of contemporary existence. Neither the extensive continuum nor the virtual provides an absolute ground for existence; they express a limited yet infinite potentiality that is neither fully exhausted nor realized by those individuals that arise out of it.

James Williams (2011: 3) describes the particular importance of Deleuze's philosophy of time succinctly in stating that 'the claim is not strictly about time as process, but rather about processes making multiple times. Times are made in multiple synthetic processes.' This synthetic dimension is particularly important as it marks out the significance of multiplicity in Deleuze's thought and the ways in which it serves to create multiple processes at any one time. Therefore, process philosophy recognises that multiplicity gives rise to multiple processes and multiple processes give rise to greater multiplicity. And times (past, present and future) and processes overlap and interrelate with one another. Deleuze reaches this point through engagement with Kant and Nietzsche to describe the possibility of a 'political subject, someone who engages in processes that not only demand a becoming-other, that is, an annihilation of the past self that he or she was, but that also put the existence of a future self at risk and thus leave the process of becoming open to success or failure' (Voss 2013: 210–11).

In *Difference and Repetition*, Deleuze (1994) identifies three ways in which syntheses of time take place. The first alludes to the summoning of the past and future into the 'living present' – for Williams (2011: 11), this first synthesis is focused on 'contraction' whereby, despite their infinity, in actualising the past and future in the present time, humans reduce the complexity of the past and the possibilities for the future. In terms of the subject, this amounts to a form of circular synthesising of the past, whereby a flattening of multiplicity takes place. In this synthesis, subjective acts are repeated habitually as a form of making sense of the present vis-à-vis a basic, synthesised version of what has already taken place in the past and a stable, relatively fixed projection of what might take place in the future. The second synthesis of time refers to Deleuze's engagement with Kant (Voss 2013: 194–7), whereby the latter is credited with freeing philosophy from the circularity of time in the first synthesis above. In this account, Kant provides a more linear projection of the passage of time whereby there can be no return to the past. Rather subjects inscribe the past with a particular meaning upon which to build understandings of the present and a more open projection of the future (albeit in a linear path). In this second synthesis, the past is memory and acts of repetition provide a synthesis of the past that are cleaved apart from actions in the present (which is yet to be synthesised) as they refer to events that have been superseded.

The third synthesis of time in Deleuze focuses on the future, which he sees as an 'assembly of events' in which each event is novel and demands a new ordering of the assembly of events. As Williams (2011: 15) makes clear, this involves an appropriation of Nietzsche's notion of 'eternal return'. In the eternal return, we do not reproduce the same that has passed and which can be navigated by habit; instead we encounter *repetition as difference*. In this depiction, 'the Nietzschean subject becomes ungrounded and free to run through all its possibilities of becoming' (Voss 2013: 212), that is, the subject is liberated from merely repeating a circular past or from being beholden to a manufactured memory of a past that cannot be revisited. Instead, the third synthesis involves looping into the past to reveal the constitutive differences that enable the construction of the subject in a particular way and opens up possibilities for 'becoming other'.

Williams points to the critical power of Deleuze's 'commitment to time as multiple processes and to the ideas that times are made with processes and that such processes make beings. They make them become, perish and return not only as active participants in processes but also as passive and cleaved subjects' (Williams 2011: 16). This highlights that Deleuze's philosophy of time is a rebuttal of both overly objective and overly subjective theories of temporality:

> There is freedom in Deleuze's philosophy of time, not in free will but in a multiplicity of open futures at work in any present and transforming all of the past. The future is not in anyone's hands, since they too are made by passive syntheses of time, but neither is the future closed down and determined. (Williams 2011: 17)

The notion of becoming is inherent in this depiction. Many commentators including Williams and Patton (2010: 104) have highlighted the opening to *The Logic of Sense* (Deleuze 1990) where Deleuze refers to Lewis Carroll's *Alice in Wonderland* to exemplify this notion. On the assumption that she continues to grow, as she grows Carroll's Alice is both bigger than she was and smaller than she will be simultaneously. Although 'it makes no sense to say that she is taller and shorter at the same time, we can say that she *becomes* taller and shorter at the same time' (Patton 2010: 104). Therefore, there is a paradoxical nature to processes of becoming which demonstrates that, for Deleuze, 'events are coextensive with becomings and that becomings exhibit contradictory properties in the absence of further specification of the temporal perspective from which we examine them' (Patton 2010: 104).

In a significant passage, discussing the concept of becoming in the work of Nietzsche, Bergson, Whitehead, Deleuze and William James, Connolly concludes that a 'philosophy of becoming thus contains speculative assumptions and concepts that may be revised in the light of future experience, experiments, and tests of coherence' (Connolly 2011: 168). For Connolly, the process of becoming requires philosophers to engage in stages of 'existential gratitude, periodic suspension, creative political action, and reflective recoil'. In typically pluralist fashion, this leads Connolly to state that navigating this terrain requires a disposition that acknowledges 'the element of contestability in your onto-philosophy' and enables humans to 'pursue relations of agonistic respect with other perspectives' (Connolly 2011: 168). Importantly, each of these stages involves 'skills' and 'dispositions' which enable these ideas around process to be translated into a political mindset that can be developed into a method for temporal politics. This is the task to which we now turn: the translation of philosophies of temporality, becoming and process into temporal political practice.

From Philosophy to Politics in Theory, Method and Practice

While process philosophy has become increasingly influential in the social sciences in recent years, it has not been as explicitly articulated in political science as in some other disciplines. Partly this is because of the challenges of applying the ontological and metaphysical implications of process philosophy to the analysis of material political issues, and partly it is because of the dominant methodological approaches in political science providing insufficient space for notions such as becoming and uncertainty to flourish within the established parameters of the discipline. My case here is that a temporal model of politics can provide a bridge between process philosophy and practical politics in a way that can have a significant impact on our understanding of and approach to some of the major political issues we face as outlined in Chapters 4 to 6. At the same time, we need to recognise that there will be distinctive opposition to such an approach both from within political science and also from other disciplines. An example of the latter is provided by cultural geographers such as Roberts (2014: 970) who, citing Brian Massumi, argues that engaging with 'Whitehead's speculative metaphysics' should 'temporarily suspend questions of politics and of political process, so as to avoid overdetermining the modes by which we might come to think, feel, and articulate a much broader range of material encounters'. On the contrary, my arguments suggest that we need to develop an engagement between process philosophy and politics precisely so that we can avoid such over-determination, in recognition that there are some political theorists engaged in precisely this kind of work (for example, Freeden 1996, 2013).

Ironically perhaps, I want to approach the task of showing how temporal politics can perform this bridging work between process philosophy and political science through a short detour into anthropological theory. In particular, I want to explore how an anthropology of time can relate to material political practices and how it can contribute to helpful dispositions in how we address temporal questions in politics. I do so as a visitor in the field of anthropology rather than someone with any specific expertise, although the important work of anthropologists such as Fabian on time have reached far beyond the confines of the discipline (Fabian 2014). Nonetheless, the work of Matt Hodges provides a very useful point of entry in his engagement with the research of Alfred Gell and Nancy Munn. The key distinction Hodges makes in terms of different modes of time is between 'A-series' time and 'B-series' time, where the former refers to subjective interpretations and experience, while the latter is objective, 'real' time (see also McTaggart 1968).

Hodges states that, in 'B-series' time, 'events exist, have definite relations
to each other, and effectively provide an objective ground for, and structure
to, the world and its "history"' (Hodges 2008: 404). In locating Gell and
Munn on time within the 'A-series/B-series' spectrum, Hodges points out
that, in *The Anthropology of Time*, Gell provides a 'moderated version' of
'B-series' time in which the '"true" nature of . . . [B-series events] is objectively inaccessible to the tools of human perception' (Hodges 2008: 404).
Hodges notes that this approach is a little unusual in anthropology, where
the emphasis tends to be more focused on 'A-series' time which concentrates
on 'the subjective, tensed existence involving past, present and future relations that comprises everyday human time perception' (Hodges 2008: 404).
While noting the unconventional disciplinary approach, Hodges has some
sympathy with Gell's perspective, but also raises some key objections. Two
are of particular significance for our purposes: first, he argues that Gell's
depiction of 'B-series' time is too linear and takes too much of what is
'real' and 'objective' in temporality at face value; the second is the cardinal
anthropological sin of generalising about temporality from a singular and
culturally specific perspective. Here, Hodges declares that Gell's model is
'brazenly cultural in character' (Hodges 2008: 405).

An alternative anthropological model is provided by Munn. Hodges
writes approvingly of her view that

> perception and experience of the past (present and future) . . . [are]
> implicated in the dynamic process of temporalization that comprises
> the living present . . . [T]emporalizing practices are . . . a dimension of
> the exercise of power, as temporality is a hinge that connects subjects
> to wider social horizons, and control over pasts and futures that are
> temporalized also influence action in the present. (Hodges 2008: 406)

However, Hodges finds neither Munn nor Gell completely satisfactory
and instead turns to philosophers such as Bergson and Deleuze to find a
way of constructing an anthropologically satisfactory way of understanding the relations between 'A-series' phenomenological time and 'B-series'
analytical time. Ultimately, he suggests that, with their disciplinary lens
on human subjects, anthropologists have been too focused on the 'A-series'
with less emphasis on the relationships between subjective interpretations
and the material environment where the subjective connects to the objective. This is the point on which he sees Gell as more useful than Munn
and it is interesting that, despite the shortcomings of his perspective,
Gell does appear to be constructing the connection between the subjective

and objective in relational terms. While Gell is criticised for approaching the subjective experience of time from a prior (and somewhat uncritical) understanding of the objectivity of 'real time', Hodges returns to Bergson 'to establish *la durée* as a basis for the study of lived experience and sociality' (Hodges 2008: 414). Moreover, in keeping with Deleuze, he argues that 'lived experience lies in a complex relationship with *la durée*, which encloses and enables it while remaining, in the last instance, inaccessible to objective human representation' (Hodges 2008: 414).

To sum up this anthropological detour, then, and in sharp contradistinction with some of the policy-oriented literature (for example, in the work of Follett in the first section of this chapter), 'there is no direction in which flux or process is moving, and there is no one river of time that flows. In this sense, *la durée* retains a universal applicability while remaining free of the totalizing impulse . . . It comprises an integrative emergent pluralism' (Hodges 2008: 415). In this Bergsonian anthropological conception of flow and becoming as the foundation of temporality, Hodges concludes that concrete temporal dynamics and the character of social change are 'a matter for contingent elucidation, rather than being indexed to the temporal ontology of *la durée*' (Hodges 2008: 416). This is the platform from which we can establish a temporal method for political practice.

Process and Becoming in Material Politics

In order to highlight the different outlook that a temporal approach to politics can bring to key material issues, let us briefly return to one of the three cases discussed in Part Two of this book. The first case concerned Indigenous politics and the relationships between First Nations peoples and the settler state. There we highlighted a number of issues around time in these relationships including the different temporal registers invoked by Indigenous peoples and settlers, the varying ways in which the connectedness and sequencing of past, present and future were understood, and divergent views on the duration of the issues at stake in the negotiation of Indigenous-settler relations. These differences have been manifest in Australia and other countries where it is only recently that the temporal dimension of the Indigenous-settler relations debate is being discussed (although it has been evident in Aboriginal and Torres Strait Islander discourses for a much longer time, of course).

Famously, Patrick Wolfe (2006: 388) contended that invasion was a structure rather than an event and this dictum has been repeated on multiple occasion in recent debates within settler colonial theory. As significant as this intervention has been in analysis of settler colonialism, it has become an almost unquestioned truth in settler colonial theory. While Wolfe was correct to emphasise the structural nature of colonisation and its enduring impact on Indigenous peoples, it might also be worth amending the dictum slightly to highlight that – in temporal terms – invasion is a structure *as well as* an event. Or, perhaps, even more tellingly, invasion is a *process* as well as an event. This is particularly pertinent if we understand the event within a processive framework that means that it is not a singular happening but an incomplete element in relations of becoming. This can then lead to a critical outlook on the notion of the event in colonisation as demonstrated by Paul Patton:

> While it is often an event of the noisy, Earth-shattering kind, this does not exclude the possibility that it is also an ongoing, silent event. Even once it has been achieved, it continues to operate inaudibly, often in ways that pass unnoticed to those not directly affected. It is an event that haunts the societies established on the territory of Aboriginal peoples, who remain caught in a form of internal exile. (Patton 2010: 110)

Therefore, colonisation cannot be identified in a singular form and reduced to a specific historical event. Rather, in Deleuzian terms, colonisation is a 'pure event' that can be 'only imperfectly actualized in the linear time of history' (Patton 2010: 103). From this perspective, colonisation is a signature term which eludes perfect definition but is realised in the everyday recurring but multiple structurings that take place within a given society. The multiplicity of colonialism is therefore one of the major challenges for those opposing it, including its victims.

For Patton, colonisation requires a simultaneous process of deterritorialisation and reterritorialisation whereby the connections between a range of social, legal, political and cultural practices and particular geographical spaces are removed and the land is recast under the auspices of a new sovereign entity. In temporal terms, the long-standing and ingrained relationships between Indigenous peoples, their practices and the territory on which they live became marginalised and replaced by the new forms of sovereignty of states which developed without recourse to the older traditional practices. These practices and beliefs were denied by ongoing mechanisms of the imposed sovereign state and continue to be so rather than simply being obliterated at first contact. Thus, this state denial does not necessarily eradicate traditional practices, but it pushes them to the margins – often out of sight (Little and McMillan 2017) and out of mind (for the historical event of the colonial encounter becomes the starting point for a 'new' history). Yet the continuation and resilience of older socio-political and legal practices reflect Patton's notion of 'internal exile'. Indigenous peoples continuing these practices and relations become the excluded inside – a constant reminder of what the sovereign settler state is not (Rancière 2010, Little 2007). This status is reinforced in the everyday structures and cadences of colonial societies rather than being reducible to a linear historical encounter.

And yet, the historical event remains important. Again, Patton's Deleuzian reflections are valuable here. Citing the influential work of John Borrows in Canada, he points out the ways in which the events of the colonial encounter can be viewed very differently according to one's stand-point. The logic of the settler state was that it was imposing order where none existed – it was establishing the rule of law as a starting point from which the state could flourish. From an Indigenous perspective, traditional legal practices, social structures and political mechanisms were swept aside by the illegal imposition of a new order. In other words, the sovereign state could only flourish because it contravened the established practices of its territory. The rule of law could only preside through its illegality. This paradox is reflected in the everyday structures of life in colonial societies and cannot be reduced to singular events. In a temporal vein, Patton makes the point that colonisation was not encapsulated in a single encounter (by British explorers planting flags in different parts of modern Australia in 1770 or 1788) but, instead, the 'reality is that such singular events, taken in isolation, are insufficient to effect even the legal event of colonization. Like declarations of war or independence, these events make sense only in *anticipation* of the process and the institution that follows. This brings us back to the elusive character of the precise moment at which the event occurs' (Patton 2010: 107, emphasis added). What is important here is that when the flag is planted, it is too early to say that colonisation has taken place, only that such a process can be *anticipated*. However, the paradoxical nature of this process is reflected in the fact that, at any point after the planting of the flag, 'it can be said that colonization has already taken place' (Patton 2010: 107).

As we saw in Chapter 4, different temporal registers co-exist in settler colonial societies, with Indigenous peoples drawing upon a much longer timeline than is part of the colonial imaginary. Part of the strategy for Indigenous peoples is to keep pre-colonial history alive, despite the efforts of the settler state to discredit prior systems of law and politics. And yet, there are points at which that pre-history is catapulted into the present. Patton uses the Mabo case in 1992 (AIATSIS 2020), where the issue of native title entered Australian law, as a case in point whereby the decision

forcibly injected the past and the pre-history largely ignored (and discred-
ited by the settler state) into the present. He states:

> The historical moment in which the [Mabo] decision took place involved
> a return to earlier events of colonization, collapsing elements of the
> colonial past into the present and making these parts of the ongoing
> elaboration of the future. At such moments, we glimpse the possibility
> of an altogether different relationship between indigenous and settler
> communities, premised on mutual recognition and equality rather than
> incorporation and subordination. (Patton 2010: 111)

Events such as the Mabo decision are reminders of the temporal disjuncture and its enduring resonance in Indigenous-settler relations in Australia.
The temporal political method of analysing these events is one that, in
grounding present political processes in greater historical awareness and
problematisations, demands that the pre-history of modern Australia is
granted its rightful place in our understanding of the decisions we take in
the present and the need for proper maintenance of relationships between
Indigenous peoples and the settler state. It demands a recognition of plurality; that there are multiple social, cultural and legal traditions in settler
colonial societies and that the settler state needs to relinquish its hubris in
proclaiming its inherent supremacy.

Again, Deleuzian analysis is useful in helping us to understand the
problem-driven approach to politics highlighted in Chapter 1. The key
distinction in understanding problems for Deleuze is the difference
between specific problems as they manifest in contemporary politics and
the broader 'problem-event' which is beyond immediate human understanding and manifests in multiple ways and remains elusive to capture by
any one instantiation of the 'problem-event'. Take debates about building
border walls or humanitarian crises on the high seas as examples of where
specific problems materialise in ways in which we might consider certain
kinds of responses to effect solutions to that specific instance. These are
not solutions to pure 'problem-events' of a more general and intangible
nature – for example, bordering, territorialisation, sovereignty – but specific instances where those 'problem-events' manifest in a particular way.
In politics, when we act on specific political problems, we are dealing with
those particular issues without resolving broader structural problems in
the world. Any particular set of actions on specific problems may *change*
the broader material 'problem-event', often in small and intangible ways,
but to address this instantiation is not the same as tackling the 'problem-
event'. Again, while tackling specific instantiations of a problem-event

may enable us to understand *better* the forces at work, the nature of these broader 'signature' problems is that their meaning and implications shift often imperceptibly in response to specific instantiations (Agamben 2009, Little 2014).

Patton (2010: 114) frames this issue in understanding political problems through the lens of colonisation and asks us to imagine the following kinds of questions: 'what is the problem to which the concept of colonization offers a solution? What are the conditions of this problem and how might a better understanding of those conditions help us to reformulate existing concepts of colonization?' In addressing these kinds of questions, he notes that there have been multiple answers leading to colonisation taking on different forms depending on contextual issues like whether treaties were signed with Indigenous peoples or the territory was merely appropriated. As colonial structures have developed, they have taken on differing forms and continue to evolve in different ways as specific instances of colonisation necessitate a variety of actions (be they to formally recognise Indigenous peoples in constitutions, apologise, repatriate territory, pay reparations and so forth). And just as different colonial societies, often containing multiple First Nations peoples, will try to reach differing partial solutions to particular instantiations of problems, so there will be multiple forms of resistance against these kinds of measures pursued under the auspices of concepts such as reconciliation and recognition. Across all these forms, the 'pure event' of colonisation remains, albeit not unchanging. As particular events such as the Mabo case impact on the nature of the pure event, we can identify 'a process of transition from one determination of colonial society to another' (Patton 2010: 116). In temporal terms, the past as well as the future is catapulted into the present, co-existing in a moment of becoming and difference, and exemplifying the multiplicity inherent in colonial relationships.

My point here is that this kind of political analysis, inflected with a significant temporal dimension, can be extended to all kinds of examples from the impacts of climate change on communities to the challenges of migration in a bordered world to the implications of particular understandings of democracy and authoritarianism. The method of temporal analysis is not just the recognition that things could have been different, but that that potential remains inherent to the multiplicity of political issues. This potential is one that may burst forth, sometimes unpredictably according to responses to events, on a range of 'pure problem events' such as colonisation, bordering and democracy. Rather than these 'problem events' being seen as singular, we need to find a form of politics that brings forth their multiplicity, that recognises their incompletion and the opportunities inherent in their becoming. This is where temporal political methodology can both help to demonstrate this multiplicity and locate specific instantiations of a problem on the broader canvas of the 'problem event'.

A Processive Approach to Temporal Politics

This chapter has focused on the importance of developing a political theory of temporality through its engagement of recent work on time in public policy and older and more recent forms of process philosophy. While some public policy scholars have embraced the notion of temporal analysis, the work is almost entirely backward-facing. Indeed, there is a strong tradition of process analysis within the field of public policy and this is evident not only in the authors discussed like Pollitt, but also in some of the recent work on bricolage in the public policy literature (e.g. Wilder and Howlett 2014). The implication of this work is that public policy making is not a simple linear system but a process involving many cross-currents and unforeseen influences and outcomes. Policies emerge from these processes rather than coming together fully formed and being implemented as initially envisaged. Focused as these analyses are on the actual policy environment in particular settings, there are often elements of incompletion and becoming at work in this literature, even if it is not always named as such. However, perhaps not surprisingly, this literature is focused on policy processes, rather than the broader way in which temporality and process come together to form a more general notion of political temporality that has specific implications for political scientists of all hues, whether they are analysts of public policy or not.

For this reason, the argument returned to process philosophy to investigate the ideas therein about temporality with a view to bringing these literatures together to develop a more general temporal method for political science. The point here was to introduce a more future-oriented dimension to the discussion and a perspective that offered guidance on political analysis and action, rather than discussion of processes remaining wholly within the domain of philosophy. Therefore, when we imagine temporal politics, we are invoking a form of analysis in which theory and practice are closely related and where the material elements give rise to new thinking just as much as the theory guides the practice. It does not privilege philosophy over practical, material politics but focuses instead on how they relate to one another. Therefore, the method of such an approach necessitates an integrated and relational perspective on political philosophy and policy processes that enables both sub-disciplines to build from each other.

Needless to say, internecine disputes within political philosophy about which traditions of thought are the best at doing so have limited value to this enterprise of engaging with material political practices. At the same time, discussions of policy issues which do not engage with these kinds of political theories and methodologies have similarly limited horizons.

8
Coda: Contested Pasts, Uncertain Futures

The argument presented in *Temporal Politics* is that political theorists need to take time and, more specifically, temporality more seriously in our consideration of our practice. No doubt, there will be much in the preceding discussion that other theorists will take exception to, but, at the very least, the fact of co-existing temporalities in the understanding of many problems in material politics is hopefully manifest. Certainly, the implications of this situation for theoretical analysis will be a matter of some disagreement, but the case remains that the events and implications of the past for the present are a matter for contestation (given such disputes already exist), and there is undeniable contention about the ways in which contemporary political actions will impact on the future. Given that any actions taken now can be confounded by other socio-political events, political action directed towards meeting the challenges of the present has uncertain ramifications for the future.

Having established these conditions as the backdrop of any political theory that is concerned with material political practice, the argument of *Temporal Politics* goes further to challenge the orthodox way in which past, present and future tend to be imagined in politics as distinct categories. In arguing for a concept of political temporality in which the flow of time is continually present in political debates, the book has made the case for an overlapping understanding of the categories of past, present and future in a more complex and contingent combination than is often the case in theoretical debates. Undoubtedly, the pathway from this foundation to the depiction of weak ontological and epistemological claims through the lens of openness and becoming will be problematic for some critics, but it is a perspective based on engagement with the practical political debates that are discussed in the second section of the book. Indeed, the case is made that these debates in contemporary politics exemplify the open, plural and contingent nature of the material issues at stake (even when these stakes might be understood and expressed much more definitively in political practice).

In some respects, the divergence between the theoretical core of the argument explained in Part One of the book and the illustrative cases discussed in Part Two could lead to the conclusion that there is just a schism between theory and practice that is too difficult to bridge. The case could be made that theorists should just get back to what they know – a mode of analysis which makes generalisable arguments based on hypothetical analyses, or strictly bracketed concerns that deliberately circumvent complexity, or that just state baldly that grubby material politics is not a topic that political philosophers should concern themselves with. The corollary of that argument is that it is not the job of theorists to address 'real world' problems and those matters can be left to others within the discipline of political science or beyond. Not surprisingly, given my statement at the outset that it is vital for political theorists to engage in material debates, the argument of *Temporal Politics* does not reach these kinds of conclusions.

Instead, the third part of the book turns to debates on time in public policy and the perspective provided by process philosophy to argue for an alternative way in which the concept of temporality can contribute to the practice of political theory. By developing a processive perspective influenced by the contested nature of the past and the uncertainty of the future, it identifies a way in which temporal politics can be conducted. To be clear, this is not a perspective that provides 'solutions' to the issues identified in the second part of the book, but I contend that it does provide a *method* of temporal politics that may enable different kinds of discussions about the issues in dispute. In keeping with the insights of Whitehead and Deleuze, such a method may facilitate new forms of creative thinking that challenge more traditional approaches. The invitation to think creatively and in a spirit of openness about key challenges in contemporary politics accords with processive accounts of political action and change. Importantly, however, these kinds of theoretical methods are also cognisant of the possibilities of failure when new ideas are applied to material issues or policy conundrums. The processive approach connected to a Bergsonian temporal politics suggests that thinking about creative action – even if it leads to failure – is preferable to the impasses that blight discussion of these issues in contemporary politics.

Perhaps most significant of all is the commitment to open-ended futures in temporal politics. This openness is based upon epistemological incompletion and the impossibility of commandeering all of the relevant knowledge about a practical issue when the key elements of it are all in a process of becoming. This does not incapacitate actors from taking action on particular issues, but merely constrains the extent to which they can fully comprehend all of the matters they engage with. Similarly, it is impossible to make definitive ontological claims in processive temporal politics because the actors involved are part of a mesh of relationships that help to inform their perspectives. However, these perspectives are not settled as humans, non-humans, institutions, policies and their environments are all forged through relationships with other entities that are also in the course of relational development. Again, this should not incapacitate political actors, but encourage them to engage with others in a relational spirit of incompletion and openness.

Returning to the analytical-continental divide, I mentioned at the outset that this book was an attempt to establish a *practice* of temporal politics that transcended the barriers between the two approaches. It was not an attempt to create a synthesis between them, but an exercise in mapping what an approach that did not adhere to one methodology or the other might look like. I am all too aware that the result is less tidy or self-contained than is usually the case in political theory. Having wrestled with this issue in the course of the book, I have reached the conclusion that such untidiness and multiplicity is actually part and parcel of the process of temporal politics. We do a disservice to temporal analysis built up from actual cases in material politics if we superimpose harmony, tidiness and cohesion for the sake of elegance. In fact, we cannot do justice to material cases and the temporal issues they invoke if we override their complexity with a superimposed desire for unity and completion. Ultimately, *Temporal Politics* demands that we relinquish such preconditions, if we are concerned to challenge the analytical-continental divide *and* develop a form of political theory that is more engaged with material politics.

Bibliography

ABC (2017), 'Indigenous advisory body rejected by PM in "kick in the guts" for advocates', 26 October, <www.abc.net.au/news/2017-10-26/indigenous-advisory-body-proposal-rejected-by-cabinet/9087856> (last accessed 16 November 2021).

Abizadeh, Arash (2008), 'Democratic Theory and Border Coercion: No Right to Unilaterally Control your Own Borders', *Political Theory* 36(1): 37–65.

Ackerly, Brooke and Rochana Bajpai (2017), 'Comparative Political Thought', in Adrian Blau (ed.), *Methods in Analytical Political Theory*, Cambridge: Cambridge University Press, pp. 270–96.

Ackleson, Jason (2005), 'Constructing Security on the U.S.-Mexico Border', *Political Geography* 24(2): 165–84.

Ackrill, Robert, Adrian Kay and Nikolaos Zahariadis (2013), 'Ambiguity, Multiple Streams, and EU Policy', *Journal of European Public Policy* 20(6): 871–87.

Adam, Barbara (1995), *Timewatch: The Social Analysis of Time*, Cambridge: Polity Press.

Adam, Barbara (2004), *Time*, Cambridge: Polity Press.

Agamben, Giorgio (2009), *The Signature of All Things: On Method*, New York: Zone Books.

Agnew, John (2008), 'Borders on the Mind: Re-Framing Border Thinking', *Ethics and Global Politics* 1(4): 175–91.

Albert, Mathias, David Jacobson and Yosef Lapid (eds) (2001), *Identities, Borders, Orders: Re-Thinking International Relations Theory*, Minneapolis: University of Minnesota Press.

Allam, Lorena (2019), 'Dodson, Burney call for government to fund National Council of Australia's First Peoples', *The Guardian*, 12 June, <https://www.theguardian.com/australia-news/2019/jun/12/national-

congress-of-australias-first-peoples-fights-for-financial-survival> (last accessed 16 November 2021).

Allam, Lorena (2020), '"Deaths in our backyard": 432 Indigenous Australians have died in custody since 1991', *The Guardian*, 1 June, <https://www.theguardian.com/australia-news/2020/jun/01/deaths-in-our-backyard-432-indigenous-australians-have-died-in-custody-since-2008> (last accessed 16 November 2021).

Allen, Barry (2013), 'The Use of Useless Knowledge: Bergson against the Pragmatists', *Canadian Journal of Philosophy* 43(1): 37–59.

Alonso, Ana Maria (1994), 'The Politics of Space, Time and Substance: State Formation, Nationalism and Ethnicity', *Annual Review of Anthropology* 23: 379–405.

Amoore, Louise (2011), 'On the Line: Writing the Geography of the Virtual Border', *Political Geography* 30(2): 63–4.

Anderson, James (2002), *Transnational Democracy: Political Spaces and Border Crossings*, London: Routledge.

Anderson, James and Liam O'Dowd (1999), 'Borders, Border Regions and Territoriality: Contradictory Meanings, Changing Significance', *Regional Studies* 33(7): 593–604.

Anthony, Thalia (2018), '"They Were Treating Me Like a Dog": The Colonial Continuum of State Harms against Indigenous Children in Detention in the Northern Territory, Australia', *State Crime Journal* 7(2): 251–77.

Appadurai, Arjan (2020), 'Globalization and the Rush to History', *Global Perspectives* 1(1): 1–7.

Appleby, Gabrielle (2019), '"A worthwhile project": Why two chief justices support the Voice to parliament, and why that matters', 1 August, <https://theconversation.com/a-worthwhile-project-why-two-chief-justices-support-the-voice-to-parliament-and-why-that-matters-120971> (last accessed 16 November 2021).

Appleby, Gabrielle and Megan Davis (2018), 'The Uluru Statement and the Promises of Truth', *Australian Historical Studies* 49(4): 501–9.

Appleby, Gabrielle and Gemma McKinnon (2017), 'Indigenous Recognition: The Uluru Statement', *LSJ: Law Society of New South Wales Journal* 37: 36–9.

Archibugi, Daniele (2008), *The Global Commonwealth of Citizens: Toward Cosmopolitan Democracy*, Princeton: Princeton University Press.

Archibugi, Daniele, Mathias Koenig-Archibugi and Raffaele Marchetti (eds) (2011), *Global Democracy: Normative and Empirical Perspectives*, Cambridge: Cambridge University Press.

Aristotle (2018), *Physics*, Cambridge, MA: Hackett.

Attwood, Bain (2009), *Possession: Batman's Treaty and the Matter of History*, Carlton, Victoria: Miegunyah Press.

Augustine (1963), *The Confessions*, London: Penguin.

Australian Human Rights Commission (AHRC) (2020), 'Indigenous Deaths in Custody', 28 December, <https://humanrights.gov.au/our-work/indigenous-deaths-custody-chapter-3-comparison-indigenous-and-non-indigenous-deaths> (last accessed 16 November 2021).

Australian Institute of Aboriginal and Torres Strait Islander Studies (AIATSIS) (2013), 'The 1938 Day of Mourning', <https://aiatsis.gov.au/explore/day-of-mourning> (last accessed 29 November 2021).

Australian Institute of Aboriginal and Torres Strait Islander Studies (AIATSIS) (2020), 'The Mabo Case', 24 September, <https://aiatsis.gov.au/explore/articles/mabo-case> (last accessed 16 November 2021).

Auxier, Randall (2002), 'Foucault, Dewey, and the History of the Present', *Journal of Speculative Philosophy* 16(2): 75–102.

Balfour, Lawrie (2011), *Democracy's Reconstruction: Thinking Politically with W. E. B. Du Bois*, Oxford: Oxford University Press.

Balibar, Étienne (2002), *Politics and the Other Scene*, London: Verso.

Bang, Henrik P. (2014), 'Foucault's Political Challenge: Where There Is Obedience There Cannot Be Parrhesia', *Administrative Theory & Praxis* 36(2): 175–96.

Bardon, Adrian (2013), *A Brief History of the Philosophy of Time*, New York: Oxford University Press.

Barkawi, Tarak and Mark Laffey (2006), 'The Postcolonial Moment in Security Studies', *Review of International Studies* 32(2): 329–52.

Barker, Timothy Scott (2012), *Time and the Digital: Connecting Technology, Aesthetics, and a Process Philosophy of Time*, Hanover, NH: Dartmouth College Press.

Barta, Tony (2008), 'Sorry, and Not Sorry, in Australia: How the Apology to the Stolen Generations Buried a History of Genocide', *Journal of Genocide Research* 10(2): 201–14.

Bastian, Michelle (2013), 'Political Apologies and the Question of a "Shared Time" in the Australian Context', *Theory, Culture & Society* 30(5): 94–121.

Beetham, David (1999), *Democracy and Human Rights*, Cambridge: Polity Press.

Behrendt, Jason (2007), 'Changes to Native Title since Mabo', *Indigenous Law Bulletin* 6(26): 13–14.

Behrendt, Larissa (2007), 'The 1967 Referendum: 40 Years On', *Australian Indigenous Law Review* 11: 12–16.

Beitz, Charles (1979), *Political Theory and International Relations*, Princeton: Princeton University Press.

Benjamin, Walter (2007), *Illuminations*, New York: Schocken Books.

Bergson, Henri (1910), *Time and Free Will*, New York: Macmillan.

Bergson, Henri (1911), *Creative Evolution*, Mineola, NY: Dover Publications.

Bergson, Henri (1977), *The Two Sources of Morality and Religion*, trans. R. A. Audra and C. Brereton with the assistance of W. H. Carter, Notre Dame, IN: University of Notre Dame Press.

Bhabha, Homi (2012), *The Location of Culture*, London: Routledge.

Bohle, Darren (2017), 'The Public Space of Agonistic Reconciliation: Witnessing and Prefacing in the TRC of Canada', *Constellations* 24(2): 257–66.

Bohman, James (2007), *Democracy across Borders*, Cambridge, MA: MIT Press.

Borrows, John (2015), 'The Durability of Terra Nullius: Tsilhqot'in Nation v. British Columbia', *UBC Law Review* 48: 701.

Boyce, James (2012), *1835: The Founding of Melbourne and the Conquest of Australia*, Melbourne: Black Inc.

Braidotti, Rosi (2011), *Nomadic Theory: The Portable Rosi Braidotti*, New York: Columbia University Press.

Braidotti, Rosi (2013), *The Posthuman*, Cambridge: Polity Press.

Bridges, Amy (2000), 'Path Dependence, Sequence, History, Theory', *Studies in American Political Development* 14(1): 109–12.

Brown, Wendy (2010), *Walled States, Waning Sovereignty*, New York: Zone Books.

Brubaker, Rogers (2017), 'Why Populism?', *Theory and Society* 46(5): 357–85.

Buchanan, Allen (2003), 'The Making and Unmaking of Boundaries: What Liberalism Has to Say', in Allen Buchanan and Margaret Moore (eds), *States, Nations and Borders: The Ethics of Making Boundaries*, Cambridge: Cambridge University Press, pp. 231–61.

Buchanan, Allen and Robert O. Keohane (2006), 'The Legitimacy of Global Governance Institutions', *Ethics & International Affairs* 20(4): 405–37.

Burke, Megan (2019), *When Time Warps*, Minneapolis: University of Minnesota Press.

Büthe, Tim (2002), 'Taking Temporality Seriously: Modeling History and the Use of Narratives as Evidence', *American Political Science Review* 96(3): 481–93.

Butler, Judith (1988), 'Performative Acts and Gender Constitution: An Essay in Phenomenology and Feminist Theory', *Theatre Journal* 40(4): 519–31.

Butler, Judith (1995), 'Melancholy Gender—Refused Identification', *Psychoanalytic Dialogues* 5(2): 165–80.

Butler, Judith (1999), *Gender Trouble*, London: Routledge.

Cabrera, Luis (2014), 'Individual Rights and the Democratic Boundary Problem', *International Theory* 6(2): 224–54.

Cairney, Paul (2012), 'Complexity Theory in Political Science and Public Policy', *Political Studies Review* 10(3): 346–58.

Cairney, Paul and Nikolaos Zahariadis (2016), 'Multiple Streams Analysis: A Flexible Metaphor Presents an Opportunity to Operationalize Agenda Setting Processes', in Nikolaos Zahariadis (ed.), *Handbook of Public Policy*, Cheltenham: Edward Elgar, pp. 87–105.

Carens, Joseph (2013), *The Ethics of Immigration*, Oxford: Oxford University Press.

Carver, Terrell and Samuel A. Chambers (eds) (2008), *Judith Butler's Precarious Politics: Critical Encounters*, New York: Routledge.

Carvounas, David (2002), *Diverging Time: The Politics of Modernity in Kant, Hegel and Marx*, Lanham, MD: Lexington Books.

Chakrabarty, Dipesh (2018), 'Anthropocene Time', *History and Theory* 57(1): 5–32.

Chakrabarty, Dipesh (2021), *The Climate of History in a Planetary Age*, Chicago: University of Chicago Press.

Chambers, Pete (2011), 'Society Has Been Defended: Following the Shifting Shape of State through Australia's Christmas Island', *International Political Sociology* 5(1): 18–34.

Chambers, Samuel and Terrell Carver (2008), *Judith Butler and Political Theory: Troubling Politics*, New York: Routledge.

Chin, Clayton (2016), 'Beyond Analytic and Continental in Contemporary Political Thought: Pragmatic Methodological Pluralism and the Situated Turn', *European Journal of Political Theory* 15(2): 205–22.

Chin, Clayton (2017), 'Challenging Political Theory: Pluralism and Method in the Work of Bernard Williams', *Public Reason* 9(1–2): 8–26.

Chin, Clayton (2018), *The Practice of Political Theory: Rorty and Continental Thought*, New York: Columbia University Press.

Chowers, Eyal (1999), 'The Marriage of Time and Identity: Kant, Benjamin and the Nation-State', *Philosophy and Social Criticism* 25(3): 57–80.

Christiano, Thomas (2006), 'A Democratic Theory of Territory and Some Puzzles about Global Democracy', *Journal of Social Philosophy* 37(1): 81–107.

Christiansen, Thomas, Fabio Petito and Ben Tonra (2000), 'Fuzzy Politics around Fuzzy Borders: The European Union's "Near Abroad"', *Cooperation and Conflict* 35(4): 389–415.

Cilliers, Paul (1998), *Complexity and Postmodernism: Understanding Complex Systems*, London: Routledge.

Cohen, Elizabeth F. (2018), *The Political Value of Time*, Cambridge: Cambridge University Press.

Colebrook, Claire (2012), 'The Art of the Future', in Alexandre Lefebvre and Melanie White (eds), *Bergson, Politics, and Religion*, Durham, NC: Duke University Press, pp. 75–97.

Coles, Romand, Mark Reinhardt and George Shulman (eds) (2014), *Radical Future Pasts: Untimely Political Theory*, Lexington: University Press of Kentucky.

Connolly, William (2011), *A World of Becoming*, London: Duke University Press.

Coulthard, Glen Sean (2014), *Red Skin, White Masks: Rejecting the Colonial Politics of Recognition*, Minneapolis: University of Minnesota Press.

Coulthard, Glen Sean and Leanne Betasamosake Simpson (2016), 'Grounded Normativity/Place-Based Solidarity', *American Quarterly* 16(2): 249–55.

Crozier, Michael and Adrian Little (2012), 'Democratic Voice: Popular Sovereignty in Conditions of Pluralisation', *Australian Journal of Political Science* 47(3): 333–46.

Curthoys, Ann, Ann Genovese and Alexander Reilly (2008), *Rights and Redemption: History, Law and Indigenous People*, Sydney: University of New South Wales Press.

Dahl, Robert (1989), *Democracy and its Critics*, New Haven: Yale University Press.

Dallmayr, Fred R. (1999), *Border Crossings: Toward a Comparative Political Theory*, Lanham, MD: Lexington Books.

Deleuze, Gilles (1990), *The Logic of Sense*, New York: Columbia University Press.

Deleuze, Gilles (1991), *Bergsonism*, New York: Zone Books.

Deleuze, Gilles (1994), *Difference and Repetition*, New York: Columbia University Press.

Deleuze, Gilles and Felix Guattari (1994), *What Is Philosophy?*, London: Verso.

Derrida, Jacques (2005), *Rogues*, Stanford: Stanford University Press.

Devetak, Richard (2004), 'In Fear of Refugees: The Politics of Border Protection in Australia', *The International Journal of Human Rights* 8(1): 101–9.

Diamond, Larry Jay and Marc F. Plattner (2016), *Democracy in Decline?*, Baltimore: Johns Hopkins University Press.

Dodson, Patrick (1993), 'Reconciliation and the High Court's Decision on Native Title', *Aboriginal Law Bulletin* 3(61): 6–10.

Donahue, Thomas J. and Paulina Ochoa Espejo (2016), 'The Analytical–Continental Divide: Styles of Dealing with Problems', *European Journal of Political Theory* 15(2): 138–54.

Donaldson, Mike (1996), 'The End of Time? Aboriginal Temporality and the British Invasion of Australia', *Time & Society* 5(2): 187–207.

Donaldson, Sue and Will Kymlicka (2011), *Zoopolis: A Political Theory of Animal Rights*, Oxford: Oxford University Press.

Donnan, Hastings and Tom Wilson (eds) (1994), *Border Approaches: Anthropological Perspectives on Frontiers*, London: University Press of America.

Downey, Leah (2020), 'Delegation in Democracy: A Temporal Analysis', *Journal of Political Philosophy*, DOI: https://doi.org/10.1111/jopp.12234.

Drezner, Daniel (2020), 'Power and International Relations: A Temporal View', *European Journal of International Relations*, DOI: https://doi.org/10.1177/1354066120969800.

Dryzek, John (2002), *Deliberative Democracy and Beyond: Liberals, Critics, Contestations*, Oxford: Oxford University Press.

Dryzek, John (2010), *Foundations and Frontiers of Deliberative Governance*, Oxford: Oxford University Press.

Dunn, John (2019), *Setting the People Free: The Story of Democracy*, Princeton: Princeton University Press.

El Amine, Loubna (2016), 'Beyond East and West: Reorienting Political Theory through the Prism of Modernity', *Perspectives on Politics* 14(1): 102–20.

El Amine, Loubna (2020), 'Political Liberalism, Western History, and the Conjectural Non-West', *Political Theory*, DOI: https://doi.org/10.1177/0090591720927802.

Elchardus, Mark and Bram Spruyt (2016), 'Populism, Persistent Republicanism and Declinism: An Empirical Analysis of Populism as Thin Ideology', *Government and Opposition* 51(1): 111–33.

Ellis, Elisabeth (2005), *Kant's Politics: Provisional Theory for an Uncertain World*, New Haven: Yale University Press.

English, Richard and Michael Kenny (eds) (1999), *Rethinking British Decline*, London: Macmillan.

Erman, Eva and Niklas Möller (2019), *The Practical Turn in Political Theory*, Edinburgh: Edinburgh University Press.

Esposito, Roberto (2012), *Terms of the Political: Community, Immunity, Biopolitics*, New York: Fordham University Press.

Euben, Roxanne (2008), *Journeys to the Other Shore: Muslim and Western Travelers in Search of Knowledge*, Princeton: Princeton University Press.

Evans, Fred (2016), 'Derrida and the Autoimmunity of Democracy', *Journal of Speculative Philosophy* 30(3): 303–15.

Fabian, Johannes (2014), *Time and the Other*, New York: Columbia University Press.

Fanon, Frantz (1986), *Black Skins, White Mask*, London: Pluto Press.

Feit, Mario (2012), 'Wolin, Time, and the Democratic Temperament', *Theory & Event*, 15(4).

Festenstein, Matthew (2016), 'Pragmatism, Realism and Moralism', *Political Studies Review* 14(1): 39–49.

Finlayson, Alan and Jeremy Valentine (eds) (2002), *Politics and Post-Structuralism*, Edinburgh: Edinburgh University Press.

Floyd, Jonathan (2009), 'Is Political Philosophy Too Ahistorical?', *Critical Review of International Social and Political Philosophy* 12(4): 513–33.

Floyd, Jonathan (2011), 'Relative Value and Assorted Historical Lessons', in Jonathan Floyd and Marc Stears (eds), *Political Philosophy versus History? Contextualism and Real Politics in Contemporary Political Thought*, Cambridge: Cambridge University Press, pp. 206–25.

Floyd, Jonathan and Marc Stears (eds) (2011), *Political Philosophy versus History? Contextualism and Real Politics in Contemporary Political Thought*, Cambridge: Cambridge University Press.

Foa, Roberto Stefan and Yascha Mounk (2016), 'The Democratic Disconnect', *Journal of Democracy* 27(3): 5–17.

Folkers, Andreas (2016), 'Daring the Truth: Foucault, Parrhesia and the Genealogy of Critique', *Theory, Culture & Society* 33(1): 3–28.

Follesdal, Andreas (2011), 'Cosmopolitan Democracy', in Daniele Archibugi, Mathias Koenig-Archibugi and Raffaele Marchetti (eds), *Global Democracy: Normative and Empirical Perspectives*, Cambridge: Cambridge University Press, pp. 96–114.

Follett, Mary Parker (1951), *Creative Experience*, New York: Smith.

Foucault, Michel (1977a), *Discipline and Punish*, New York: Random House.

Foucault, Michel (1977b), 'The Political Function of the Intellectual', *Radical Philosophy* 17: 12–14.

Foucault, Michel (1986), 'Kant on Enlightenment and Revolution', *Economy and Society* 15(1): 88–96.

Foucault, Michel (1997), 'What Is Enlightenment?', in Sylvère Lotringer and Lysa Hochroth (eds), *The Politics of Truth*, New York: Semiotext(e), pp. 101–34.

Foucault, Michel (1998), 'Polemics, Politics and Problematizations', in *Essential Works of Foucault, Vol. 1: Ethics*, ed. Paul Rabinow, New York: New Press, pp. 381–90.

Foucault, Michel (2001), *Fearless Speech*, Los Angeles: Semiotext(e).

Foucault, Michel (2010), *The Government of Self and Others: Lectures at the Collège de France, 1982–1983*, Basingstoke: Palgrave Macmillan.

Fraser, Nancy (2008), *Scales of Justice*, New York: Columbia University Press.

Freeden, Michael (1996), *Ideologies and Political Theory: A Conceptual Approach*, Oxford: Oxford University Press.

Freeden, Michael (2009a), 'Failures of Political Thinking', *Political Studies* 57(1): 141–64.

Freeden, Michael (2009b), 'What Fails in Ideologies?', *Journal of Political Ideologies* 14(1): 1–9.

Freeden, Michael (2013), *The Political Theory of Political Thinking: The Anatomy of a Practice*, Oxford: Oxford University Press.

Freeden, Michael and Andrew Vincent (eds) (2013), *Comparative Political Thought: Theorizing Practices*, London: Routledge.

Galston, William A. (2010), 'Realism in Political Theory', *European Journal of Political Theory* 9(4): 385–411.

Gaus, Gerald (2019), 'What Might Democratic Self-Government in a Complex Social World Look Like?', *San Diego Law Review* 56(4): 967–1012.

Geuss, Raymond (2008), *Philosophy and Real Politics*, Princeton: Princeton University Press.

Geyer, Robert and Samir Rihani (2010), *Complexity and Public Policy*, London: Routledge.

Gilabert, Pablo and Holly Lawford-Smith (2012), 'Political Feasibility: A Conceptual Exploration', *Political Studies* 60(4): 809–25.

Gilroy, Paul (2019), '"Rhythm in the Force of Forces": Music and Political Time', *Critical Times* 2(3): 370–95.

Glaser, Barney G. and Anselm L. Strauss (2017), *The Discovery of Grounded Theory: Strategies for Qualitative Research*, London: Routledge.

Godrej, Farah (2009), 'Response to "What Is Comparative Political Theory?"', *Review of Politics* 71: 567–82.

Godrej, Farah (2011), *Cosmopolitan Political Thought: Method, Practice, Discipline*, Oxford: Oxford University Press.

Goodall, Heather (1996), *Invasion to Embassy: Land in Aboriginal Politics in NSW, 1770–1972*, Sydney: Allen & Unwin.

Goodhand, Jonathan (2012), 'Bandits, Borderlands and Opium Wars: Afghan State-Building Viewed from the Margins', in Hastings Donnan and Tom Wilson (eds), *A Companion to Border Studies*, Sydney: John Wiley, pp. 332–53.

Goodin, Robert (2007), 'Enfranchising All Affected Interests, and its Alternatives', *Philosophy & Public Affairs* 35(1), 40–68.

Goodin, Robert (2010), 'Global Democracy: In the Beginning', *International Theory* 2(2): 175–209.

Goodin, Robert and Charles Tilly (eds) (2006), *The Oxford Handbook of Contextual Political Analysis*, Oxford: Oxford University Press.

Gooley, Cameron (2020), 'NT Treaty Commission eyes 2022 submission of final report with consultations to commence', ABC News, 16 July, <https://www.abc.net.au/news/2020-07-16/nt-treaty-commissioner-mick-dodson-releases-discussion-paper/12459072> (last accessed 16 November 2021).

Graham, Mary (1999), 'Some Thoughts about the Philosophical Underpinnings of Aboriginal Worldviews', *Worldviews: Global Religions, Culture and Ecology* 3(2): 105–18.

Gunnell, John (1998), *The Orders of Discourse: Philosophy, Social Science and Politics*, Lanham, MD: Rowman & Littlefield.

Habermas, Jurgen (1994), 'Three Normative Models of Democracy', *Constellations* 1(1): 1–10.

Halewood, Michael (2005), 'On Whitehead and Deleuze: The Process of Materiality', *Configurations* 13(1): 57–76.

Halewood, Michael (2011), *A. N. Whitehead and Social Theory*, London: Anthem Press.

Hampsher-Monk, Iain (2011), 'Politics, Political Theory and its History', in Jonathan Floyd and Marc Stears (eds), *Political Philosophy versus History? Contextualism and Real Politics in Contemporary Political Thought*, Cambridge: Cambridge University Press, pp. 105–27.

Hampshire, Stuart (2000), *Justice Is Conflict*, Princeton: Princeton University Press.

Hanchard, Michael (1999), 'Afro-Modernity: Temporality, Politics, and the African Diaspora', *Public Culture* 11(1): 245–68.

Hassan, Robert and Ronald E. Purser (eds) (2007), *24/7: Time and Temporality in the Network Society*, Stanford: Stanford University Press.

Hayward, Katy (2020), 'Why It Is Impossible for Brexit Britain to "Take Back Control" in Northern Ireland', *Territory, Politics, Governance* 8(2): 273–8.

Held, David (1995), *Democracy and the Global Order*, Cambridge: Polity Press.

Held, David (2007), 'Reframing Global Governance: Apocalypse Soon or Reform!', in David Held and Anthony McGrew (eds), *Globalization*

Theory: Approaches and Controversies, Cambridge: Polity Press, pp. 250–9.

Hirst, Paul Q. and Grahame Thompson (2009), *Globalization in Question: The International Economy and the Possibilities of Governance*, Cambridge: Polity Press.

Hodges, Matt (2008), 'Rethinking Time's Arrow: Bergson, Deleuze and the Anthropology of Time', *Anthropological Theory* 8(4): 399–429.

Holland, Eugene W. (2011), *Nomad Citizenship: Free-Market Communism and the Slow-Motion General Strike*, Minneapolis: University of Minnesota Press.

Hom, Andrew R. (2018), 'Timing Is Everything: Towards a Better Understanding of Time and International Politics', *International Studies Quarterly* 62(1): 69–79.

Hom, Andrew R. (2020), *International Relations and the Problem of Time*, Oxford: Oxford University Press.

Honig, Bonnie (2001), 'Dead Rights, Live Futures: A Reply to Habermas's "Constitutional Democracy"', *Political Theory* 29(6): 792–805.

Honig, Bonnie and Marc Stears (2011), 'The New Realism: From Modus Vivendi to Justice', in Jonathan Floyd and Marc Stears (eds), *Political Philosophy versus History? Contextualism and Real Politics in Contemporary Political Thought*, Cambridge: Cambridge University Press, pp. 177–205.

Honneth, Axel (2015), *The Struggle for Recognition*, Cambridge: Polity Press.

Hooker, Juliet (2016), 'Black Lives Matter and the Paradoxes of U.S. Black Politics: From Democratic Sacrifice to Democratic Repair', *Political Theory* 44(4): 448–69.

Hoy, David (2012), *The Time of our Lives: A Critical History of Temporality*, Cambridge, MA: MIT Press.

Huber, Jakob (2017), 'Pragmatic Belief and Political Agency', *Political Studies* 66(3): 651–66.

Hutchings, Kimberley (2013), *Time and World Politics: Thinking the Present*, Manchester: Manchester University Press.

Idris, Murad (2016), 'Political Theory and the Politics of Comparison', *Political Theory*, DOI: https://doi.org/10.1177/0090591716659812.

Idris, Murad (2020), 'The Kazanistan Papers: Reading the Muslim Question in the John Rawls Archives', *Perspectives on Politics*, DOI: https://doi.org/10.1017/S153759272000239X.

Ignatieff, Michael (1996), 'Articles of Faith', *Index on Censorship* 5: 110–22.

Iparraguirre, Gonzalo (2016), 'Time, Temporality and Cultural Rhythmics: An Anthropological Case Study', *Time & Society* 25(3): 613–33.

Iqtidar, Humeira (2016), 'Redefining "Tradition" in Political Thought', *European Journal of Political Theory* 15(4): 424–44.

James, William (1910), 'Bradley or Bergson?', *Journal of Philosophy, Psychology and Scientific Methods* 7(2): 29–33.

Jankélévitch, Vladimir (2012), 'Bergson and Judaism', in Alexandre Lefebvre and Melanie White (eds), *Bergson, Politics, and Religion*, Durham, NC: Duke University Press, pp. 217–45.

Jehangir, Hamza Bin (2019), 'Class, Subjectivity, and the Political in Pakistan: Bridging the Practice-Theory Divide in Comparative Political Theory', PhD thesis, University of Melbourne, <http://minerva-access.unimelb.edu.au/handle/11343/224218> (last accessed 16 November 2021).

Jehangir, Hamza Bin and Adrian Little (2020), 'Temporality and Comparative Political Theory', unpublished manuscript.

Jenco, Leigh (2007), '"What Does Heaven Ever Say?" A Methods-Centered Approach to Cross-Cultural Engagement', *American Political Science Review* 101(4): 741–55.

Jenco, Leigh (2016), 'New Pasts for New Futures: A Temporal Reading of Global Thought', *Constellations* 23(3): 436–47.

Jervis, Robert (2000), 'Timing and Interaction in Politics: A Comment on Pierson', *Studies in American Political Development* 14(1): 93–100.

Johnson, Corey, Reece Jones, Anssi Paasi, Louise Amoore, Alison Mountz, Mark Salter and Chris Rumford (2011), 'Interventions on Rethinking "the Border" in Border Studies', *Political Geography* 30(2): 61–9.

Kant, Immanuel (1998), *Critique of Pure Reason*, Cambridge: Cambridge University Press.

Kauffman, Stuart (2008), *Reinventing the Sacred: A New View of Science, Reason and Religion*, New York: Basic Books.

Keating, Paul (2001), 'Redfern Park Speech 10 December 1992', *Indigenous Law Bulletin* 5(11).

Kingdon, John (1995), *Agendas, Alternatives and Public Policies*, New York: HarperCollins.

Knuuttila, Simo (2001), 'Time and Creation in Augustine', in Eleonore Slump and Norman Kretzmann (eds), *The Cambridge Companion to Augustine*, Cambridge: Cambridge University Press, pp. 103–15.

Koenig-Archibugi, Mathias (2011), 'Is Global Democracy Possible?', *European Journal of International Relations* 17(3): 519–42.

Koenig-Archibugi, Mathias (2012), 'Fuzzy Citizenship in Global Society', *Journal of Political Philosophy* 20(4): 456–80.

Konrad, Victor and Heather N. Nicol (2011), 'Border Culture, the Boundary between Canada and the United States of America, and the Advancement of Borderlands Theory', *Geopolitics* 16(1): 70–90.

Koopman, Colin (2009a), *Pragmatism as Transition: Historicity and Hope in James, Dewey and Rorty*, New York: Columbia University Press.

Koopman, Colin (2009b), 'Two Uses of Genealogy: Michel Foucault and Bernard Williams', in Carlos Prado (ed.), *Foucault's Legacy*, New York: Continuum, pp. 90–108.

Koopman, Colin (2010), 'Bernard Williams on Philosophy's Need for History', *The Review of Metaphysics* 64: 3–30.

Koopman, Colin (2011a), 'Genealogical Pragmatism: How History Matters for Foucault and Dewey', *Journal of the Philosophy of History* 5: 531–59.

Koopman, Colin (2011b), *Genealogy as Critique: Foucault and the Problems of Modernity*, Bloomington: University of Indiana Press.

Kurlantzick, Joshua (2013), *Democracy in Retreat: The Revolt of the Middle Class and the Worldwide Decline of Representative Government*, New Haven: Yale University Press.

Kyle, David and Marc Scarcelli (2009), 'Migrant Smuggling and the Violence Question: Evolving Illicit Migration Markets for Cuban and Haitian Refugees', *Crime, Law and Social Change* 52(3): 297–311.

Kymlicka, Will (1998), 'Is Federalism a Viable Alternative to Secession?', in Percy Lehning (ed.), *Theories of Secession*, London: Routledge, pp. 11–150.

Lane, Melissa (2011), 'Constraint, Freedom, and Exemplar: History and Theory without a Teleology', in Jonathan Floyd and Marc Stears (eds), *Political Philosophy versus History? Contextualism and Real Politics in Contemporary Political Thought*, Cambridge: Cambridge University Press, pp. 128–50.

Lawlor, Leonard (2010), 'Intuition and Duration: An Introduction to Bergson's "Introduction to Metaphysics"', in Michael Kelly (ed.), *Bergson and Phenomenology*, London: Palgrave, pp. 25–41.

Lawlor, Leonard and Valentine Moulard-Leonard (2020), 'Henri Bergson', in *The Stanford Encyclopedia of Philosophy* (Fall 2020 Edition), (ed.) Edward N. Zalta, <https://plato.stanford.edu/archives/fall2020/entries/bergson> (last accessed 16 November 2021).

Lawson, Tom (2014), *The Last Man: A British Genocide in Tasmania*, London: I.B. Tauris.

Lefebvre, Alexandre (2012), 'Bergson and Human Rights', in Alexandre Lefebvre and Melanie White (eds), *Bergson, Politics, and Religion*, Durham, NC: Duke University Press, pp. 193–215.

Lefebvre, Alexandre (2013), *Human Rights as a Way of Life: On Bergson's Political Philosophy*, Stanford: Stanford University Press.

Lefebvre, Alexandre and Melanie White (eds) (2012), *Bergson, Politics, and Religion*, Durham, NC: Duke University Press.

Lehning, Percy B. (ed.) (1998), *Theories of Secession*, London: Routledge.

Letters Patent (n.d.), <https://adelaidia.history.sa.gov.au/subjects/letters-patent> (last accessed 16 November 2021).

List, Christian and Mathias Koenig-Archibugi (2010), 'Can There Be a Global Demos? An Agency-Based Approach', *Philosophy & Public Affairs* 38(1): 76–110.

Little, Adrian (2007), 'Between Disagreement and Consensus: Unravelling the Democratic Paradox', *Australian Journal of Political Science* 42(1): 143–59.

Little, Adrian (2008), *Democratic Piety: Complexity, Conflict and Violence*, Edinburgh: Edinburgh University Press.

Little, Adrian (2010), 'Democratic Melancholy: On the Sacrosanct Place of Democracy in Radical Democratic Theory', *Political Studies* 58(5): 971–87.

Little, Adrian (2012), 'Political Action, Error and Failure: The Epistemological Limits of Complexity', *Political Studies* 60(1): 3–19.

Little, Adrian (2014), *Enduring Conflict: Challenging the Signature of Peace and Democracy*, New York: Bloomsbury.

Little, Adrian (2015a), 'The Complex Temporality of Borders: Contingency and Normativity', *European Journal of Political Theory* 14(4): 429–47.

Little, Adrian (2015b), 'Performing the Demos: Towards a Processive Theory of Global Democracy', *Critical Review of International Social and Political Philosophy* 18(6): 620–41.

Little, Adrian (2015c), 'Reconstituting Realism: Feasibility, Utopia and Epistemological Imperfection', *Contemporary Political Theory* 14(3): 276–313.

Little, Adrian (2017), 'Fear, Hope and Disappointment: Emotions in the Politics of Reconciliation and Conflict Transformation', *International Political Science Review* 38(2): 200–12.

Little, Adrian (2018), 'Contextualizing Concepts: The Methodology of Comparative Political Theory', *The Review of Politics* 80(1): 87–113.

Little, Adrian (2020), 'The Politics of Makarrata: Understanding Indigenous–Settler Relations in Australia', *Political Theory* 48(1): 30–56.

Little, Adrian and Moya Lloyd (eds) (2009), *The Politics of Radical Democracy*, Edinburgh: Edinburgh University Press.

Little, Adrian and Kate Macdonald (2013), 'Pathways to Global Democracy? Escaping the Statist Imaginary', *Review of International Studies* 39(4): 789–813.

Little, Adrian and Terry Macdonald (2016), 'Towards a Problem-Based Approach to Normative Political Theory', paper presented at European

Consortium for Political Research, Charles University, Prague, September 7–10.

Little, Adrian and Mark McMillan (2017), 'Invisibility and the Politics of Reconciliation in Australia: Keeping Conflict in View', *Ethnopolitics* 16(5): 519–37.

Little, Adrian and Umut Ozguc (2022), 'The Politics of Becoming and the Ethos of Open Societies: Rethinking More-Than-Human Borders', *Geopolitics*, forthcoming.

Little, Adrian and Nick Vaughan-Williams (2017), 'Stopping Boats, Saving Lives, Securing Subjects: Humanitarian Borders in Europe and Australia', *European Journal of International Relations* 23(3): 533–56.

Lloyd, Moya (1999), 'Performativity, Parody, Politics', *Theory, Culture & Society* 16(2): 195–213.

Lloyd, Moya (2007), *Judith Butler: From Norms to Politics*, Cambridge: Polity Press.

Longo, Matthew (2017), *The Politics of Borders: Sovereignty, Security and the Citizen after 9/11*, Cambridge: Cambridge University Press.

McCall, Cathal (2011), 'Culture and the Irish Border: Spaces for Conflict Transformation', *Cooperation and Conflict* 46(2): 201–21.

Macdonald, Kate (2011), 'Global Democracy for a Partially Joined-Up World', in Daniele Archibugi, Mathias Koenig-Archibugi and Raffaele Marchetti (eds), *Global Democracy: Normative and Empirical Perspectives*, Cambridge: Cambridge University Press, pp. 183–209.

Macdonald, Kate (2014), *The Politics of Global Supply Chains: Power and Governance beyond the State*, Cambridge: Polity Press.

Macdonald, Terry (2008), *Global Stakeholder Democracy: Power and Representation beyond Liberal States*, Oxford: Oxford University Press.

Macdonald, Terry (2011), 'Citizens or Stakeholders?', in Daniele Archibugi, Mathias Koenig-Archibugi and Raffaele Marchetti (eds), *Global Democracy: Normative and Empirical Perspectives*, Cambridge: Cambridge University Press, pp. 47–68.

McIntosh, Christopher (2015), 'Theory across Time: The Privileging of Time-Less Theory in International Relations', *International Theory* 7(3): 464–500.

McNevin, Anne (2011), *Contesting Citizenship: Irregular Migrants and New Frontiers of the Political*, New York: Columbia University Press.

McNevin, Anne (2020), 'Time and the Figure of the Citizen', *International Journal of Politics, Culture, and Society*, DOI: https://doi.org/10.1007/s10767-020-09358-4.

Macoun, Alissa (2011), 'Aboriginality and the Northern Territory Intervention', *Australian Journal of Political Science*, 46(3): 519–34.

McTaggart, J. M. E. (1968), *The Nature of Existence*, 2 vols, Cambridge: Cambridge University Press.

Mamdani, Mahmood (2020), *Neither Settler nor Native*, Cambridge, MA: Harvard University Press.

March, Andrew (2009), 'What Is Comparative Political Theory?', *The Review of Politics*, 71: 531–65.

Marchetti, Raffaele (2011), 'Models of Global Democracy', in Daniele Archibugi, Mathias Koenig-Archibugi and Raffaele Marchetti (eds), *Global Democracy: Normative and Empirical Perspectives*, Cambridge: Cambridge University Press, pp. 22–46.

Margolis, Joseph (2017), *Pragmatism Ascendent: A Yard of Narrative, a Touch of Prophecy*, Stanford: Stanford University Press.

Markell, Patchen (2003), *Bound by Recognition*, Princeton: Princeton University Press.

Marrati, Paola (2012), 'James, Bergson, and an Open Universe', in Alexandre Lefebvre and Melanie White (eds), *Bergson, Politics, and Religion*, Durham, NC: Duke University Press, pp. 299–312.

Mearsheimer, John J. and Stephen M. Walt (2013), 'Leaving Theory Behind: Why Simplistic Hypothesis Testing Is Bad for International Relations', *European Journal of International Relations* 19(3): 427–57.

Meilaender, Peter C. (1999), 'Liberalism and Open Borders: The Argument of Joseph Carens', *International Migration Review* 33(4): 1062–81.

Michaelsen, Scott and David E. Johnson (eds) (1997), *Border Theory: The Limits of Cultural Politics*, Minneapolis: University of Minnesota Press.

Mignolo, Walter D. and Catherine E. Walsh (2018), *On Decoloniality: Concepts, Analytics, Praxis*, Durham, NC: Duke University Press.

Miller, David (2009), 'Democracy's Domain', *Philosophy & Public Affairs* 37(3): 201–28.

Miller, David (2010), 'Against Global Democracy', in Keith Breen and Shane O'Neill (eds), *After the Nation?*, London: Palgrave Macmillan, pp. 141–60.

Miller, David (2012), *Justice for Earthlings*, Cambridge: Cambridge University Press.

Mills, Charles W. (2014), 'White Time: The Chronic Injustice of Ideal Theory', *Du Bois Review* 11(1): 27–42.

Mills, Charles W. (2020), 'The Chronopolitics of Racial Time', *Time & Society* 29(2): 297–317.

Minow, Martha (2000), 'The Hope for Healing: What Can Truth Commissions Do?', in Robert Rotberg and Dennis Thompson (eds), *Truth v Justice: The Morality of Truth Commissions*, Princeton: Princeton University Press, pp. 235–360.

Moffitt, Ben (2016), *The Global Rise of Populism: Performance, Political Style, and Representation*, Stanford: Stanford University Press.

Moreton-Robinson, Aileen (2015), *The White Possessive: Property, Power, and Indigenous Sovereignty*, Minneapolis: University of Minnesota Press.

Morris, Randall C. (1991), *Process Philosophy and Political Ideology*, Albany: SUNY Press.

Mouffe, Chantal (2005), *On the Political*, London: Verso.

Mountz, Alison (2011), 'Border Politics: Spatial Provision and Geographical Precision', *Political Geography* 30(2): 65-6.

Muldoon, Paul (2017), 'A Reconciliation Most Desirable', *International Political Science Review* 38(2): 213-27.

Nagy, Rosemary (2020), 'Settler Witnessing at the Truth and Reconciliation Commission of Canada', *Human Rights Review* 21: 219-41.

Nakata, Sana (2015), *Childhood Citizenship, Governance and Policy: The Politics of Becoming Adult*, London: Routledge.

Näsström, Sofia (2011), 'The Challenge of the All-Affected Principle', *Political Studies* 59(1): 116-34.

Neville, Robert Cumming (2004), 'Whitehead and Pragmatism', in Janusz A. Polanowski and Donald W. Sherburne (eds), *Whitehead's Philosophy: Points of Connection*, Albany: SUNY Press, pp. 19-40.

Newman, David (2006), 'Borders and Bordering: Towards an Inter-disciplinary Dialogue', *European Journal of Social Theory* 9(2): 171-86.

Nichols, Robert (2020), *Theft Is Property: Dispossession and Critical Theory*, London: Duke University Press.

Nightingale, Andrea Wilson (2011), *Once out of Nature: Augustine on Time and the Body*, Chicago: University of Chicago Press.

Nine, Cara (2008), 'The Moral Arbitrariness of State Borders: Against Beitz', *Contemporary Political Theory* 7(3): 259-79.

Norris, Pippa (2014), *Democratic Deficit: Critical Citizens Revisited*, Cambridge: Cambridge University Press.

Norris, Pippa and Ronald Inglehart (2019), *Cultural Backlash: Trump, Brexit, and Authoritarian Populism*, Cambridge: Cambridge University Press.

Ochoa Espejo, Paulina (2012), 'Creative Freedom: Henri Bergson and Democratic Theory', in Alexandre Lefebvre and Melanie White (eds), *Bergson, Religion, and Politics*, Durham, NC: Duke University Press, pp. 159-73.

Ochoa Espejo, Paulina (2020), *On Borders: Territories, Legitimacy and the Rights of Place*, Oxford: Oxford University Press.

O'Dowd, Liam (2002), 'Transnational Integration and Cross-Border Regions in the European Union', in James Anderson (ed.), *Transnational*

Democracy: Political Spaces and Border Crossings, London: Routledge, pp. 111–28.

Ohmae, Kenichi (1999), *The Borderless World*, New York: HarperCollins.

Orren, Karen and Stephen Skowronek (1996), 'Institutions and Inter-currence: Theory Building in the Fullness of Time', *Nomos* 38: 111–46.

Orren, Karen and Stephen Skowronek (2004), *The Search for American Political Development*, Cambridge: Cambridge University Press.

Ørsted-Jensen, Robert (2011), *Frontier History Revisited: Colonial Queensland and the 'History War'*, Brisbane: Lux Mundi Publications.

Osborne, Thomas (2003), 'What Is a Problem?', *History of the Human Sciences* 16(4): 1–17.

Overwijk, Jan (2020), 'Paradoxes of Rationalisation: Openness and Control in Critical Theory and Luhmann's Systems Theory', *Theory, Culture & Society*, DOI: https://doi.org/10.1177/0263276420925548.

Owen, David (2016), 'Reasons and Practices of Reasoning: On the Analytic-Continental Distinction in Political Philosophy', *European Journal of Political Theory* 15(2): 172–88.

Ozguc, Umut (2020), 'Borders, Detention, and the Disruptive Power of the Noisy Subject', *International Political Sociology* 14(1): 77–93.

Parel, Anthony and Ronald C. Keith (eds) (2003), *Comparative Political Philosophy: Studies under the Upas Tree*, Oxford: Lexington Books.

Parker, Noel and Nick Vaughan-Williams (2009), 'Lines in the Sand? Towards an Agenda for Critical Border Studies', *Geopolitics* 14(3): 582–7.

Patten, Alan (2014), 'Democratic Secession from a Multinational State', in *Equal Recognition: The Moral Foundations of Minority Rights*, Princeton: Princeton University Press, pp. 232–68.

Patton, Paul (2000), *Deleuze and the Political*, London: Routledge.

Patton, Paul (2010), *Deleuzian Concepts*, Stanford: Stanford University Press.

Pierson, Paul (2000), 'Not Just What, but When: Timing and Sequence in Political Processes', *Studies in American Political Development* 14(1): 72–92.

Pierson, Paul (2004), *Politics in Time: History, Institutions and Social Analysis*, Princeton: Princeton University Press.

Pollitt, Christopher (2008), *Time, Management, Policy*, Oxford: Oxford University Press.

Popper, Karl (2020), *The Open Society and its Enemies*, Princeton: Princeton University Press.

Portschy, Jürgen (2020), 'Times of Power, Knowledge and Critique in the Work of Foucault', *Time & Society*, DOI: https://doi.org/10.1177/0961463X20911786.

Power, Carl (2012), 'Bergson's Critique of Practical Reason', in Alexandre Lefebvre and Melanie White (eds), *Bergson, Politics, and Religion*, Durham, NC: Duke University Press, pp. 174–92.

Prigogine, Ilya (1997), *The End of Certainty: Time, Chaos, and the New Laws of Nature*, New York: Free Press.

Rahman, Smita A. (2014), *Time, Memory, and the Politics of Contingency*, London: Routledge.

Rancière, Jacques (2006), *Hatred of Democracy*, London: Verso.

Rancière, Jacques (2010), *Dissensus: On Politics and Aesthetics*, London: Continuum.

Rawls, John (1993), *Political Liberalism*, New York: Columbia University Press.

Referendum Council (2017), Final Report of the Referendum Council and Terms of Reference, <https://www.referendumcouncil.org.au/final-report.html#toc-anchor-forewordfrom-the-co-chairs> (last accessed 16 November 2021).

Rehfeld, Andrew (2006), 'Towards a General Theory of Political Representation', *The Journal of Politics* 68(1): 1–21.

Rehfeld, Andrew (2009), 'Representation Rethought: On Trustees, Delegates, and Gyroscopes in the Study of Political Representation and Democracy', *American Political Science Review* 103(2): 214–30.

Rehfeld, Andrew (2011), 'The Concepts of Representation', *American Political Science Review* 105(3): 631–41.

Revelli, Marco (2019), *The New Populism: Democracy Stares into the Abyss*, London: Verso.

Reynolds, Henry (1981), *The Other Side of the Frontier: Aboriginal Resistance to the European Invasion of Australia*, Ringwood: Penguin Books.

Ricoeur, Paul (2008), *Time and Narrative*, vol. 3, Chicago: University of Chicago Press.

Rifkin, Mark (2017), *Beyond Settler Time: Temporal Sovereignty and Indigenous Self-Determination*, Lanham, MD: Duke University Press.

Roberts, Tom (2014), 'From Things to Events: Whitehead and the Materiality of Process', *Environment and Planning D: Society and Space* 32: 968–83.

Robinson, Keith (ed.) (2009), *Deleuze, Whitehead, Bergson: Rhizomatic Connections*, London: Palgrave.

Rogers, Thomas James and Stephen Bain (2016), 'Genocide and Frontier Violence in Australia', *Journal of Genocide Research* 18(1): 83–100.

Rollo, Toby (2018), 'Back to the Rough Ground: Textual, Oral and Enactive Meaning in Comparative Political Theory', *European Journal of Political Theory*, DOI: https://doi.org/10.1177/1474885118795284.

Rorty, Richard (1995), 'Philosophy and the Future', in Herman J. Saatkamp (ed.), *Rorty and Pragmatism: The Philosopher Responds to his Critics*, Nashville: Vanderbilt University Press, pp. 197–206.

Rosenau, James (1990), *Turbulence in World Politics*, Princeton: Princeton University Press.

Rosenau, James (1997), *Along the Domestic–Foreign Frontier: Exploring Governance in a Turbulent World*, Cambridge: Cambridge University Press.

Roy, Srila (2009), 'Melancholic Politics and the Politics of Melancholia: The Indian Women's Movement', *Feminist Theory* 10(3): 341–57.

Runciman, David (2018), *How Democracy Ends*, New York: Basic Books.

Sabl, Andrew (2011), 'History and Reality: Idealist Pathologies and "Harvard School" Remedies', in Jonathan Floyd and Marc Stears (eds), *Political Philosophy versus History? Contextualism and Real Politics in Contemporary Political Thought*, Cambridge: Cambridge University Press, pp. 151–76.

Sanders, Will (2018), *Mabo and Native Title: Origins and Institutional Implications*, Canberra: Centre for Aboriginal Economic Policy Research (CAEPR), Australian National University.

Saward, Michael (2006), 'The Representative Claim', *Contemporary Political Theory* 5(3): 297–318.

Saward, Michael (2010), *The Representative Claim*, Oxford: Oxford University Press.

Scholte, Jan Aart (2014), 'Reinventing Global Democracy', *European Journal of International Relations* 20(1): 3–28.

Schuppert, Fabian (2011), 'Climate Change Mitigation and Intergenerational Justice', *Environmental Politics* 20(3): 303–21.

Seglow, Jonathan (2005), 'The Ethics of Immigration', *Political Studies Review* 3(3): 317–34.

Seibt, Johanna (ed.) (2003), *Process Theories: Crossdisciplinary Studies in Dynamic Categories*, New York: Kluwer.

Sewell, William (1996), 'Three Temporalities: Toward a Sociology of the Event', CRSO Working Paper 448, available at <https://deepblue.lib.umich.edu/handle/2027.42/51215> (last accessed 16 November 2021).

Shapiro, Ian and Sonu Bedi (eds) (2006), *Political Contingency: Studying the Unexpected, the Accidental, and the Unforeseen*, New York: New York University Press.

Shapiro, Michael (2016), *Politics and Time*, Cambridge: Polity Press.

Sharma, Sarah (2014), *In the Meantime: Temporality and Cultural Politics*, Durham, NC: Duke University Press.

Sheingate, Adam (2014), 'Institutional Dynamics and American Political Development', *Annual Review of Political Science* 17(1): 461–77.

Sherburne, Donald W. (2004), 'Whitehead, Descartes and Terminology', in Janusz A. Polanowski and Donald W. Sherburne (eds), *Whitehead's Philosophy: Points of Connection*, Albany: SUNY Press, pp. 3–18.

Simmons, A. John (2010), 'Ideal and Nonideal Theory', *Philosophy and Public Affairs* 38(1): 5–36.

Simon, Joshua (2020), 'Institutions, Ideologies and Comparative Political Theory', *Perspectives on Politics* 18(2): 423–38.

Simpson, Audra (2014), *Mohawk Interruptus: Political Life across the Borders of Settler States*, London: Duke University Press.

Simpson, Leanne Betasamosake (2017), *As We Have Always Done: Indigenous Freedom through Radical Resistance*, Minneapolis: University of Minnesota Press.

Skrimshire, Stefan (2019), 'Deep Time and Secular Time: A Critique of the Environmental "Long View"', *Theory, Culture & Society* 36(1): 63–81.

Sleat, Matt (ed.) (2018), *Politics Recovered: Realist Thought in Theory and Practice*, New York: Columbia University Press.

Song, Sarah (2012), 'The Boundary Problem in Democratic Theory: Why the Demos Should Be Bounded by the State', *International Theory* 4(1): 39–68.

Stokes, Susan (2007), 'Region, Contingency, and Democratization', in Ian Shapiro and Sonu Bedi (eds), *Political Contingency: Studying the Unexpected, the Accidental and the Unforeseen*, New York: New York University Press, pp. 171–202.

Stout, Margaret and Carrie M. Staton (2011), 'The Ontology of Process Philosophy in Follett's Administrative Theory', *Administrative Theory & Praxis* 33(2): 268–92.

Stuhr, John J. (1997), *Genealogical Pragmatism: Philosophy, Experience, and Community*, Albany: SUNY Press.

Sum, Ngai-Ling (2000), 'Rethinking Globalisation: Re-Articulating the Spatial Scale and Temporal Horizons of Trans-Border Spaces', in Kris Olds et al. (eds), *Globalisation and the Asia-Pacific: Contested Territories*, London: Routledge, pp. 124–39.

Thelen, Kathleen (2000), 'Timing and Temporality in the Analysis of Institutional Evolution and Change', *Studies in American Political Development* 14(1): 101–8.

Thomson, Alex (2005), 'What's to Become of Democracy to Come?', *Postmodern Culture* 15(3).

Tilly, Charles (1988), 'Future History', *Theory & Society* 17(5): 703–12.

Tormey, Simon (2014), *The End of Representative Politics*, Cambridge: Polity Press.

Traverso, Enzo (2017), *Left-Wing Melancholia*, New York: Columbia University Press.

Tully, James (2008), *Public Philosophy in a New Key*, vol. 1, Cambridge: Cambridge University Press.

Uluru Statement (2017), *The Uluru Statement from the Heart*, <https://ulurustatement.org/the-statement> (last accessed 16 November 2021).

Urry, John (2002), *Global Complexity*, Cambridge: Polity Press.

Valentini, Laura (2009), 'On the Apparent Paradox of Ideal Theory', *Journal of Political Philosophy* 17(3): 332–55.

van Beek, Ursula (2019), *Democracy under Threat: A Crisis of Legitimacy?*, London: Palgrave Macmillan.

Vaughan-Williams, Nick (2009), *Border Politics: The Limits of Sovereign Power*, Edinburgh: Edinburgh University Press.

Vaughan-Williams, Nick (2016), 'Borders', in Aoileann Ní Mhurchú and Reiko Shindo (eds), *Critical Imaginations in International Relations*, London: Routledge, pp. 11–27.

von Vacano, Diego (2015), 'The Scope of Comparative Political Theory', *Annual Review of Political Science* 18: 465–80.

Voss, Daniela (2013), 'Deleuze's Third Synthesis of Time', *Deleuze Studies* 7(2): 194–216.

Walker, Rob. B. J. (1993), *Inside/Outside: International Relations as Political Theory*, Cambridge: Cambridge University Press.

Ware, Alan (2020), 'Democracy through Time: Identity Politics and Future Generations', *The Political Quarterly* 91(4): 814–24.

Warren, Mark (2017), 'A Problem-Based Approach to Democratic Theory', *American Political Science Review* 111(1): 39–53.

Warren, Mark and Melissa Williams (2014), 'A Democratic Case for Comparative Political Theory', *Political Theory* 42(1): 26–57.

Watson, Irene (2014a), *Aboriginal Peoples, Colonialism and International Law: Raw Law*, London: Routledge.

Watson, Irene (2014b), 'Re-Centring First Nations Knowledge and Places in a Terra Nullius Space', *AlterNative: An International Journal of Indigenous Peoples* 10(5): 508–20.

Weir, Jessica (2009), *Murray River Country: An Ecological Dialogue with Traditional Owners*, Canberra: Aboriginal Studies Press.

Whitehead, Alfred North (1978), *Process and Reality*, New York: Free Press.

Whitt, Matt (2014), 'Democracy's Sovereign Enclosures: Territory and the All-Affected Principle', *Constellations* 21(4): 560–74.

Widder, Nathan (2008), *Reflections on Time and Politics*, University Park: Pennsylvania State University Press.

Wilder, Matt and Michael Howlett (2014), 'The Politics of Policy Anomalies: Bricolage and the Hermeneutics of Paradoxes', *Critical Policy Studies* 8(2): 183–202.

Williams, Bernard (2005), *In the Beginning Was the Deed: Realism and Moralism in Political Argument*, Princeton: Princeton University Press.

Williams, James (2011), *Gilles Deleuze's Philosophy of Time*, Edinburgh: Edinburgh University Press.

Williams, Melissa S. (ed.) (2020), *Deparochializing Political Theory*, Cambridge: Cambridge University Press.

Williams, Michael C. (2005), *The Realist Tradition and the Limits of International Relations*, Cambridge: Cambridge University Press.

Wilson, Thomas (1994), 'Symbolic Dimensions to the Irish Border', in Hastings Donnan and Thomas Wilson (eds), *Border Approaches: Anthropological Perspectives on Frontiers*, Lanham, MD: University Press of America, pp. 101–18.

Wilson, Thomas and Hastings Donnan (eds) (1998a), *Border Identities: Nation and State at International Frontiers*, Cambridge: Cambridge University Press.

Wilson, Thomas and Hastings Donnan (1998b), 'Nation, State and Identity at International Borders', in Wilson and Donnan (eds), *Border Identities: Nation and State at International Frontiers*, Cambridge: Cambridge University Press, pp. 1–30.

Wolfe, Patrick (2006), 'Settler Colonialism and the Elimination of the Native', *Journal of Genocide Research* 8(4): 387–409.

Young, Iris Marion (2000), *Inclusion and Democracy*, Oxford: Oxford University Press.

Zürn, Michael (2004), 'Global Governance and Legitimacy Problems', *Government and Opposition* 39(2): 260–87.

Index

EU representative:
Easy Access System Europe
Mustamäe tee 50, 10621 Tallinn, Estonia
Gpsr.requests@easproject.com

www.ingramcontent.com/pod-product-compliance
Lightning Source LLC
Chambersburg PA
CBHW071739270326
41928CB00013B/2739